BRESCIA COLLEGE
LONDON ONTARIO

Elizabeth Barrett and Robert Browning

This book is for my parents,
Charles and Vivian Sanders

Cathedral and Campanile from the Palazzo Pitti.

Cathedral and Campanile from the Palazzo Pitti, engraving from a drawing by P.H. Delamotte, *The Makers of Florence* (1885) by Mrs. [Margaret] Oliphant, Frontispiece

People say of you and me. . . that we love the darkness
and use a sphinxine idiom in our talk. . . .

(EBB, 1845)

***

"Ah, but if you knew how time has dragged, days, nights!
    All the neighbor-talk with man and maid—such men!
All the fuss and trouble of street sounds, window-sights:
    All the worry of flapping door and echoing roof; and then,
All the fancies. . . Who were they had leave, dared try
    Darker arts than that almost struck despair in me?
If you knew but how I dwelt down here!" quoth I:
    "And was I so much better off up there?" quoth She.

(RB, 1872)

Elizabeth Barrett and Robert Browning

A Creative Partnership

MARY SANDERS POLLOCK
Stetson University, USA

ASHGATE

Published by
Ashgate Publishing Limited
Gower House
Croft Road
Aldershot
Hampshire GU11 3HR
England

Ashgate Publishing Company
Suite 420
101 Cherry Street
Burlington, VT 05401-4405
USA

Ashgate website: http//www.ashgate.com

British Library Cataloguing in Publication Data
Pollock, Mary Sanders
    Elizabeth Barrett and Robert Browning : a creative
    partnership. - (The nineteenth century series)
    1.Browning, Elizabeth Barrett, 1806-1861 - Influence
    2. Browning, Robert, 1812-1889 - Influence 3.English poetry
    - 19th century - History and criticism
    I.Title
    821.8'09

Library of Congress Cataloging-in-Publication Data
Pollock, Mary Sanders, 1948-
    Elizabeth Barrett and Robert Browning : a creative partnership / Mary Sanders Pollock.
    p. cm. -- (The nineteenth century series)
    Includes bibliographical references (p.) and index.
    ISBN 0-7546-3328-4 (alk. paper)
    1. Browning, Elizabeth Barrett, 1806-1861--Criticism and interpretation. 2. Browning,
    Robert, 1812-1889--Criticism and interpretation. 3.
    Authorship--Collaboration--History--19th century. 4. Browning, Elizabeth Barrett,
    1806-1861--Marriage. 5. Browning, Robert, 1812-1889--Marriage. 6. Married
    people--Great Britain--Biography. 7. Poets, English--19th century--Biography. I. Title. II.
    Nineteenth century (Aldershot, England)

PR4194.P654 2003
821'.809--dc21   2002043899

ISBN 0 7546 3328 4

Printed and bound in Great Britain by Biddles Ltd, *www.biddles.co.uk*

Contents

The Nineteenth Century General Editors' Preface

The aim of the series is to reflect, develop and extend the great burgeoning of interest in the nineteenth century that has been an inevitable feature of recent years, as that former epoch has come more sharply into focus as a locus for our understanding not only of the past but of the contours of our modernity. It centres primarily upon major authors and subjects within Romantic and Victorian literature. It also includes studies of other British writers and issues, where these are matters of current debate: for example, biography and autobiography, journalism, periodical literature, travel writing, book production, gender, non-canonical writing. We are dedicated principally to publishing original monographs and symposia; our policy is to embrace a broad scope in chronology, approach and range of concern, and both to recognize and cut innovatively across such parameters as those suggested by the designations 'Romantic' and 'Victorian'. We welcome new ideas and theories, while valuing traditional scholarship. It is hoped that the world which predates yet so forcibly predicts and engages our own will emerge in parts, in the wider sweep, and in the lively streams of disputation and change that are so manifest an aspect of its intellectual, artistic and social landscape.

Vincent Newey
Joanne Shattock

University of Leicester

List of Illustrations

Acknowledgments

Books result from creative partnerships among authors and communities. The staff of the Armstrong Browning Library at Baylor University have created for me, along with many other scholars, a sense of community; this library has also helped fund my research. I am especially grateful to Rita Patteson, Cynthia Burgess, and Mairi Rennie. I am also grateful for the assistance of Ruth R. Rogers and Mariana S. Oller at the Margaret Clapp Library of Wellesley College, and to the Southern Regional Education Board for funding my research there. At the DuPont-Ball Library of Stetson University, Jane Bradford has been consistently generous with her time and help since I began working on this book, and Sims Klein has been most helpful during the final stages.

I am no less indebted to other colleagues at Stetson, especially John Pearson, Terri Witek, Bryan Gillespie, Thomas J. Farrell, Karen Kaivola, Gary Bolding, and Lou Brakeman. Dialogue with them has strengthened my research in a variety of ways. Without Cathy Burke's commitment, generosity, and editing skills, my task at one point would have seemed impossible. Roberta Favis and Ann Burlin have given me indispensable aid in preparing the illustrations. Over the years, Stetson University has supported this project with sabbatical leaves and research grants. I am grateful for this institutional support, and in particular I thank the Deans of the College of Arts and Sciences for promoting my work.

This book has also benefitted from the criticism of colleagues elsewhere, including Sandra Donaldson, Adrienne Auslander Munich, Beverly Taylor, and the expert staff and readers at Ashgate Publishing. From them, I have received much needed encouragement and correction. Other friends and colleagues read entire early drafts: Lynn Moss Sanders, Amy Johns, and the late H. Patsy Boyer, whose marginal notes enabled me to have one more conversation with her after her death in 2000. I am grateful to David Latané, the editor of *Victorians Institute Journal*, for permission to reprint portions of an article which appeared in Vol. 27.

My debt to Nancy Vosburg is greatest of all: she has inspired me, argued with me, and read every word of this book several times. I also thank the rest of my family for offering me several models of collaborative relationship. And finally, I thank Rory, who studiously reminded me to look up and play.

Introduction

A matched pair, the Gordigiani portraits of the Brownings, seated in their heavy gold frames, dominate the walls of the National Portrait Gallery, where they reside with the portraits of other Victorian writers.[1] The Brownings' position in this room is emblematic: together, they have dominated the twentieth-century imaginative view of the Victorian period. Their story fascinates us: it has been scrutinized in realistic fiction, celebrated on stage, spun out into sentimental biographies, deconstructed in postmodern love stories.[2] Ironically, ever since the publication of their love letters in 1899, the Brownings have inspired the popular imagination not as poets working on a life-long project, but as a sentimental diptych - even though the work of writing was at the core of their relationship.[3]

More obviously, the work of writing was always at the core of the Brownings' separate lives. Fifteen-year-old Elizabeth Barrett noted in an autobiographical essay that, when she was ten, her "poetry was entirely formed by the style of written authors and I read that I might write" (*Correspondence* 1.350). Thus ensued decades of struggle with literary tradition: how to become part of it, how to distinguish herself from it. In an essay about Thomas Chatterton which is at least as revealing about himself as his subject, Robert Browning writes that "Genius almost invariably begins to develop itself by imitation [. . .] and its object is to compete with, or prove superior to, the world's already recognized idols [. . .]". The next

---

[1] Arrangements of the portraits in the National Portrait Gallery change, of course, but the size and frame design of the Browning portraits call attention to them wherever they are placed.

[2] Fictional treatments of the Brownings are, of course, legion. Probably the most influential in terms of the popular imagination has been Rudolph Besier's 1930 psychological (and sentimental) play, *The Barretts of Wimpole Street*, which was made into a film. Henry James' "The Private Life," in which Browning appears as a personality split between everyday ordinariness and poetic intensity, has an obvious appeal for academic readers. Most recently, A. S. Byatt has moved from Browning criticism to fictional treatments of the poets, especially in *Possession* (1990).

[3] Although she does not argue that the courtship correspondence should not have been published, Patricia O'Neil suggests in *Robert Browning and Twentieth-Century Criticism* that the availability of the letters has harmed the literary reputations of both Brownings--damage which began with the earliest reviews.

stage in the development of a literary gift is to "create, and imitate no longer" (*Essay on Chatterton* 111). From childhood, both these poets were profoundly aware of literary influence as contemporary and historical context, both nurturing and stifling. In this sense of influence, they did not influence each other. Instead, I believe, their working relationship was a continuous conversation about balancing the demands of their craft, the requirements of their readers, the debts they owed because of their respective gifts, and the practicalities of working. Perhaps because she was a woman in the masculine world of literature, Barrett Browning was particularly responsive when Browning encouraged her to create her own new literary forms. Through his faith in her work, he granted her permission to experiment, and her great mature work, *Aurora Leigh*, testifies to his support. In contrast, Browning always consciously asserted himself against tradition, but the confusing polyvocality of his early work and the strangeness of his literary forms alienated readers. Elizabeth Barrett enabled him to reconsider the transaction between author and audience which is essential if the written conversation is to continue. She read his work with minute attention, helped him revise it without betraying his own voice or his vision of the world, and urged him to be accessible. To her Browning owed the popularity which finally became his after her death. When the Brownings actually appear in each other's work, they do so as "the audience in the poem."[4]

The Brownings' life together from 1845 to 1861 was a collaboration. During their courtship and marriage, Elizabeth Barrett Browning wrote the most mature and original poetry of her career; at the same time, Robert Browning persisted in developing his vigorous and demanding experimental poems, in spite of the critics who had not yet learned how to read them. The Brownings' life was an ongoing dialogue of mutual influence, agreement and disagreement, love and rivalry. In studying the poetry they wrote during their years together, I try to show how their working relationship enabled each to develop assurance and a greater range of expression. My comparison of these two closely-linked careers shows, too, that literary men and women in the nineteenth century had similarly vexed, if distinctly different, relationships to tradition. The Brownings benefited enormously - but differently - from their relationship. Elizabeth Barrett Browning found that her own voice emerged most clearly in works more dialogic in form and language, more engaged with the contemporary world, than the language of her early poems. Given the strictures of her life before she met him, such language and such engagement could only have

---

[4] The term comes from the title of Dorothy Mermin's 1983 study.

come about in Robert Browning's presence. And through Elizabeth, Robert Browning was able to relax the adversarial stance toward his models and his readers, establishing a more cooperative, though still never easy, relationship with his audience.

Before they encountered each other, Elizabeth Barrett and Robert Browning had worked in what amounted to separate social vacuums, which diffused and defused their creative power. Both were petted and precocious - and artistically isolated. Hope End, the extravagant home Elizabeth Barrett's father built with the family wealth accumulated by generations of Jamaican planters, was geographically isolated in the Malvern Hills. Browning's childhood home in the London suburb of Camberwell, though not isolated in the same way, was made so comfortable for him by his indulgent parents that he never formed the kinds of social ties that most children do. Unrestrained by their parents, both poets learned voraciously. When she was a child, Elizabeth tried to pattern herself after Byron and, in her desire for genius and fame, "went out one day with my pinafore full of little sticks, (& a match from the housemaids cupboard) to sacrifice to the blue-eyed Minerva" (*Correspondence* 11.319). With his father, six-year-old Robert played Homeric games under the furniture (the cat was Helen of Troy) and a few years later eschewed meat and God in imitation of Shelley. "Development," a poetic retrospective in *Asolando* (1889), recounts the way Browning's father first taught him Homer's stories through games, then read with him Pope's translations, and finally oversaw the young poet's study of the original Greek - more satisfying to the poet, ultimately, than any dry lesson from the pages of the *Nicomachean Ethics* or Friedrich Wolf's analysis of the *Iliad* as a product of oral tradition. But there were limits to the pedagogical effectiveness and the cultural riches offered in the homes of both children - and both were still hungry for teachers when they met.

As teenagers, Barrett and Browning moved tentatively out of their social isolation into similar precocious, almost enmeshed friendships with older adults of the opposite sex - in Barrett's case, with the blind classical scholar Hugh Boyd, in Browning's, with Eliza and Sarah Flower, the talented daughters of the radical journalist Benjamin Flower. After these friendships faded, and well into their thirties, both Barrett and Browning remained domestically dependent on their parents, highly aware of but uninitiated into the complexities of adult sexuality, still unsure about how their work would relate to literary tradition and to their readers, and still, despite their productivity as poets, attempting to gain more control over poetic language and form. Both were so committed to their work that they would certainly have continued to grow as artists - but they would not have developed in the same way. Apart, they would not have become the writers we know now as "Robert Browning" and "Elizabeth Barrett Browning."

The pattern of changes in their poetry after 1845, when they began their famous correspondence, suggests that for each of them development as a human being and a poet depended on contact with the creativity and intellectual power of the other. The early twentieth-century Russian theorist Lev Vygotsky's work on educational development suggests that children develop as they are pulled forward by their teachers into ever greater intellectual, creative, and psychic depths, "zones of proximal development," which define abilities "that have not yet matured but are in the process of maturing, functions that will mature tomorrow but are currently in an embryonic state," functions that "could be termed the 'buds' or 'flowers' of development rather than the fruit" (*Mind in Society* 87). The teacher pulls the child through these zones in dialogue. Thus the educational process is always social, whether its content is algebra or etiquette. Mental growth is not simply a function of age; it does not ascend a fixed set of developmental rungs, but expands in an open-ended process through which the subject learns and develops in continual dialogue with her social surroundings.

If the young J. S. Mill suffered an excess of such pulling, the young Barrett and Browning suffered a dearth of it. As a result, each lacked the confidence of being understood. Similar as Barrett and Browning were in ability, bourgeois background, and poetic interests, each also needed to be pulled forward by the different strengths of the other and taught by the other's complementary magisterial qualities. Clyde de L. Ryals remarks that, until their flight to Italy forced them into worldly maturity, both Barrett and Browning had lived in a state of "prolonged childhood" (*The Life of Robert Browning* 90).[5] Thus, their chronological maturity did not make this dialogic process any less necessary, and each eagerly cast the other in the role of teacher.

Anyone reading these poets together confronts the fact that their critical history is unequal. This disparity is most apparent in the condition of the *oeuvres* themselves: three modern editions of Browning's collected works are available; for Barrett Browning, only *Sonnets from the Portuguese*, *Casa Guidi Windows* and *Aurora Leigh* are available in editions published according to contemporary scholarly standards. Furthermore, there are long silences with regard to Barrett Browning, who was popular during her

---

[5] Several other biographers, particularly Betty Miller (*Robert Browning: A Portrait*, 1952) and Daniel Karlin (*The Courtship of Robert Browning and Elizabeth Barrett*, 1987), have also made the argument that the Brownings' psychic development depended upon each other.

lifetime, revived in the 1970s by the project of feminist criticism, and read since then primarily (though not solely) in terms of the intellectual and creative work of women. Although modern criticism has seldom explored other aspects of Barrett Browning's work,[6] Browning's poetic language has always been scrutinized - since Mill reacted with dismay to the twenty-year old poet's *Pauline* in 1833 - from a variety of perspectives. Whereas Browning's contemporary Tennyson strove for transparency, Browning's meaning always floats between possibilities. If his contemporaries usually balked at the effort his poetry required, and the next generation of Browning readers undertook to smooth out the language and extract a unitary meaning, then later critics have embraced Browning's polyvocality, his irony, his indeterminacy. There are many ways to describe Browning's poetic language. Some of the most productive since the mid-twentieth century have been W. David Shaw's dialectical readings of the poetry; Herbert Tucker's deconstructionist approach; and most recently Donald S. Hair's research into Browning's own linguistic and philosophical studies, which suggests that what Browning termed late in life "parleyings" - open-ended conversations among author, subject/s, and audiences inside or outside the poem - may be a kind of metagenre which explains Browning's poetic language from the beginning.

Within the last twenty years, a number of critics have also read individual works by both Robert Browning and Elizabeth Barrett Browning from the theoretical perspective of Mikhail Bakhtin, a contemporary of Vygotsky whose dialogic theory posits, like Vygotsky's, the social construction of all linguistic activity. Bakhtin's work explores how writers exploit these properties of language to enrich the aesthetic experience, represent metaphorically the way language really works, and involve the reader. Because Bakhtin has so much to say about dialogue in both literature and extra-literary speech acts, his theory provides a useful lens through which to examine the work of *both* poets, together, in historical context. Bakhtin's work also addresses the central tropes shared by both poets, particularly that of translation. One of the basic assumptions of Vygotsky's and

---

[6] Although it focuses on gender, Tricia Lootens' *Lost Saints: Silence, Gender, and Victorian Literary Canonization* (1996) begins by noting a shift in Barrett Browning's critical history which allows her to examine Barrett Browning's reception within mainstream trends, as well as with respect to other women writers. Other recent critical work which focuses on issues other than gender issues include Antony H. Harrison's work on Barrett Browning's epic as a response to imperialism in *Victorian Poets and the Politics of Culture: Discourse and Ideology* (1998).

Bakhtin's milieu - and an increasingly compelling idea in the postmodern age - is that the individual's mind and language are the products of interactions with other people and with history; since we constantly experience new things, our minds continue to develop and our language continues to change.[7] For them, dialogue is the essential fact of human identity because it is the essential force in language: as long as it remains alive, language - even literary language on the printed page - can never be completely fixed, but must instead be fluid, inhabited by various voices and meanings in agreement or in conflict. For Bakhtin, the literary genre which most successfully captures this aspect of living language is the novel, which happened to be, in England as well as Russia, what he calls the "dominant" of the Victorian age. The poetry of the Brownings tends toward this dominant in different ways. The critical tradition of attention to Browning's language is important for a reader who wishes to come to terms with Robert Browning alone, but Bakhtin's more flexible theory provides the principle frame of reference for this book, explicitly or implicitly. Because Bakhtin's work comprehends writing and speech, the word and the work, literary and extraliterary speech acts, and the constitution of human relationships through language, the poems of both Brownings are highly responsive to it.

From the beginning of their acquaintance, the two poets were attracted by the possibility of mutual exchange, and after they met and moved to Italy, their poetry mirrored even more clearly the intensified personal and erotic dialogue between them. If, through their private dialogue, the Brownings contributed to each other's emotional and intellectual growth, the concern of this study is how that growth is reflected in their writing. After the poets began to work together in early 1845, Elizabeth Barrett, especially, began to write a more confident and fluid language. In Bakhtin's terminology, her work started to become more "novelistic" - more flexible and open to the potential of language for change and renewal in the presence of a reader, a listener, a partner in dialogue. At least on the surface, Barrett's earlier work fitted nicely within the lyric tradition she

---

[7] Vygotsky and Bakhtin consciously follow Marx, of course. Their line of psychological and linguistic inquiry breaks away from Kantian metaphysics in minimizing the importance of inherent psychological structures and also breaks away from the behaviorists and Freud by socializing, rather than privatizing, psychological phenomena and by focusing on the conscious rather than the unconscious. In his experiments in pedagogy, Vygotsky's immediate antagonist was Piaget. Vygotsky and Bakhtin also break away from Saussure's conceptions about the internal structures of language, which are fundamental to so much twentieth-century thinking about language.

inherited, but she was not content with the position relegated to women poets. Novel reading had been a passion since her childhood, and with her husband's encouragement, the novel would provide a way out of the poetic place she had been assigned. For Browning, on the other hand, the reader became more real as a result of Barrett's mediation; and Browning's increased awareness of the reader's needs is also an issue addressed in the works of Bakhtin, for whom the conscious (and conscientious) reader has the last word about meaning. Robert Browning's early work had already represented a radical departure from the lyric self-centeredness of his Romantic predecessors: in his early non-dramatic poems, he often mimicked the narrative complexity of the novel. But, unable to convey the breadth of his new conceptions, he stalled, isolated as a poet, until he found in Elizabeth Barrett the aware, sympathetic and communicative reader he needed. In the great poems of his middle years with Elizabeth, he learned to make his poetry accessible to readers, thus extending the dialogue from its location within the poem to a pragmatic position outside its borders as well.

Cross-generational literary influence studies have long been a staple of literary scholarship, although such influence is difficult to prove. Feminist scholarship, on the other hand, has emphasized the work of women writers, whose lives have usually been lived most fully within domestic settings, and whose works therefore lend themselves to a different kind of comparatism, to lateral comparisons among artists living together in the same domestic environment, for instance. The domestic environment, as distinguished from the cultural or historical environment foregrounded in traditional comparative studies, suggests a different kind of influence, which has been the subject of several important biographical studies in the last decade, including an important article on the Brownings, "The Domestic Economy of Art: Elizabeth Barrett and Robert Browning" by Mermin, and Julia Markus's fine 1995 biography of the Brownings.[8] My work builds on theirs, focusing on the major works the Brownings wrote during their years together.

---

[8] Markus's title is *Dared and Done: The Marriage of Elizabeth Barrett and Robert Browning*. Family biographies, such as the classic joint biography of the Brontës by Fanny Ratchford, *The Brontës' Web of Childhood* (1941), and a recent one by Juliet Barker, *The Brontës* (1994), have been popular for a long time. Lately, biographers have also begun to study the intimate relationships of artist and writer couples. Among the best works of this kind is *Significant Others: Creativity & Intimate Partnership* (1993), a collection of biographical essays edited by Whitney Chadwick and Isabelle de Courtivron.

Examining the ways in which two intimately connected artists affect each other's work is of the utmost importance in understanding creative process and in fully appreciating the work of the individual artists themselves. As Myra Jehlen pointed out two decades ago in a *Signs* article, "Archimedes and the Paradox of Feminist Criticism" (1981), if feminist scholars would adopt "a radical comparatism," studying the works of women writers within the masculinist literary tradition, then the influence of tradition on female *and* male writers would become more understandable (79). Jehlen's suggestion applies as well to scholars who study male authors, for they, too, live and work within a gendered literary tradition and a gendered social environment. Indeed, this was an early trend in Browning studies, exemplified by an essay written on the "Married Poets" by Elizabeth's friend Mary Russell Mitford in 1852. Early in the twentieth century, Lillian Whiting published *The Brownings: Their Life and Art*. In 1929, a joint biography by Osbert Burdett helped to perpetuate the sentimental Browning myth by characterizing the two poets as types of the masculine and feminine. More recently, Mary Rose Sullivan has written convincingly about episodes of mutual literary influence between the Brownings.[9] In general, however, comparative critical studies of literary productions by men and women are still lacking, and my own work will, I hope, help to fill this gap in Browning studies.

This book is a comparative study of the Brownings' poetry written between 1845 and 1861. The influence they had on each other was powerful but not dominating. Although his respect for Elizabeth Barrett Browning's work was enormous, Robert Browning did not copy or borrow from it, nor did Elizabeth borrow from Robert's work, despite her admiration for it, and despite her consciousness that she owed her mature power to the freedom she experienced in her life with him. Instead, the two poets supported and criticized each other, urged each other forward, and drew inspiration from common interests. A parallel examination of their works, written in the different keys of their histories and personalities, allows us to hear differences, but also allows us to hear how the work of each resonated with the poetry of the other.

The literary relationship between these two began before they met in 1844, when Browning read Barrett's description in "Lady Geraldine's Courtship" of his own poetry, as a

---

[9] Sullivan's articles are "Some Interchange of Grace" (1987), about *Saul* and the *Sonnets*, and "Elizabeth Barrett Browning and the Art of Collaboration" (1991), which explains that the Brownings never collaborated in the usual sense because Barrett Browning's earlier attempts to do so had been problematic.

'Pomegranate,' which, if cut deep down the middle,
Shows a heart within blood-tinctured, of a veined humanity [. . .].

The attraction resulted partly from their mutual scholarly interests. Barrett and Browning were impressively self-educated, and both were particularly interested in classical and modern languages. In the poetry of both, English is continually infiltrated by other languages and the realities these other languages represent. Before they met, the poetry of Elizabeth Barrett and Robert Browning already sounded alike. Both habitually stretched meter to its limits; both experimented with rhyme, favoring various incomplete rhymes. Both brought the sounds of poetry closer to the sounds of speech. Although they deployed different poetic forms, there was considerable overlap in their choices. Both experimented with masks and impersonations, and they wrote dramatic monologues, probably even before they read each other's poetry. Both meditated on the relationship between the art of their time and the traditions which gave rise to it, and both were interested in marginal or grotesque characters and situations. A parallel study of these two poets increases our understanding of how each was circumscribed by the limitations of gender - and how they helped each other to renegotiate their gendered roles as poets and lovers. Barrett Browning's readers have typically noticed how her work reflected and affected gender ideologies; our understanding of Browning's work will become more profound as more scholars also consider his work in this context.[10]

It is not surprising that, even before they met, the two poets were conscious of being in a dialogue with each other. After they met, the Brownings created an environment which fostered the poetic impulses they had in common. And during their years together, their poetry became, in different ways, increasingly dialogic. Engaged in daily intimate dialogue, they became more aware of the productive frictions within language and between languages, the productive conflicts within and among artistic forms, the energy released by challenging literary tradition, and the nature of the "interindividual word."[11] This was the "flower" of their mutual development: they confirmed in each other the impulse toward poetic

---

[10] Indeed, John Woolford's *Robert Browning in Contexts* (1998) suggests a new trend, of which my own study is a part.

[11] Bakhtin uses the term "inter-individual word" in "The Problem of the Text" (121) to emphasize that the meaning of a word is not simply the idea invested in it by the speaker and not simply the way it is understood by the listener, but that the meaning of the word is suspended in the space among sender, receiver, and past meanings of the word.

language that could, as Bakhtin says of the novel, represent "an indeterminacy, a certain semantic openendedness, a living contact with unfinished, still-evolving contemporary reality" ("Epic and Novel" 7).

Out of this relationship came two bodies of poetry which, though distinct, nevertheless reflect a belief in literary language as a profound and endless drama. In Bakhtin's words,

> The author [. . .] has his own inalienable right to the word, but the listener also has his rights, and those whose voices are heard in the word before the author comes upon it also have their rights (after all, there are no words that belong to no one). The word is a drama in which three characters participate [. . .]. ("The Problem of the Text" 122-23)

Together, they came to a deeper understanding that socially determined meaning is a necessary dimension of poetry. And by the time they wrote their major works - Barrett Browning's *Aurora Leigh* (1856) and Browning's *Men and Women* (1855) and *The Ring and the Book* (1868-69) - the poetry of each resonates with the poetry of the other.

The comparison I wish to make requires examination of four different periods in the Brownings' lives. To underscore how profoundly they affected one another, I have focused in the first chapter on the early careers of the two poets. I have done this partly in order to avoid the usual temptation which besets both close and casual readers - that is, to read backwards from the major works of canonical writers, finding in the early writing sure promise of the later. What strikes me about both the Brownings is in fact the difference between the work before and after 1845, not the continuity. Second, it goes without saying that the period of the Brownings' courtship is important in understanding their poetry because some of their most striking compositions come from this short and intense period, and because this period of less than two years set the course of their artistic development for the rest of their lives; Chapters 2 and 3 address the poetry they produced during this time. Most of this book focuses on the years in Italy (Chapters 4 through 7). In an afterword, I treat an episode in Robert Browning's creative life after Elizabeth's death.

Saul, the focal point of Chapter 3, was published as a fragment at Barrett's urging in 1845. Browning had stalled in working on this poem partly because it attempts to negotiate among conflicting, but always erotically charged, artistic representations of the characters David and Saul; in addition, *Saul* is a provocative mix of genres which Browning was unable to merge until the early 1850s, after he had begun work on the new monologues of *Men and Women*. While reading *Saul*, among Browning's other works in progress, Barrett was secretly transforming the traditional masculinist sonnet sequence through the poems in *Sonnets from the Portuguese*, which, as Loy Martin has shown, in many ways resemble the dramatic monologues Browning published in his 1845 collection, *Dramatic Lyrics and Romances*.[12] Although she is still far from the novelized language of her great work, the sonnets, as I show in Chapter 4, signal a change in Barrett's lyrical approach, moving away from the "unitary and singular language" Bakhtin associates with most poetic genres. In these poems, she begins to develop a kind of doubleness as she positions herself both inside and outside the traditional sonnet sequence. Unlike the conventional sonneteer, she is female; and she refers ironically to the conventions of the sonnet sequence itself, which usually serves as a substitute for rather than a prelude to physical love. But so little did Barrett trust that this new poetic idiom could be understood that she showed the poems to no one, not even Robert Browning, until three years after she had completed them.

After the Brownings left England together in September, 1846, they underwent profound changes in outlook, work habits, and creative process. In Chapter 5, I show that in *Christmas-Eve and Easter-Day* (1850), Browning departs from his usual style to compose a major work exploring religious controversies in a personal voice. The subject of these two interlocking poetic essays is faith; Browning undertook the project when exile and marriage, fatherhood, productive disagreements with Barrett Browning on religious and political issues, and the death of his mother challenged his own faith. Like *Casa Guidi Windows*, Barrett's poem of the same period, *Christmas-Eve and Easter-Day* is atypical. In order to write discursively, Browning had to redirect the impulses which originally had drawn him to the dramatic mode - his interest in psychology and his hesitation about revealing in poetry his private feelings. From the mine of literary history, he drew up the ancient form of Menippean satire, a serio-comic, proto-novelistic genre so alien to the tastes of his Victorian reading public that they complained of obscurity - the typical objection to much of his earlier poetry as well. In *Casa Guidi Windows*, written between 1848 and 1851, Barrett Browning also departs from her usual subject matter to examine what it means to be a woman poet witnessing the Risorgimento. As I show in Chapter 6, at the end of the poem, the focus becomes blurred: the ambiguity of Barrett Browning's own role as woman/ poet parallels the indeterminacy of the move for Italian reunification, and she has not yet fully integrated historical authority into her own female poetic voice. The poem is less unified than most of her work.

---

[12] *Browning's Dramatic Monologues and the Post-Romantic Subject* (1985).

By 1853, however, Barrett Browning was well on her way to completing *Aurora Leigh*, which was finally published in 1856, and Browning would soon be writing the poems which would become *Men and Women*, published a year earlier than his wife's great work.[13] The period in which these poems were composed is the focal point of Chapters 7 and 8. Both poets had overcome the creative disorganization of their early years in Italy. At the height of their powers, both were experimenting successfully, and Browning had a clearer sense of audience than ever before. The title character of Barrett Browning's novel poem is a woman poet whose characteristic internal and social languages are dialogic. Into her poetry, Aurora Leigh learns to introduce heteroglossia - multiple viewpoints, multiple layers of language, multiple meanings - and this new way of creating enriches and deepens her literary expression, much as Barrett Browning's work developed. Like the prose Victorian novel, this long poem layers different narratives and encloses many literary and extraliterary genres such as letters and diaries. Like other realistic novels, *Aurora Leigh* is also an attempt to represent the real lives of women in Victorian society - and so it challenges the conventions and subject matter of mainstream Victorian poetry. During this time, Browning returned to the dramatic monologue - the poetic genre in which he had worked most successfully between 1836 and 1845. As he had developed it, the dramatic monologue resembles the novel in its psychological complexity and the way it represents individual voices. By 1855, when he published *Men and Women*, Browning's poems were more varied and complex, and they spoke to each other in more complex ways. Like *Aurora Leigh*, they take up a range of subjects which challenge contemporary assumptions about life, art, and the gender polarities which troubled Victorian society. Some of them, such as "Old Pictures in Florence," fictionalize the poet himself.

After the publication of her major work in 1856, Elizabeth Barrett Browning's chronic illnesses reasserted themselves, taking a toll on her productivity and the quality of her life. But despite her illnesses, she continued to write shorter works which critiqued both domestic life and the political lives of nations. In *Poems before Congress* (1860) and *Last Poems* (1861), she granted herself greater expressive freedom than ever before.

---

[13] Dating most of the poems in *Men and Women* on the basis of external evidence is virtually impossible because this evidence is self-contradictory, and dating them according to internal evidence is risky. However, according to the Introduction to *Men and Women* (Oxford 1995) by Ian Jack and Robert Inglesfield, the only poem in the collection indubitably written before 1853 is "The Guardian Angel." Most of the poems were probably composed between 1853 and 1855 (ix-xiv).

The brevity of such works as "Lord Walter's Wife" and "Mother and Poet" should not obscure their technical virtuosity and their generic similarity to the dramatic monologues which Browning had published in 1855, and which he continued to write for his next collection, *Dramatis Personae* (1863).

Elizabeth Barrett Browning's presence never quite abandoned Browning. After her death in 1861, Browning's later work overtly or covertly continues to suggest her influence. The tribute to her at the conclusion to the introductory section in *The Ring and the Book* is simply the best known of many works and passages alluding to Elizabeth:

O lyric Love, half-angel and half-bird
And all a wonder and a wild desire, --
Boldest of hearts that ever braved the sun [. . .]
Never may I commence my song, my due
To God who best taught song by gift of thee,
Except with bent head and beseeching hand --
That still, despite the distance and the dark,
What was, again may be; some interchange
Of grace, some splendour once thy very thought,
Some benediction anciently thy smile [. . .]. (I.1391-93, 1403-09)

The strength of the Brownings' dialogue is especially clear in a joyous poem Browning wrote ten years after his wife's death - *Balaustion's Adventure*, a novel poem about the "interchange of grace" which comes from a story well told. The story and the meaning are multi-layered. The witty and attractive heroine, a refugee from Athens whose name, Balaustion, means "flower of the wild pomegranate," "tells" Euripides' latest play to the people of a war-weary city. Balaustion's account of *Alkestis*, the story of a wife who sacrifices her life for her husband's and is then literally rescued from the underworld, brings hope and healing to the populace and to her own Athenian shipmates. As I will suggest in the last chapter, the *Adventure* reflects, in the mirror of art, much about the Brownings' relationship as poets, storytellers, scholars, rivals, and married lovers.

The iconic significance of these two poets diminishes in proportion to what we know about their working relationship. That loss, I believe, represents an incalculable gain. No longer an emblem of Victorian romantic love, they become an example of two people who enable each other to live against the odds, to thrive, love, and create art.

In the waning days of 1844, when Browning read about himself in Barrett's new book, how did he know what they might become for one another? Why, on 10 January, 1845, did he risk declaring love to a woman he had never met? That now famous declaration itself suggests the answer:

> I love your verses with all my hear, dear Miss Barrett, -- and this is no off-hand complimentary letter that I shall write,--whatever else, no prompt matter-of-course recognition of your genius and there a graceful and natural end of the thing: since the day last week when I first read your poems, I quite laugh to remember how I have been turning and turning again in my mind what I shouid be able to tell you of their effect upon me -- for in the first flush of delight I thought I would this once get out of my habit of purely passive enjoyment, when I do really enjoy, and thoroughly justify my admiration -- perhaps even, as a loyal fellow-craftsman should, try and find fault and do you some little good to be proud of hereafter! -- but nothing comes of it al l-- so into me has it gone, and part of me has it become, this great living poetry of yours, not a flower of which but took root and grew [. . .]. After all, I need not give up the thought of doing that, too, in time; because, even now [. . .] I can give a reason for my faith in one and another excellence, the fresh strange music, the affluent language, the exquisite pathos and true new brave thought--but in this addressing myself to you, your own self, and for the first time, my feeling rises altogether. I do, as I say, love these Books with all my heart--and I love you too [. . .]. (*Correspondence* 10.17)[14]

Browning loved the texture, wealth, and strangeness of Barrett's poetic language. He admired her feeling and her intellect. Most of all, her poetry spoke directly to him, involved him, included him in a dialogue which he could only imagine as open-ended, and which demanded a response.

Barrett answered the next day, in kind: "Such a letter from such a hand! Sympathy is dear -- very dear to me: but the sympathy of a poet & such a poet, is the quintessence of sympathy to me!" She, too, hoped the dialogue would not end: "if ever you emerge without inconvenient effort from your 'passive state,' & will <u>tell</u> me of such faults as rise to the surface & strike you as important in my poems [. . .] you will confer a lasting obligation on me, and one which I shall value so much, that I covet it at a distance" (*Correspondence* 10.18-10). Thus began a conversation about poetry which lasted, in love and rivalry, eros and argument, for the rest of her life, and in many ways the rest of Robert Browning's.

With every stage of this conversation, each poet became more integrated as an artist: Barrett, by bringing together in her works the political with the emotional and the aesthetic; and Browning, by entering into a more open,

---

[14] Both Brownings frequently used a two-dot ellipsis to indicate a slight pause. When such ellipses are *not* enclosed with brackets, that is because they are part of the original text. The ellipses in the quotations above represent my deletions.

authentic exchange with his readers, which resulted finally in greater clarity, with greater moral and aesthetic complexity.

Chapter 1

Art and Inexperience
1806-1844

The last manifesto of the Romantic age, Shelley's *Defense of Poetry*, proclaims that "Poetry ever communicates all the pleasure which men are capable of receiving; it is ever still the light of life; the source of whatever of beautiful, or generous, or true can have place in an evil time." Shelley goes on to claim that the spirit of poetry has been responsible for "the abolition of personal and domestic slavery, and the emancipation of women from a great part of the degrading restraints of antiquity," and finally he declares that poetry is the "influence which is moved not, but moves. Poets are the unacknowledged legislators of the World" (493, 496, 508).[1] Shelley's polemic was written as a private joke with his friend Peacock in 1821; there is an element of play in his exaggeration which often escapes readers unaware of the context. Still, the *Defense* does express a Romantic view of the poet similar to that in Wordsworth's 1802 Preface to *Lyrical Ballads* and Coleridge's *Biographia Literaria*, published in 1817, and serves as a theoretical description of Byronic practice. The Romantics did believe that poetry - and the person of the poet - should have a powerful impact on public life.

Although Shelley's essay ranks with the theoretical pronouncements of Wordsworth and Coleridge as a description of the Romantic project, by the time Mary Shelley finally published her husband's essay in 1840, its premises presented a problematic model, seductive yet impractical. In the decades after Shelley's death, neither poets nor their public could still believe that spiritual and moral enlightenment automatically derived from contemplation of the beautiful and the true: Browning's boyhood ambition had been fired by Shelley's poetry, but Shelley was an inadequate model for him by the time Browning was twenty. By the time Elizabeth Barrett and Robert Browning had come to literary maturity, pleasure was considered a secondary characteristic of poetry.

---

[1] *A Defense of Poetry* in *Shelley's Poetry and Prose*, ed. Donald H. Reiman and Sharon B. Powers. A Norton Critical Edition.

i. Elizabeth Barrett Moulton Barrett

Barrett commented in the Preface to her 1844 *Poems* that "Poetry has been as serious a thing to me as life itself; and life has been a very serious thing: there has been no playing at skittles for me in either. I never mistook pleasure for the final cause of poetry; nor leisure, for the hour of the poet" (104).[2] Though they felt that poetry carried distinct moral and ethical weight, most Victorian poets and readers believed that the lessons of art worked indirectly, within the privacy of the individual human heart. Few credited poets with the moral, spiritual, or political power of Shelley's Utopian analysis. Elizabeth Barrett, for one, was a careful and critical reader of Shelley. Although attracted to his poetry, she questioned his sentiments, his logic, and, in reference to *Prometheus Unbound*, his competence as a Greek scholar.[3]

Indeed, in one of her most quintessential Victorian statements, "The Poet's Vow," Barrett suggests the opposite of the Shelleyan impulse - that, if pursued with exclusive dedication, poetry can be destructive. In five parts, reminiscent of Coleridge's "The Rime of the Ancient Mariner" and Mary Shelley's *Frankenstein*, Barrett's ballad "The Poet's Vow" narrates the story of a poet who withdraws from human life in order to contemplate nature and to create, godlike, his own works. Striking an explicitly feminist note, the poet's fiancée Rosalind refuses to be "bought and sold" when she is "given" by the poet, along with his ancestral hall, to his more conventional (and more moral) friend Sir Roland. Only too late does the poet realize his own responsibility toward other human beings and learn the truth that human life is part of a continuum with nature: splitting off the "human" from the natural, the artistic and intellectual from the spiritual and emotional, inevitably results in death. Rosalind dies of sorrow, her poet of remorse and grief; over their grave, Sir Roland considers:

"That God's own unity compresses
    (One into one) the human many,
And that his everlastingness is
    The bond that is not loosed by any:
That thou and I this law must keep,
    If not in love, in sorrow then, --

---

[2] Unless otherwise noted, all quotations from Barrett Browning's poetry and essays are from *The Works of Elizabeth Barrett Browning* (1994), Ed. Karen Hill.

[3] For insight into Barrett's reading of Shelley, see her published marginalia in "Elizabeth Barrett's Commentary on Shelley" by James Thorpe.

Though smiling not like other men,
   Still, like them we must weep."

Instead of emphasizing the sheer power of the imagination and assuming the vatic stance of the Romantic poets, during the early years of Victoria's reign, poets were more involved, suggests Mermin, in a struggle "to make a source of power [. . .] for [. . .] poetry out of [the] experience of constriction, exclusion, renunciation, and rebellion." According to Mermin's analysis, it is a fortunate irony of history that because a woman's lot and a poet's were felt in similar terms during the Victorian period

> [. . .] it was possible for [Barrett] to create the first major female voice in English poetry out of the specifically female struggle to enter the poetic tradition. ("Elizabeth Barrett Browning through 1844," 714).

But if Barrett's historical moment enabled her to express the struggle of the artist to draw power from pain and conflict, then history was in other respects unkind to her. The idea that poetry can be made out of individual struggle is essentially historical, and with the development of historical consciousness came additional problems for intellectual women: women were not a part of recorded history; they did not see themselves in history, and they were not seen. The first victim in Barrett's parable about the Romantic poet is, after all, the woman who has loved him. If the male poets of the nineteenth century suffered from "anxiety of influence," then women poets suffered from the lack of influence, and a perception that female literary tradition was very thin. Barrett worried the question of the female writer over and over, and she described her own sense of deprivation in 1845, in a letter to the critic Henry Fothergill Chorley:[4]

> England has had many learned women, not merely readers but writers of the learned languages, in Elizabeth's time & afterwards, -- women of deeper acquirements than are common now in the greater diffusion of letters: and yet where were the poetesses? The divine breath which seemed to come & go, &, ere it went, filled the land with that crowd of true poets whom we call the old dramatists, . . why did it never pass even in the lyrical form over the lips of a woman? How strange! And can we deny that it was so? I look everywhere for Grandmothers & see none. It is not in the filial spirit I am deficient, I do assure you -- witness my reverent love of the grandfathers! -- (*Correspondence* 10.14)

---

[4] On the whole, Chorley, who wrote for the *Athenaeum*, had a balanced view of both the Brownings. In 1851, he anonymously suggested Elizabeth Barrett Browning as a competitor with Tennyson for the post of poet laureate.

Two contemporary women poets, Letitia Landon (LEL) and Felicia Hemens, were, in fact, the subject of several poems by Elizabeth Barrett and of frequent speculation in Barrett's conversations with various correspondents. In fact, her remarks to Chorley about a female literary tradition are part of the explanation she offers him for this lack of a female "line" in poetry: Barrett anticipates Virginia Woolf's argument in *A Room of One's Own* that the lack of a female literary tradition requires an explanation beyond the cliché that women are intellectually deficient. Women did, she felt, write genuine poetry which was unsupported by their cultural environment and therefore not as good as it could have been. She continues in her letter to Chorley:

> Of poor LEL, for instance I could write with <u>more</u> praiseful appreciation than you can. It appears to me that she had the gift, though in certain respects, she dishonored the art -- & her later lyrics are, many of them, of great beauty & melody [. . .]. (*Correspondence* 10.14)

Elsewhere, in Barrett's view, LEL was more sinned against than sinning, her commercialized and inferior art the result of her own difficult life. The problem, then, was more complex than a lack of grandmothers, or even undue attention to the grandfathers. Christina Crosby has theorized that the nineteenth-century rise of historical consciousness in itself created a more extreme sense of sexual difference, that:

> Constructing history as the necessary condition of human life, as so many nineteenth-century texts do, ensures that "man" can emerge as an abstraction, can know himself in history, find his origin there and project his end -- but only if there is something other than history, something intrinsically unhistorical. "Women" are the unhistorical other of history. (*The Ends of History* 1)

It is not coincidental that historical consciousness accompanied the split between the public and private spheres and the relegation of women to the private, and that reactions against this ideology came to be termed "the woman question." For women, the self became even more critically other than before; the concept of individual subjectivity - the basis of what is most distinctive about nineteenth-century Western thought - is thus problematized for women. During her youth, Barrett actually witnessed a paradigm shift - the growing ascendancy of masculine individuality and subjectivity as cultural values. And because female subjectivity was not an articulated value, she therefore also witnessed herself becoming more marginalized.

Reading her *oeuvre* from start to finish, one can trace, through the early years, a continually more acute awareness of this marginalization, which reveals itself in the split between the lyrical and discursive impulses in her poetry, the division of the intellectual from the emotional. In an excellent and much-needed study of her early work, Antony H. Harrison argues that these "substantial and aesthetically polished" early poems by Elizabeth Barrett reveal an acute and sophisticated political awareness (75) and notes that reviewers of *The Seraphim* praised her "masculine" intelligence. Nevertheless, noting the consistency with which Barrett separates emotion from reason in her work underscores how her poetry became more profound and more dialogic after her long, living conversation with Robert Browning began. Although, as we shall see, in later years, the rifts within her poetry gradually healed, at first she was sensitive to the way her work was perceived, and feared equally the roles of bluestocking and poetess. Typically, in Barrett's early work, the scholar/ translator is separated from the lyric poet so that Barrett's considerable learning openly informs the imitations of Greek drama, but breathes not a whisper in the ballads and occasional lyrics. The sonnets and other lyric poems about abstract human experiences such as "Vanities," "Bereavement," and "Consolation" are qualitatively different from the appealing ballads which she herself took less seriously. During these early years, Barrett almost never contaminated genres with features from other genres, despite the theoretical disposition to do so which she expressed in *An Essay on Mind*. Her early work was entirely monologic, its ironies openly expressed. She was self-censored and, in Bakhtin's term, "single-voiced." Despite ample evidence in this early work that she wished to break out of the bounds of tradition, she stayed, for the most part, within the boundaries of received literary form. Barrett waited longer than most major poets to find a voice which expressed her self, her experience, her perspective, and her own particular music. Not until relatively late in her career was Barrett able to write in the flexible style that we now associate with her best poetry - because during her young adulthood, Barrett's was a poetic of concealment rather than communication. When Barrett was a child, the only poetic tradition of which she was aware was the male tradition. Even when she discovered contemporary women poets, she was still unable to depend on maternal strength in either art or daily life, so she continued to trust in patriarchal models.

Part of Barrett's future growth as a poet would depend upon her ability to reclaim the feminine and trust in it. And it is a happy irony that her connection with Robert Browning made this possible. With him, she would learn to trust her own strength and became part of the world. In the world, she would find, not only women who needed someone to speak for them, but other women, too, who thought and worked with strength and power for honorable ends.

Elizabeth Barrett Moulton Barrett was born on March 6, 1806, near the home of her maternal grandparents in the County of Durham. She was the first child of Edward Moulton Barrett and Mary Graham-Clarke, the daughter of a Newcastle merchant. Three years after her birth, Edward moved his family to a fanciful and isolated mansion in the Malvern Hills prophetically named Hope End (after the small valley which enclosed it), which he had built with family wealth accumulated by generations of Jamaican sugar planters. Here, Elizabeth passed an idyllic childhood, surrounded by younger brothers and sisters and adoring parents.

Early likenesses of Elizabeth taken by her mother, a talented portraitist, suggest humor, energy, intelligence, and a mischievous temperament. Almost everything in her early life, including the talent and intellect of her mother, who directed her earliest studies, seemed to support her creative impulses. By her own account, she ran wild in the woods surrounding her home and rode her pony Minnie. Her father paid the printing costs for her earliest forays into publication, though his praise was sometimes grudging.[5] The tutor employed for her younger brother Edward ("Bro") gave equal time to the sister's classical education, and she also pursued her studies independently in her father's large library.[6]

After a healthy childhood, Elizabeth seemed devastated by puberty after her favorite sibling Bro left for school, and baffled physicians could not agree about the nature of her complaints. Although Elizabeth did not lapse immediately into invalidism, she lost most of the quick social impulses of her childhood and increasingly devoted her energy to books. In 1826,

---

[5] Barrett wrote about her early life, not only in her correspondence with Browning, but in several autobiographical essays included in *The Brownings Correspondence*. The untitled essay in which she fictionalizes herself as "Beth" shows Barrett to have been energetic, witty, and affectionate (*Correspondence* 1. 360-62). One of the crises of her youth, recounted in another untitled autobiographical essay (*Correspondence* 1.358-60), was Edward Barrett's harsh response to "The Development of Genius," on which she labored almost a year when she was twenty. The Byronic speaker resembles that of Browning's speaker in *Pauline*.

[6] In the preface to a posthumous edition of his wife's poems, Browning wrote, "In point of fact, she was self-taught in almost every respect" (*Poems by Elizabeth Barrett Browning, Selected and Arranged by Robert Browning*, iv). Browning stressed Barrett Browning's intellectual vigor and pointed out that she had been unaided in fundamental ways as she struggled to become a poet.

Barrett met and began a correspondence with the elderly scholar Sir Uvedale Price, who was charmed by her first collection of poetry, *An Essay on Mind, with Other Poems*. Their correspondence was devoted almost entirely to poetry and scholarship, and, in one twelve-page letter to Price - one of her earliest pieces of literary theory - Barrett challenges Price's authority on matters of Greek, Latin, and English prosody ("The Art of Scansion"). It is obvious from the sprightly style of these letters that Barrett had begun to channel her childhood mischief and playfulness into scholarship and poetry. Shortly after her friendship with Price had begun, she also became acquainted with the blind classical scholar Hugh Boyd, with whom she developed a much deeper relationship. Boyd encouraged her study of Greek and her facility for translation; he also found her useful as a reader and came to depend on her scholarly acumen. She persisted in this friendship for several years, despite Boyd's heavy emotional demands and the resistance of her own family as well as his.

In 1827, the Barrett family was shocked by the sudden death of Elizabeth's maternal grandmother, followed by the even more profound loss of Elizabeth's mother less than a year later. The example of her mother's lost and buried gifts must have been terrifying: years after her mother died, she wrote to her future husband that Mary Moulton Barrett had been "One of those women who can never resist, -- but, in submitting & bowing on themselves, make a mark, a plait, within, a sign of suffering" (*Correspondence* 13.305-06). Throughout the ten years after his wife's death, family tensions continued to rise as Edward Moulton Barrett suffered serious financial losses, which he kept secret from his children.[7] The sale of Hope End and the family's removal to London in 1837 was sudden and unexpected, as was the death of Elizabeth's brother Sam from a fever in Jamaica in February 1840. But the most serious blow was Bro's drowning only six months later at Torquay, where Elizabeth had been sent for the sea air. She felt the more guilty because she had insisted that Bro stay with her, even after their father had summoned him back to London. In the house on Wimpole Street, overcome by grief and guilt, she shut herself in a third-story room with sealed windows and two thick doors. Since she had vowed never again to break up the family in search of better health, this course was for her the only acceptable defense against the London weather, pollution, and noise. Barrett's health and spirits continued to decline. She became addicted to opium, the only available relief from physical pain, and

---

[7] Since the beginning of the century, Cuban sugar had gradually driven down the price of the Jamaican product; the abolition of slavery in the British colonies in 1833 was the last in a series of reverses suffered by this industry, which had enriched the English middle class, including the Barrett and Browning families.

emotionally dependent on her father, who held her hands in prayer every evening before he retired to bed. She ate almost nothing, and had it not been for her golden-haired spaniel Flush, a gift from Mitford, she might have relaxed her hold on life altogether. But since she was not burdened with any of the domestic duties expected of her sisters, Elizabeth could now devote herself entirely to the life of the mind, cultivating an enormous correspondence, reading widely, and admitting only a select few from the busy London world of letters into her presence.[8]

During this time, she continued to study prosody. She pursued her reading of Hebrew, Latin, Italian, German, and, especially, Greek. She translated some works for publication (and still more for practice) and collected translations of Italian sonnets in a notebook, which would become an important resource for her mature poetry in the years that followed.[9] In order better to understand the rhythms of Italian and the processes of translation, she even wrote several poems in Italian.[10] Like Browning, Barrett devoted much of her attention during these formative years to metrical and rhythmic experiments. She also schooled herself in various poetic forms and genres: the collections published in 1838 and 1844 include discursive poems on poetry and art, imitations of Greek tragedy (*A Drama of Exile* and *The Seraphim*, each the centerpiece of a volume), an adaptation of Chaucer's "Knight's Tale," half a dozen hymns, fifteen long ballads, over thirty sonnets, numerous other lyrics, and dramatic monologues, which she was already writing before Robert Browning had published a word.

A glance at the early poetry is essential for full appreciation of the later poetry and for an understanding of how much Elizabeth Barrett Browning's poetic maturity was affected by her dialogue with Robert Browning. If she had not lived to write *Sonnets from the Portuguese* or *Aurora Leigh*, the

---

[8] A number of good biographies treat Barrett's London years; the most helpful is Margaret Forster's *The Life and Loves of a Poet: Elizabeth Barrett Browning* (1988).

[9] Phillip D. Sharp's 1981 masters thesis, "Elizabeth Barrett Browning and the Wimpole Street Notebook" and his 1985 dissertation, "Poetry in Process: Elizabeth Barrett Browning and the Sonnets Notebook" (Lousiana State University), are unpublished. Providing text and commentary of one of Barrett's working notebooks for a period of some two decades, Sharp's work shows the deliberateness of Barrett's poetics and the depth of her scholarship, unsuspected by most readers.

[10] Unpublished manuscripts of the Italian poems are in the Armstrong Browning Library at Baylor University.

early poetry would have given her a place in the history of Victorian poetry perhaps no more significant than that of Hemens or Landon.

As a very young poet, Elizabeth Barrett imitated Pope, and her first published work (one for which her father paid the printing costs) was *The Battle of Marathon* (1820), a precocious miniature epic in heroic couplets. "Happily it is not now, as it was in the days of Pope, who was so early in thinking himself 'the greatest genius of the age'," she announces in the Preface; "Now, even the female may drive her Pegasus through the realms of Parnassus [. . .]" (1). And drive she did, at a cheerful bouncing pace through four books - an impressive piece of juvenilia.

An Essay on Mind (1826) reveals to a remarkable degree Elizabeth Barrett's intellectual approach to poetry - an approach which needs to be borne in mind from the beginning, since her reputation for emotionalism is unjustified by her early poetic practice. In this two-book essay in heroic couplets, which was the centerpiece of her second published collection, Barrett continues to imitate Pope, entering deliberately into the contemporary debate about the nature and function of poetry with the weapons of the masters, including the male persona and the occasional Alexandrine with which Pope himself occasionally punctuated his essays in verse. In the following passage from Book II, Barrett argues that poetry is synthetic, that it merges rational thought with human feeling in a unique way. The human heart, she says, is always "kindled" at:

> Some sound which brings high musings in its track,
> Or calls perchance the days of childhood back
> In its dear echo, when, without a sigh,
> Swift hoop and bounding ball were first laid by,
> To clasp in joy, from schoolroom tyrant free,
> The classic volume on the little knee,
> And con sweet sounds of dearest minstrelsy,
> Or works of sterner lore; the young brow, fraught
> With a calm brightness which might mimic thought,
> Leant on the boyish hand -- as, all the while,
> A half-heaved sigh, or ay th'unconscious smile,
> Would tell how, o'er that page the soul was glowing
> In an internal transport, past the knowing! (pp. 44-45)

The epigrammatic quality of the heroic couplet both lent itself to and encouraged the logical rhythm of Barrett's dialectical argument.

Barrett did not hesitate to bring her scholarship and creativity into a good argument with her contemporaries or with the authorities of the past. As she explains in the Preface, one of her most important theses is that rules prescribing the parameters and content of genres are invalid and that poetic genres, in particular, may evolve:

> I am [. . .] aware how often it has been asserted that poetry is not a proper vehicle for abstract ideas -- how far the assertion may be correct, is with me a matter of doubt. We do not deem the imaginative incompatible with the philosophic, for the name of Bacon is on our lips; then why should we expel the argumentative from the limits of the poetic? If indeed we consider Poetry as Plato considered her, when he banished her from his republic; or as Newton, when he termed her "a kind of ingenious nonsense"; or as Locke, when he pronounced that "gaming and poetry went usually together"; or as Boileau, when he boasted of being acquainted with two arts equally useful to mankind -- "writing verses and playing at skittles," we shall find no difficulty in assenting to this opinion. But while we behold in poetry the inspiritings to political feeling, the "momentum aere perennius" of buried nations, we are loathe to believe her unequal to the higher walks of intellect: when we behold the works of the great though erring Lucretius, the sublime Dante, the reasoning Pope -- when we hear Quintilian acknowledge the submission due from Philosophers to Poets, and Gibbon declare Homer to be "the law-giver, the theologian, the historian, and the philosopher of the ancients," we are *unable* to believe it. Poetry is the enthusiasm of the understanding; and, as Milton finely expresses it, there is "a high reason in her fancies."(29)[11]

True to the form she will follow throughout this work, Barrett sets up the terms of her argument at the beginning of this passage: poetry as rational inquiry (thesis) versus poetry as nonrational expression (antithesis). She lines up her authorities on either side to reach, with Milton, a synthesis of the two points of view - that poetry partakes of both the rational and the nonrational, that it is, in other words, a complete mode of human inquiry, flexible enough to express far more than Plato and his intellectual descendants have been willing to admit. In Book II, after an extended poetic exploration of this argument (which appears in condensed form in the Preface), she concludes that:

> Poesy's whole essence, when defined,
> Is elevation of the reasoning mind,
> When inward sense from Fancy's page is taught,
> And moral feeling ministers to Thought.
> And hence the natural passions all agree
> In seeking Nature's language -- poetry.

---

[11] Unless otherwise noted, all quotations from Barrett Browning's works, except *Casa Guidi Windows* and *Aurora Leigh*, are from the Wordsworth edition.

The Preface concludes with a tactful yet self-assured request that the reader excuse any faults in the work as the result of "my narrow capacity, as opposed to the infinite object it would embrace" (30). Barrett clearly implies here that, since no human mind is adequate to the task of generalizing about the final causes of mental activity, she has as much business doing it as anyone - and more, since, as a poet herself, she can reasonably discourse upon mind's highest activity - poetry.

Although Pope was certainly the most important formative figure for Barrett's earliest poetry, her thinking was not circumscribed by the limits of his. Forbidden by her father to read Fielding and Gibbon, she substituted the *philosophes* and Mary Wollstonecraft. (Of course, on the sly, she continued to read Gibbon's works, and novels as well.) In *A Vindication of the Rights of Woman* (1792), Wollstonecraft had described the triviality of ordinary female education, the absorption of wives into the legal identities of their husbands, institutionalized violence against women, and the perverse images of women which informed masculinist literature. Her arguments became part of Barrett's intellectual frame of reference and inform many of Barrett's narrative poems, which only at first glance seem to be exercises in sentimentality for a relatively uneducated female reading public. In reading Wollstonecraft and observing the power dynamics of her own family, Barrett saw that, just as individual expression was becoming more valued than ever before, individual women were systematically deprived of autonomy. Wollstonecraft presented a threat and a promise.

Barrett's unpublished fragment *Essay on Woman*, a poem in heroic couplets written in 1822 when she was sixteen, attacks not so much women's political, economic, and educational disenfranchisement - Wollstonecraft's primary concerns - as the historical and cultural marginalization of women. Pope had become her adversary, and in *Essay on Woman*, even more than *The Battle of Marathon*, she pits her heroic couplets against his. Following Wollstonecraft's critique of the misogynous tradition in English poetry, including an analysis of some of Pope's most offensive lines, Barrett begins her own poem at Pope's historical moment. After explaining how the practice of poetry creates powerful images of man, Barrett then shifts her gaze from man to woman:

> But while we hail him potent, and devine [sic]
> Shall gentle woman claim no humble line? (Moser 11)

In a metaphysical pun, Barrett laments that because women are not masters of the poetic line, there is no female line in poetry, no tradition of women poets. Consequently, poetry does not offer a proper description of the female subject, much less a model which can "bend to nobler thoughts the

British fair!" With youthful confidence, Barrett then suggests, "Be it mine to exert my humble case/[. . .] Found the proud path, where Glory's breezes fan," so that woman "stands the equal of her Master Man" (11). The question, she asks, is whether man will:

> Smother each flash of intellectual fire,
> And bid Ambition's noblest throb expire?
> Pinion the wing, that yearns for glory's light,
> Then boast the strength of thy superior flight? (12)

The fragment ends with an invocation of Genius, to whom the poet asks a rhetorical question: has "thy sacred influence never stole,/ With radiance unobscured, on Woman's soul?" An answer is implied in the last line: "Comnena, Dacier, More, DeStael, reply!" (12) By invoking women of science, scholarship, drama, and fiction, Barrett suggests that her ambition to found a "female line" in poetry is historically feasible, although the present is hostile.

Deborah Byrd argues that Barrett did not finish "Essay on Woman" because she accepted the hierarchy of genres posited by Western masculine cultural tradition. Unable fully to credit the ballads and topical poems written by contemporary women poets such as Landon and Hemens, Barrett felt "the burden of proving that women could excel in poetic composition rested squarely on her shoulders" (28). But Barrett's situation was even more complex than Byrd suggests. The struggle turned out to be more difficult than she imagined it would be, not because attempts were made to "smother" her "intellectual fire," and not only because she felt her female models were inadequate, but because she also found herself fighting against the patriarchal poetic tradition - and simultaneously internalizing it as she struggled to write serious poetry. The young poet was literally at war with herself, and the battle front was the traditional, neo-classical field of the heroic couplet of "Essay on Woman," which Barrett employed to her fullest satisfaction when writing about "masculine" subjects with a masculine persona. It was ironic that, although she argued against ossified literary genres, she did not engage in generic experiments until much later.

After Pope, Barrett's most important early models were Milton and the Romantic poets, whose works dominated the literary scene during her childhood. Writing to Mitford in 1841, Barrett expresses an admiration for Byron which began in childhood and lasted throughout her life: "L^d. Byron with all his wrongs & his sins -- & he had many of both -- seems to me worth ten Walter Scotts, as a <u>man to be loved</u>" (*Correspondence* 5, 98, Barrett's italics). This from a poet who loved novels and argued about them constantly with Mitford. Barrett's earliest poems are typically composed within the neoclassical forms which characterize Byron's early work, such as *English Bards and Scotch Reviewers*, (1809), and after this early phase, she began, in her twenties, to write stories in verse, just as Byron had done, notably in the wildly popular tales of the Mediterranean. In Barrett's early work, these impulses - the intellectual and the emotional, the discursive and the lyrical or narrative - are as distinct and separate as they are in Byron's poetry.

The split in Barrett's early work is related to gendered assumptions, still evident in our own critical practice at the end of the twentieth century, about genre. She was, and wished to be considered, intellectual. She wished for and yet avoided emotional expression in her discursive work. Like most poets, publishers, and readers of her time, she seemed to feel that writing the discursive poetry she associated with Pope (and the intellectual side of Byron) was a male activity (in *An Essay on Mind* she even presents herself as male), and that emotional poetry was a female mode of expression, despite Byron's indulgence in it.[12] Thus, as a poetic personality she could be a poetess, like L.E.L. or Felicia Hemens; she could be anonymous (and male); or she could be detached and gender neutral. Consequently, the speakers in *The Seraphim* (1838) and *A Drama of Exile* (1844), the dramatic poems of which Barrett was most proud, are angels, neither male nor female. "An Essay on Woman," the one early discursive poem in which she speaks as a woman, remained unfinished and unpublished in her lifetime. The two sides of her poetic character did not comfortably co-exist.

But even though, after *An Essay on Mind*, Elizabeth Barrett's discursive voice became gradually more subdued, she did not set aside her theoretical concerns. Instead, she split off the argumentative impulse, channeling her opinions about poetry into prose essays and, more covertly, her sexual politics into the "female genres," short lyrics and ballads for periodicals and gift albums, often marketed toward a female readership. These poems, the major dramatic poems, the essays, and the vast correspondence constitute an enormous literary output, in which a few particularly significant motifs appear over and over again, almost always covertly, almost never wholly expressing the impulse behind them, running the risk that, as Julia Kristeva writes in *Strangers to Ourselves*, "By dint of saying things in various ways, one just as trite as the other, just as approximate,

---

[12] In *Godiva's Ride*, Mermin suggests that, for nineteenth-century women writers, Byronism was a "psychological impulse to be cherished and an artistic problem they had to resolve. Byron's self assertion, his reckless defiance of tyranny and convention, gave an essential impetus to women who had to defy cultural authority and override the convention of feminine self-suppression to write" (11).

one ends up no longer saying them" (275). In the sonnet entitled "Insufficiency" (1844), Barrett herself writes:

> When I attain to utter forth in verse
> Some inward thought, my soul throbs audibly
> Along my pulses, yearning to be free [. . .].
> But, like a wind-exposed distorted tree,
> We are blown against for ever by the curse
> Which breathes through Nature. Oh, the world is weak!
> The effluence of each is false to all,
> And what we best conceive we fail to speak.

Until her relationship with Robert Browning began in 1845, Barrett's willingness to engage in public discourse about social issues and about aesthetic issues in poetry, which had been so strong in her youth, gradually diminished, as did her physical health. As an intellectual presence and a physical being, she was becoming a shadow of herself.

The speaker of *An Essay on Mind* is male. Cross-dressing in this and other poems is one of Elizabeth Barrett's most conflicted and significant tropes; to study this motif in the early poetry is to see Barrett addressing in a covert way the issue of gender construction in art that had inspired her youthful passion. In the juvenilia, of course, the poet herself was a cross-dresser, but this masculine disguise was no longer possible after she began publishing under her own name, and the male persona was no longer desirable when she began writing more "feminine" poetry. "The Romaunt of the Page," published in 1839 in the gift album Finden's *Tableaux*, narrates the story of a woman who is murdered while disguised as her husband's page. That same year, Barrett discovered the novels of George Sand, whose life and works inspired her to write two sonnets about the cost of exercising personal and literary authority beyond what custom allows women. In *Poems* of 1844, only two short lyrics ("The Prisoner" and "Insufficiency") separate them from "The Romaunt of the Page," which Barrett republished in the same volume. In both the ballad and the sonnets to Sand, cross-dressing is deployed as a way of exploring the relationships among gender, empowerment, and identity. These three poems constitute one of the most provocative moments in her work.

The idea of George Sand was irresistible. Unlike any other woman Barrett knew of, this Byronic French novelist had successfully broken out of her literary and real-life confinement through the outrageous yet simple strategy of wearing men's clothes; she was the subject of racy gossip, and she wrote daring novels which engaged with some of Elizabeth Barrett's dearest concerns about the rights and treatment of women. Thus, Barrett's own struggles with the conflicting roles of woman and poet could be cathected onto the figure of George Sand. The question that Barrett worries from every angle is what Sand's strategy costs - in reputation, moral fiber, and peace of mind.

In the first, "To George Sand: A Desire," she hails her subject as "Thou large-brained woman and large-hearted man." Ostensibly, Barrett's desire is that "some mild miraculous thunder" will announce to the world the "nobler nature" that is obscured by Sand's unusual behavior, and that somehow,

> thou to woman's claim
> And man's, mightst join beside the angel's grace
> Of a pure genius sanctified from blame,
> Till child and maiden pressed to thine embrace
> To kiss upon thy lips a stainless fame.

In her study of Sand's impact on British literature, Patricia Thompson has suggested that Barrett's "desire" has also an erotic component that eventually found its way into her best work. The last quatrain of the sonnet, which I have quoted above, supports Thompson's suggestion, but Barrett's reaction to Sand is actually more complicated. Throughout this sonnet is developed a series of circus images which suggest that Barrett also felt, perhaps unconsciously, both envy and sexual superiority.[13] The soul of her hero, Barrett writes, "amid the lions/ Of thy tumultuous senses, moans defiance." And the poet wishes that "miraculous thunder" would run:

> Above the applauded circus, in appliance
> Of thine own nobler nature's strength and science,
> Drawing two pinions, white as wings of swan,

---

[13] I wish to thank Nancy Vosburg for arguing with me about this poem, and also to thank the students in my Victorian literature classes during the last few years for their contribution to my understanding of it. Nancy has written that "by 'unsexing' George Sand, Barrett can then justify her desire for her, can confess her 'love' (spiritual love). In a sense, she's not struggling so much with Sand's androgynous behavior, but with her own gender issues, her own assimilation of gender norms which constitute barriers to her desire. If there is condescension (I'm still doubting), it's a nod to her own limitations." These two sonnets inspire more different reactions than any other poems I teach. Some of my students have read them as lesbian love poems; some see this positively and others (of course) negatively. Some read the sonnets as unqualified tributes, others as insults. Some students are satisfied to accept the ambiguity and go on.

From thy strong shoulders, to amaze the place
With holier light.

Then Sand would appear, not as a lion, nor even a swan, but as a sexless angel, recalling the stern figures who dominate *The Seraphim* and *A Drama of Exile*.

Barrett's ambivalence is configured differently in the second sonnet, "To George Sand: A Recognition." This poem begins "True genius, but true woman," the "but" suggesting that Barrett still finds the two identities impossible to reconcile. The hint of sexual superiority is gone, replaced by fellow feeling. No longer is George Sand held primarily responsible for her internal conflict; instead, it is society's fault that she is at war with herself, that despite her man's clothes she is torn between her woman's body/ woman's nature and the destiny of her genius:

Thy woman's hair, my sister, all unshorn
Floats back dishevelled strength in agony,
Disproving thy man's name.

By the end of the poem, Barrett has changed the terms of the first line, asserting that it is not in spite of Sand's genius, but because of it that the "woman-heart" is unmistakably revealed. Nevertheless, because the world oppresses her, Sand still cannot be at rest:

Till God unsex thee on the heavenly shore
Where unincarnate spirits purely aspire!

Barrett's last word, then, is that an embodied woman cannot be a genius or poet with complete integrity, whether because of woman's essential nature or her circumscribed existence. In writing these sonnets, Barrett was exploring her own ambivalence more than reaching for a genuine understanding of George Sand.[14]

In "The Romaunt of the Page," Barrett deals with her gender/ writing conflict less directly, but perhaps more radically and certainly with less ambivalence. The poem consists of forty-four stanzas, each six to ten lines; the narrative is broken twice, near the beginning and at the end, by verse paragraphs describing the activities at a nearby convent. In its oriental setting and the reckless heroism of the main character, the story recalls Byron's tales published two decades earlier.

---

[14] In a 1995 article on Barrett Browning and Thomas Hardy, Linda Shires accounts for Barrett's ambivalence as a reaction to display and commodification as well as Sand's gender transgressions (202-05).

A woman follows her husband to "the holy war in Palestine," disguised as his page. One night, when the knight praises the page's valor, the page asks a boon - to be told about the knight's bride. In response, the knight explains that she is the daughter of an old family friend who died fighting for the honor of the knight's father. To honor the memory of the older man and comfort his widow, the young knight agrees to marry their daughter, literally in the dark, over the widow's deathbed. Since he then leaves immediately, the knight does not know whether his bride is "dark or bright." He only knows of her filial piety: he remembers that when the marriage ceremony ended, the bride kissed her dead mother's lips before she kissed his living ones. At the end of the knight's tale, the page weeps and reciprocates the knight's gesture by telling a story of his own about his "sister," who followed her husband into battle. But to his disappointment, the knight retorts that any woman who does such a thing is "unwomaned." Finally, understanding that her conception of marriage differs irreconcilably from her husband's, the page/ wife sees no way out. Although at the end of the poem she expresses hope that her knight's new wife will be to his taste when he finally meets her, there is some irony in this hope: as the Paynims suddenly attack, she asks under her breath:

'Have I renounced my womanhood,
    For wifehood unto <u>thee</u>?'

Since the answer is yes, she urges her knight to flee and refuses to tell the attackers where he has gone. In retaliation:

They cursed her deep, they smote her low,
They cleft her golden ringlets through;
    The Loving is the Dying.

She dies outside a convent wall and is sung to rest when the nuns happen to celebrate a funeral mass for their Abbess inside the wall. Having transgressed patriarchal limits, even in death the page cannot be celebrated within conventional boundaries: the singers of her funeral dirge are unaware of her death.

Unlike the sonnets to George Sand, "The Romaunt of the Page" concerns the romantic past rather than the present, action rather than writing, but at its center are two competing texts: a traditional tale of the knight who marries a pious maiden for the honor of his family (the "right" story) versus the page's tale of fluid gender boundaries, unselfish love, and a terrible death (the "wrong" story). The conclusion to this tale - that loving means dying - is written with violence on the body of the page.

In her study of Barrett Browning's love poetry, Glennis Stephenson suggests that the page/ wife dies because her husband's view of marriage is so different from her own belief that "A wife should take an active role in the relationship and share all the trials [. . .]"(32). Mermin's reading of the poem in an article about Barrett Browning's narrative poems suggests that Barrett had a darker purpose. Mermin particularly notes the irony of the page's suicidal last stand: in her incompetent husband's service, she has already saved his life three times! A frequent theme in the critical literature on Barrett's early work is the suggestion that she displaced upon such tragic female figures her own anxiety about her failure to fulfill a woman's role, even while she was a financial success as a poet - in other words, that she feared psychic transvestitism. And it is certainly possible to detect this theme by reading Barrett's early poetry through the lens provided by some of the late poetry, such as "Mother and Poet," a dramatic monologue written only months before Barrett Browning died, in which the speaker is the Risorgimento poet, Laura Savio. In this poem, Savio grapples with the realization that her patriotic poetry has led indirectly to the deaths of both her sons in the struggle for a free, unified Italy, and that her role as nurturer of her country conflicts with her role as the mother of these two beloved sons.

However, in *Aurora Leigh* and her later political poems, Barrett drops the cross dressing trope. If cross-dressing has provided Barrett a way to explore the role of the woman poet in a man's literary world, why does it disappear from her later work? The answer can be found, I think, by reading the late poetry through the lens of the earlier works, rather than the other way around.

In *Vested Interests*, Marjorie Garber argues that cross-dressing should be looked at, not through; for the mask of the cross-dresser is "a space of possibility," a "third term" which "puts into question [. . .] identity, self-sufficiency, self-knowledge" (11). Applied to the case of Barrett's cross-dressers, Garber's argument suggests, perhaps, that we should focus more completely on this rich metaphorical vehicle before resolving it into a particular, limiting tenor - that, like the masculine dress of Joan of Arc or Shakespeare's Rosalind, or the women's clothes of Byron's nubile Don Juan when he hides in the seraglio, the masks are the meaning, and not simply convenient details which advance plot or argument. (In this as in other respects, Barrett's early work is not unlike that of Robert Browning.)

What is so unsettling about Barrett's characterization of George Sand is that the novelist's identity cannot be resolved into the stereotype of a single gender - and that Barrett recognizes in this indeterminacy the source of Sand's power and her vulnerability. The cross dressing in "Romaunt of the

Page" signifies something different. At first reading of the poem, the page is valiant and loyal, despite his youth and small size, and completely convincing in his male gender role until more than halfway through the narrative. Even then, when the page begins to shed tears at the knight's moving story, the explanation for the tears - his claim that the knight's story reminds him of his sister who dressed as a page to follow her husband's Crusade - is perfectly plausible. Within the time frame of the poem, in fact, the page is neither male nor female, but, like George Sand, indeterminate, in between, and vulnerable because of this between-ness. Only at the actual moment of death is the indeterminacy resolved into the female:

> She felt the scimitar gleam down,
>   And met it from beneath
> With smile more bright in victory
>   Than any sword from sheath, --
> Which flashed across her lip serene,
> Most like the spirit-light between
>   The darks of life and death

The last sentence is grammatically blurred (again, like Browning's typical trait of grammatical ambiguity), and, in perhaps the most provocative moment of the poem, the page's smile almost literally assimilates the gleam of the curved sword.

According to Garber, the transvestite always represents the nexus between gender anxiety and anxiety of another kind - of race, class, or ethnicity. In Barrett's case, as I have already suggested, cross-dressing reveals the connection between gender and the always already vexed activity of writing. The "mask" itself is both the scene and subject of writing. Barrett is concerned with the meaning of the woman's masculine dress, her tell-tale mane of hair like a lion's, and her role as a circus performer. She is fascinated by the appurtenances of the "page" - a barely concealed reference to the paper on which Barrett inscribes her poems. The clothes and the performances are not simply metaphors. At the heart of the narrative is a grim pun: the female (literary) page in a man's world is as vulnerable as a female (military) page in a man's war.

In an article on genre in Emily Dickinson and HD in *Shakespeare's Sisters*, the classic 1979 anthology of feminist criticism on woman poets, Jeanne Kammer surmises that "For the woman poet, perhaps, the model is oracle, not bard; the activity seeing, not singing" (164). But important as the investigation of the gender/ genre connection is, to approach Barrett Browning's lifework from this direction only is to elide the even more basic problem with which she struggled as a young poet - and that is whether she should be wielding a pen at all. Like almost every other woman writer of the nineteenth century, Barrett expressed the struggle through the trope of cross-dressing. Unlike many of these women writers, and unlike the page or Barrett's hyperbolic version of George Sand, Barrett Browning eventually won the struggle, though not without battle scars and a few false starts.

Barrett's early years were more than a period of false starts, however. Throughout her career, she insisted that only the narrow-minded would attempt to prescribe generic conventions, that literary genres have to evolve, just as all human culture evolves, and that women could be poets as well as men. Nevertheless, if Barrett's theory about the nature and purpose of poetry remained consistent, her poetic practice gradually became more fluid and ironic, and more fully reflected the theory. The dialectical organization of her early discursive poetry, with its carefully constructed oppositions and resolutions, eventually gave way to a habit of dialogue, to the practice of entertaining, not merely two opposing voices resolving themselves into a single truth, but multiple, nuanced voices from which might emerge richer and less categorical discourse. Because she saw poetry as a way of mediating between the best that was thought and the best that was felt, she eventually began to combine poetry about everyday life and feeling - ballads and short lyrics in the manner of the poetesses whose work she took lightly - with serious poetry about classical subjects and abstract ideas - discursive works in the manner of Pope and long poems on religious, philosophical, or political themes. The most significant result of this combination was, of course, *Aurora Leigh*, published only five years before she died.

Reading the late poetry through the lens provided by the early work requires, I think, a reversal of Kammer's conclusion that women poets wish to see rather than sing. For Barrett desired to be the *bard*, not the oracle, to *sing* as well as see. She expressed this desire and enacted it. Her lifelong project, which was both personal and artistic, could be expressed in Rachel Blau DuPlessis' words about women artists, who struggle:

> To translate ourselves from our disguises. The enthralled sexuality, the knife-edge brilliance, the intellectual dowdiness, evasions, embarrassments, imprecisions, deferments; smug primness with which there is no dialogue. (*The Pink Guitar* 2)

ii. Robert Browning

The ordinary sense of "dialogue" is a conversation in which the words of each participant derive part of their meaning from intention and part from context. Unlike the dialectic, which theoretically ends with synthesis, Bakhtin asserts in his analysis of Dostoevsky that true dialogue is interminable:

> Dialogue here is not the threshold to action, it is the action itself. [. . .] in dialogue a person not only shows himself outwardly, but he becomes for the first time that which he is -- and, we repeat, not only for others but for himself. To be means to communicate dialogically. When dialogue ends, everything ends. (*Problems of Dostoevsky's Poetics* 252)

In dialogue, it is enough to share meanings and intentions. Literary dialogue is the representation of shared meanings and intentions. As such, dialogue is a trope, albeit an extremely complicated one. The representation of conversation can be dialogic, as can verbal irony, the layering of meanings and intentions within a single word. Dialogue is also expressed through literary form or genre.

Robert Browning strove to represent shared meanings and intentions in his poetry before he had experienced them in his life. He intuitively understood the importance of literary and conversational dialogue, and yet the dialogism in many of his early poems is so intricate that his readers closed the book, leaving him with an experience of silence and isolation more profound than his childhood had prepared him for.

Browning grew up surrounded by cultural riches, family, and nature - bounded within the beautiful gardens created by his mother and the fields surrounding Camberwell, the small village on the outskirts of London where he was born in the spring of 1812. Like the Moulton Barretts, the Browning family experienced politics and religion as a part of daily life. The great crisis in the life of Robert Browning the elder, a gentle, eccentric scholar and artist, had been his horrified observations of slavery in Jamaica, where he had been sent by his father on family business. Sarah Anna Wiedemann Browning, ten years her husband's senior, loved gardening and music, but her great passion was religion, and the rest of the family, including Robert's younger sister Sarianna, joined her in worship at the dissenting chapel where she was a member.

The humans in the Camberwell household were not entirely sufficient unto themselves, however. They lived with a large menagerie of pets - including the usual dogs, cats, and horses, as well as numerous insects and reptiles, a hedgehog, and an owl. And they valued their relationships with a few members of the extended family and a few close friends. One luxury was Robert senior's library of six thousand volumes, where the education of his children took place. If Elizabeth Barrett had been thrown upon her father's library as almost her only educational resource, Robert Browning spent his early years in the family library partly by choice, with lessons from his father and occasional tutors. As a small child, he was too precocious to benefit greatly from his two trial periods at school. Later, when he was sixteen, his father enrolled him in the University of London, but he quit after a few weeks in attendance.

Browning's interests in art and music were lifelong and pronounced, but his imagination and narrative desire were from the beginning expressed primarily in words. In 1837, he had written to an early friend and admirer, the young French count Amédée de Ripert Monclar, "I cannot remember the time when I did not make verses and think verse-making the finest thing in the world [. . .]" (*Correspondence* 3.264). Indeed, Browning's father, like Barrett's, paid the costs for publishing most of his child's works. And, like some of Barrett's childhood efforts, Browning's earliest poetry was inspired by his reading of the Romantics, first Byron and Coleridge, later Shelley. Unlike Barrett, however, at each stage of his poetic development Browning refused to forgive the infelicities of the previous stage, so nothing of his juvenilia has survived except two poems from a manuscript volume entitled "Incondita" (Latin translation: disorderly, confused), which he burned almost as soon as he wrote it.

When Browning began to venture from the small closed world of his family, he did not go far, but sought out another family similar to his own - gifted, earnest, attractive, and enmeshed - who would encourage his literary ambitions. When he was fourteen, Browning met Sarah and Eliza Flower, seven and nine years older than he. They were the daughters of the radical journalist and editor Benjamin Flower, and their multifarious talents would have had an obvious appeal to a boy as intellectually versatile as Robert Browning. Eliza was the composer of hymn music and political songs, Sarah the author of "Nearer, my God, to Thee" and an actress whose repertoire included Shakespeare. The age difference between young Robert Browning and his two new friends paralleled the gap between Browning's parents, and it would be repeated in his future relationships as well.[15]

---

[15] The close ties between the Browning parents and children, suggested by the repetition of their names, were replicated many years later within Robert Browning's own marriage to Elizabeth Barrett, especially after the birth of their son Pen. Pen's given name, Robert Weidemann Barrett Browning, shows how closely he, too, was scripted into the family drama. His self-chosen nickname

Unfortunately, the two young women seemed unsure whether to treat him as a younger brother or to fall in love with him. Several years later, after her father had died and Eliza had established herself in the household of the dissenting minister W. J. Fox, Browning re-opened his friendship with her. Fox, too, admired Browning's poetry, and he wrote one of the few reviews of Browning's first published work *Pauline* (1833). In his enthusiasm, Fox passed the poem along to John Stuart Mill, whose often-quoted negative criticism of it proved to be decisive in Browning's later poetic development.[16]

In the winter of 1834-35, Browning and the "set," a group of young men living in Hampstead area, launched a short-lived publication *The Trifler*, but the effort was soon given up, and the friends - Christopher and Joe Dowson, Alfred Domett, Fred and William Young, and Joseph Arnould - would eventually take up careers in commerce and government.[17] The set did support Browning's efforts on stage, however. Given the poor reception of his plays, the presence of his friends must have been doubly welcome.

Browning's first critically successful work was *Paracelsus*, the dramatic poem published in 1835 which established his presence on the literary scene. The work gave him access to the famous actor manager William Macready, who offered in 1837 to produce *Strafford*, the poet's closest approach to dramatic success, but the play was the first in a series of Browning's failing attempts to support his poetry by writing for the theatre.

---

suggests a struggle to differentiate himself from his famous parents -- while the name also represents the instrument which made them famous.

[16] In Mill's long summary statement at the end of the poem, he claims, "I know not what to wish for him, but that he meet with a real Pauline" (I. 1022). Harsh though Mill's remark may have been, Browning was in a sense striving for that very thing.

Unless otherwise noted, I have quoted from the two-volume *Poems*, edited by Pettigrew and Collins. (The Oxford edition by Jack and Inglesfield, however, contains more generous and reliable notes.)

[17] In *Browning's Youth* (1977), John Maynard notes that Browning's life began within a "secluded, inwardly turned [. . .] family" (50), but follows this statement with a detailed narrative of the poet's "set" in the 1830s and 40s. The sheer detail of Maynard's account suggests that, in his twenties and thirties, Browning experienced a full and satisfying social milieu, but Maynard notes that "The set and his own family really was nonetheless a class, what in popular Marxism would be termed the bourgeois intelligentsia, [which] also no doubt limited the range of Browning's response to the condition of his time" (112). He also admits that Browning "was sometimes prey to a sense of the isolated, only too sensitive self, which is at once the precondition and the price of intensified inner awareness" (130).

About this time, Browning also came to know Euphrasia Fanny Haworth, eleven years his senior - another older, educated woman to admire him. But the period of this friendship coincided with the bleakest years in his career: Macready became increasingly impatient as Browning urged upon him more plays. *Sordello*, Browning's long and intricate poem on the Italian Renaissance, was turning out to be a grueling exercise in writing and revision. Finally, when it was published in 1840, the reviews were not simply negative but hostile. Fanny could admire *Sordello* no more than the reviewers, although in it, Browning refers to his "English Eyebright," a literal translation of her name into English.

And so, for a time, Browning was thrown back upon his family, or upon friends such as Monclar, whose strongest connection with the literary life of London was Browning himself. As a young poet, then, he had to settle for an unhealthy diet of lavish praise from family and friends or attacks from strangers. By his late twenties, he had still found no place to settle, no authority upon which he could rely, no genre adequate to his own conception of what he should write, no clear sense of limits or possibilities. Deeply rooted as a son and brother, Browning was rootless as a poet. But it was inconceivable to him to give up the struggle: in 1841, he began to publish his poems in a series of pamphlets, enigmatically entitled *Bells and Pomegranates*. In the eighth of the series, to appease his puzzled readers, he explains that the title is meant to suggest

> an alteration, or mixture, of music with discoursing, sound with sense, poetry with thought; which looks too ambitious, thus expressed, so the symbol was preferred [. . .] . (I.1069)

The series was received without fanfare, and only a few readers understood its value. Elizabeth Barrett was one of them.

Like many young poets, including Elizabeth Barrett, Robert Browning taught himself to write by composing in the manner of other poets, and a late work, *Parleying with Certain People of Importance in Their Day* (1887), shows that writing against other artists remained central - and consciously so - to his work throughout his long and productive life. Furthermore, Browning habitually tried to make sense of his own efforts by placing them in dialogue with other works and himself in dialogue with other artists. For example, his analysis of Thomas Chatterton's life and tragic death, published in 1842, is in a sense an apologia for himself. The story of Chatterton's suicide by poisoning in 1770 inspired Browning to consider the typical pattern of, and necessary conditions for, artistic development:

> Genius almost invariably begins to develop itself by imitation. It has, in the short-sightedness of infancy, faith in the world; and its object is to compete with, or prove superior to, the world's already recognised idols [. . .] . This done, there grows up a faith in itself: and, no longer taking the performance or method of another for granted, it supersedes these by processes of its own. It creates, and imitates no longer. Seeing cause for faith in something external and better, and having attained to a moral end and aim, it next discovers in itself the only remaining antagonist worthy of its ambition, and in the subduing what at first seemed its most enviable powers, arrives at the more or less complete fulfilment of its earthly mission. (111)

Imitation, then originality: in Browning's analysis, this is the normal and typical pattern of creative growth. Unable to overcome the hostility of the literary community, either in his native Bristol or later in London, Chatterton never learned to move from imitation to the exercise of his own original and spectacular poetic gifts. Whereas Chatterton was isolated by provincial background, poverty, social class, lack of education, and human loneliness, Robert Browning faced none of these obstacles, and he made the transition from imitation to originality very quickly. But in spite of Browning's relative advantages, his poetic development was also difficult: there is nothing simple even in Browning's schematic rendering of a poet's coming of age. Indeed, his spirit of confrontation with tradition resulted in a self-deconstructive poetic voice which his early Victorian readers found incomprehensible. Though their circumstances and their works differed, the misunderstanding which greeted Chatterton's efforts must have seemed similar to Browning's own experience.

As a boy, Browning took up the Romantic poets one by one. Although it is difficult to reconstruct his poetic development, two poems from the ill-fated "Incondita" escaped the fire. One of the poems shows that, like Barrett, Browning was first drawn to Byron, though apparently more for Byron's worldly experience than for his neoclassical taste or radical politics. In the lyrical narrative "The first born of Egypt," an anonymous speaker tells the story (from Exodus XI-XII) of the visit to Egypt by the angel of death, who destroyed all first-born Egyptian sons as punishment for the Israelites' enslavement. As he would do in his more mature poetry, Browning already emphasizes, not plot, but reactions to events. The poem presents various perspectives of the Egyptians, from Pharaoh to the lowliest prisoner in his dungeons. Despite this premonition of Browning's later work, both the language and the narrative pose in "The first born of Egypt" are those of a young poet struggling to find his own voice. The narrator, a world-weary traveler, echoes Byron:

> It was a fearful thing -- that hour of night --
> I have seen many climes, but that dread hour
> Hath left its burning impress on my soul
> Never to be erased. (28-31)

Even more obviously derivative is the other surviving poem, "The Dance of Death," almost a parody of Coleridge's "Fire, Famine and Slaughter." Like Coleridge's poem, "The Dance of Death" is a dramatic dialogue in tetrameter couplets among personified forces which periodically wreak havoc upon human life. Instead of "Fire, Famine and Slaughter," Browning describes ailments - Fever, Pestilence, Ague, Madness, Consumption.

The history of how these poems were preserved is as revealing as the poems themselves. After he had collected the poems of "Incondita," Browning showed them to Eliza and Sarah Flower; Sarah copied the two poems which still survive into a letter to Fox.[18] In spite of their seniority and accomplishments, the sisters claimed to be in awe of Robert's formidable intelligence, and yet the commentary on his poems in Sarah's playful letter to Fox reveals a less reverent and altogether more complex attitude:

> shall I tell you whose MINE these gems come from? -- and yet I wish they were mine with all my soul -- and Im sure it would be worth all my soul if they were -- "bah" -- forgive me and if you knew what a bad muddling cold I have had you would -- They are "the boy" Robert Brownings aet. 14!! -- and so they as well as he can speak for themselves [.] (*Correspondence* 2.348)

If these words express admiration and rivalry, and hint at Browning's talkative nature, Sarah's postscript suggests with amused condescension his adolescent visions of glory:

---

[18] Since Browning wanted to suppress the *Incondita*, the provenance of the poems as we now have them is naturally complicated: the first published version was brought to the *Cornhill Magazine* in January 1914 by Bertram Dobell. Sarah's letter survives only in Dobell's handwritten copy, now in the Library of the University of Toronto. These poems were preserved not because they were good, but because Browning wrote them, and, ultimately, they were offered to the public for the same reason. And if it makes perfect sense to present every last scrap of verse by a great poet who will never write more because he is dead, it makes a very different kind of sense to preserve scraps of verse by a living teenager. Even at fourteen years of age, it seems Browning exercised the kind of power in his personal relationships which could scarcely be challenged, though certainly it might be resented. The letter, with the poems, is included in "Supporting Documents," *Correspondence* 1.348-52.

I must say a little word about that boys poems. he is mad to publish them --
You know there is a whole book full from which these two are extracted. What
ought he to do? I have copied them verbatim. -- I wonder what you will think
of them -- When I came to "Ague" thinks I my boy you are sending people to
the hundreds of Essex & the Fens of Lincolnshire [--] dangerous ground -- but
as if he had seen the evil he has introduced classical allusion so thoroughly to
avoid all thought of the ridiculous [. . .] . (352)

Here are the lines in question, from "The Dance of Death":

My influence is in the freezing deeps
Where icy power of torpor sleeps,
Where the frigid waters flow
My marble chair is more below. (43-46)

Sarah's suppression of her own critical impulse in the last sentence quoted
above is interesting: clearly she saw something ridiculous in the poem if
she could comment that Browning had avoided all thought of it. The
Flower sisters were in a position to help Browning learn the work of poetry,
yet Sarah withheld the judgements he needed to hear. Her reluctance to
criticize was evidently typical of the adults who encountered this
formidable boy.

William Wordsworth and S. T. Coleridge had each other and Dorothy
Wordsworth. Lord Byron had Robert Charles Dallas, Shelley, and Hunt,
sporting and political confederates, and a circle of intellectually
sophisticated women friends. Percy Shelley had Byron, Peacock, Hogg,
Hunt, and the Godwins. Mary Godwin Shelley came from a brilliant
literary family, married a brilliant literary man, and came by his literary
friends, too, at an early age. All (except Dorothy Wordsworth and Mary
Shelley, of course) were university men, participants in a centuries-old
culture of male love, friendship, rivalry, and support. Even Keats, the
London apothecary's apprentice, cultivated a wide gallery of friends who
were involved in the arts - poets, painters, publishers - and he found in
Tom, George, and Georgiana Keats conversants and correspondents of
enormous intelligence and tact. Elizabeth Barrett found in Price and Boyd,
if not literary verve, at least literary authority; and in her family she found
enough interest to feel connected to a literary community. She was
unequivocally relegated to the margins of that community, but she knew
where she stood.

In some ways, Browning was more isolated: schooled at home as a boy,
a stranger to the university as a young man, he found that his connections to
the world of letters were contingent and fragile. His friend Macready

belonged to the world of the theatre, but Macready soon lost patience with the young poet. Browning knew Mill only second-hand, through Fox, and Mill's now notorious notes on Browning's juvenile poem *Pauline* were based on a misreading which undermined the poet's confidence. Monclar was sophisticated, and warmly impressed by Browning, but his English was so much weaker than Browning's French that most of their correspondence was carried on in French. The Flower sisters and Fannie Haworth usually praised Browning lavishly or kept silent; at their most negative, they expressed confusion. Browning probably did not meet his good friend Alfred Domett, whose first two collections of poems appeared in 1834 and 1839, until after the publication of his own first three works. His Silverthorne cousins, flamboyant and interesting, were not scholarly, and Browning's aunt, Christina Silverthorne, enthusiastically paid the publishing costs for *Pauline* without reading it.[19] As Daniel Karlin puts it, "Browning was cleverer than his parents, cleverer than his sister, cleverer than the minister of his local church (one of whose lengthy sermons so maddened him as a boy that he gnawed the top of his pew)" (Woolford and Karlin, 76).

Browning's essay on the boy poet Thomas Chatterton (1752-70) begins with the thesis that genius dawns in imitative works, but his analysis of literary development continues with the argument that genius must encounter a receptive and yet critical environment in order to grow. Indeed, Browning asserts, "had there only happened to be a single individual of ordinary intelligence among [Chatterton's] intimates, the event must assuredly have fallen out differently" (117). The passion of the argument perhaps derives from Browning's sense that he himself had encountered less than ideal conditions. Chatterton, he claims, intended the Rowley forgeries as a first step in a literary career. When the boy poet presented some of them to the novelist and antiquary Horace Walpole, Walpole could not or did not detect the original genius of the forgeries and took them as the genuine works of the lost poet "Rowley," just as Chatterton had presented them to him. One of Chatterton's acquaintances actually saw the boy "antiquating" (117) parchment; another heard him claim that he could copy the style of any English poet (117); his Bristol patrons, Barrett and Cary, were convinced that Chatterton was utterly incapable of producing Rowley's works. "With such as these there was no fellowship possible for Chatterton" (118). Thus, in Browning's view, Chatterton was driven to

---

[19] Alfred Domett was the model for "Waring" (1842). "May and Death" (1862) was written in memory of James Silverthorne, and it was to him that Browning owed the gift of *Queen Mab*. George Silverthorne was Browning's best man at his marriage to Elizabeth Barrett.

suicide by the misunderstanding of literary men who should have smoothed the way with their teaching.[20]

Understanding the isolation which Browning describes in the Chatterton essay is essential in coming to terms with Browning's own early poems; in assessing the importance of Browning's courtship and marriage to another poet; and even in reading his mature works. If Barrett's literary coming of age was marked by the need to assert her rights as a female poet, Browning's early literary development was marked by stresses that were different from hers, but understandable to her because he, too, had to learn to speak to those who could not hear or understand. When he wrote the innocently derivative poems of "Incondita" at the age of fourteen (Barrett's age when she wrote "The Development of Genius," also highly imitative of current Romantic models), Browning was evidently troubled neither by the fear of being misunderstood nor by the need to assert his independence from his literary progenitors. However, by the time he was twenty, when he wrote *Pauline*, Browning had became conscious of both the problem of the audience and the twin processes of creative affiliation and differentiation.

In *The Visionary Company*, Harold Bloom argues that the Romantic poets suffered from the necessity of defining themselves against the tradition of English poetry, in particular against the epic and revolutionary tradition of Milton. In his essay on "Childe Roland to the Dark Tower Came," Bloom notes a similar Oedipal dynamic of affiliation and differentiation at work in Browning's poem. I would suggest that Browning's struggle to differentiate himself from his Romantic predecessors was more intense than the struggles of the Romantics because of Browning's isolation. As a young poet, Browning had to substitute the virtual community of Western literary tradition for the actual community of the literary world. If Browning had been part of a sophisticated literary circle in his youth, as almost every one of the Romantics was, he would surely have been able to claim an identity with greater confidence and passion. Instead, he perceived his struggle to define himself within and against literary tradition as a private and isolated event, while he was in fact more dependent upon Western literary tradition for his identity than were the Romantics. Without the sense of belonging to a generation, how can one rebel against the older generation? Without a sense of community, how is it possible to communicate? Browning's isolation exacerbated for him the problem of audience which every young writer must solve.

Indeed, the protagonists of *Pauline* (1833), *Paracelsus* (1835), and *Sordello* (1840) are not supernatural or demonic. They are not Byronic

---

[20] In tone, if not in language, Browning's analysis of poetic development anticipates Lev Vygotsky's theory of educational development.

heroes. They fail in their visionary quests for knowledge and transcendence, not because they are misunderstood or self-abandoned, or because they are driven by the will to reach beyond the limits of human power and experience, but because they do not understand how to touch the human nature which seems to be within their reach - and if this is also a failing of the demonic Romantic, it is not his principal failing. The *Pauline* poet, Paracelsus, Sordello - all are even more lost in solipsistic tangles than Victor Frankenstein, Alastor, Manfred, or the Ancient Mariner. The isolation of Browning's protagonists prevents them from loving or accepting love, but it does not prevent them from understanding the importance of love. They are shut out of the garden, gazing over the wall.

Pauline is a transitional poem. It can be read as the last piece of Browning's juvenilia or the first of his published works. The poems of Browning's youth have given critics more pause, perhaps, than the youthful works of any other English poet because, in them, Browning displays mature power in his deployment of the English language, depth of knowledge, and intensity of thought - yet these works are formally disorganized and discursively confusing. About *Pauline*, specifically, critics seem equally divided over the status of the speaker: in terms of the language Browning borrowed from Coleridge for his essay on Shelley (1852), is the speaker Browning himself, speaking as a "subjective" poet, or is he a dramatic character, the creation of an "objective poet"? Although John Stuart Mill claimed to worry about the sanity of a young man who could write such a self-divided work, in *Becoming Browning*, Clyde Ryals suggests that Browning's poetic practice is consistently based on the possibility that "these two modes of poetic faculty [the subjective and the objective] might [. . .] be combined" (6). In any case, the poem participates in Browning's lifelong habit of dramatizing himself, even when he seems to be speaking in his own voice. This was his approach in the two earliest extant poems, and it would be his strategy later on in major works such as *Christmas-Eve and Easter-Day*, many shorter poems, and, typically, the long works of his old age as well.

In *Pauline*, a young poet describes, apparently in real time (J.W. Harper 63), the history of his ambitions, hopes, dreams, and doubts. The sensibility of the speaker is an exaggeration of the self-reflexive romantic hero, and the genre, within the frame defined by headnotes and a footnote, is that of the greater Romantic lyric: the speaker's memory is triggered by the present, the present finds new meaning in light of the memory, and the speaker looks forward to the future with insight and renewed hope. However, Mill overlooked the frame, which identifies *Pauline*, not as a lyric at all, but as an early and somewhat crude dramatic monologue. In a letter to Monclar (1842), Browning confirms that he was writing in this genre, when he says with a wry self-awareness that *Pauline* was to have been the first installment in a series of works about a poet, a playwright, a composer, and an orator. "The Abortion in question was the '*tentative*' of 'the Poet'[. . .] -- who would have been more legitimately 'myself' than most of the others, but I had planned a very delicious and romantic life for him" (*Correspondence* 3.265).

Unfortunately for the speaker of *Pauline*, the "delicious and romantic life" of the poet does not seem to have materialized. The poem begins with the suggestion that Romantic self-consciousness equals self-destructiveness. At the end, the speaker claims to have learned the value of love, truth, and God, and he reasserts his connection with Shelley, the "Sun-treader" whose influence he has struggled to integrate into his own nature. Finally, he also asks for his lover's support and guidance: "So, love me -- me, Pauline [. . .]/ Never leave loving!" (903-04). Despite the speaker's final claim of connectedness, one is left doubting that he will thrive or even survive as a poet or a human being, for he has admitted that the fire is dead within him, and though he asks for love, he seems incapable of giving it.

One problem for the developing poet is, of course, the conflict endemic in modern Western culture - Bloom's "anxiety of influence." Yet Browning's Romantic models had already expressed a revolutionary break with their predecessors; rebelling consciously against those who had already rebelled in such compelling terms would have been difficult for him, if not impossible, to carry out overtly. In his essay "Notes for a History of Victorian Poetic Genres," Avrom Fleishman suggests that, not only "Browning's early failures," but many of the works of Tennyson, Clough, Hopkins, Arnold, and Swinburne also demonstrate alienation "in the root form of impeded communication" (367). Their experiments, Fleishman argues, emerge from their awareness of history and their "felt needs for personal standing-ground, rather than from willed oppositional stances" (373). Thus, paradoxically, Browning's individual history intensified his loneliness and at the same time linked him with the other major poets of the age.

During the five years between the ages of fourteen and nineteen, Browning clearly experienced a transition from identification with the Romantic poets to differentiation from them, if not outright revolt. And if *Pauline* is not strictly autobiographical, the speaker in *Pauline* does resemble Browning in many ways. The fictional neophyte poet is confused and confusing as he rejects his Romantic predecessors, struggles to differentiate himself from them, and yet continues to love the example they have left him. To them, indeed, he owes his very definition of the poet as subjective intelligence, and he claims in the manner of Shelley that:

I am made up of an intensest life,
Of a most clear idea of consciousness
Of self, distinct from all its qualities,
From all affections, passions, feelings, powers;
And thus far it exists, if tracked, in all:
But linked, in me, to self-supremacy,
Existing as a centre to all things [. . .]
And to a principle of restlessness
Which would be all, have, see, know, taste, feel, all --   (268-74, 277-78)

But his feelings for Shelley's example are mixed:

I was thine in shame,
And now when all thy proud renown is out,
I am a watcher whose eyes have grown dim
With looking for some star which breaks on him
Altered and worn and weak and full of tears. (225-29)

If Shelley is indicated in descriptions of the "Sun-treader" and by the biographical certainty that Browning's teenage poetic passions were fired by reading his work, the language of this passage suggests, more subtly and ironically, an additional debt to Keats. In "On First Looking into Chapman's Homer," Keats speaks in his own voice about the discovery of two poets, Homer and his translator Chapman. The discovery of Chapman's Homer, Keats claims, makes him feel "like some watcher of the skies/ When a new planet swims into his ken" (10-11). Browning's veiled allusion to Keats suggests that, in some ways, Browning's affiliation with him was even more complicated than his relationship with Shelley, for whereas Keats can claim an uncomplicated inheritance of poetic joy and power from both Homer and Chapman, Browning's speaker expresses, again and again, the ambivalence which Browning seems to have felt:

I to rise and rival him?
Feed his fame rather from my heart's best blood,
Wither unseen that he may flourish still. (558-59)

And in fact, to Shelley is given the place of power at the end of the poem:

Sun-treader, I believe in God and truth
And love; and as one just escaped from death

Would bind himself in bands of friends to feel
He lives indeed, so, I would lean on thee! (1020-24)

The language here is as revealing of Browning's predicament as anything he ever wrote. Shelley must be mentor, literary father, friend, and equal, but no figure, even a man of such mythic proportions as Shelley, could, even in imagination, respond to so many and such conflicting demands.

The isolation of Browning's position is also revealed in the form of the poem. As David G. Riede suggests in an article on Browning's generic experiments, because it exaggerates the confessional mode in romantic poetry, *Pauline* "problematizes [and calls] into question the authority and value of the Romantic egotistical sublime" (50). As a dramatic monologue, the poem is similar to some of Browning's later great works. In *Pauline*, a speaker plumbs the depths of his own thought in the presence of an auditor who will judge what he says. But whereas, in his later works, Browning often realizes the auditor's presence in the poem by means of the speaker's paraverbal reactions and rhetorical shifts, in this early work, the auditor seems hermetically sealed off from the speaker. Mermin argues in *The Audience in the Poem* that Browning's mature power resulted from his integration of an audience into the poem itself. But in *Pauline*, the audience still hovers around the edges: the young poet/speaker talks to his lover Pauline, not to communicate, but in order to understand himself. His is the infantile egocentric speech (over a thousand lines of it) of a child struggling for self-articulation. According to Vygotsky's analysis of egocentric speech, children understand themselves in the world and learn how to negotiate in it by talking to themselves out loud, but only in the presence of others ("Tool and Symbol in Child Development" 24-30). Like the young child, learning through deployment of language, Browning's protagonist must have an auditor in order to speak. Even though he claims to be "thine forever" (860), Pauline exists in the poem only as a critical ear and responds only in a footnote - in French - as if distanced even further from the text. She has her revenge, however, for the distance at which she is kept: she explains at great length, with exaggerated condescension, that she would advise the poet to burn this muddled composition if she could be certain that it contained nothing of merit. (Indeed, Browning claimed to Monclar that he had destroyed "Pauline, Part 2," just as he had consigned "Incondita" to the flames when he was fourteen.) Pauline concludes with an analysis (here "translated" by Browning) of the poet's philosophy as she understands it, and by appending this note, Browning deconstructs the speaker in a move that predicts the rich combination of sympathy with judgment, loneliness with genuine dialogue, humor with allegiance to ethical good which characterizes the irony of his mature work:

I believe that in what follows he refers to a certain examination that he once made of the soul, or rather of his own soul, to discover the succession of goals which it would be possible for him to attain, and of which each one, once obtained, would be a sort of plateau from which one could discern other ends, other projects, other pleasures, that should in their turn be surmounted. The conclusion was that oblivion and sleep ought to end everything. This idea, which I do not perfectly grasp, is perhaps as unintelligible to him as to me. (I.1027)

This deconstruction is far more direct and, for the twentieth-century reader, unmistakable, than the judgments passed by the auditors in the later dramatic monologues. Despite her disclaimer, Pauline understands her lover very well, and her voice frames his words in such a way that his mood and temper become clear. Her remarks capture perfectly the tone of Sarah Flower, if not her expressed opinions, and suggest that Browning was worried about the way his poetic efforts were perceived by others, externalizing these (hypothetical) opinions as those of a fictional editor/auditor, as if to diminish their power. In publishing the poem, Browning was trying to form a relationship with anonymous readers, but by publishing a poem which was even more self-referential than the works of his romantic exemplars, he made such a relationship virtually impossible.

When he looked back on *Pauline* years later, Browning saw the poem as part of the process of learning how to be a poet. Four years after its publication, he refers to it in a letter to Monclar as the remaining "crab [. . .] of the stately Tree of Life in my fool's Paradise" (*Correspondence* 3.265). A few years later, he wrote to Elizabeth Barrett, "I was unluckily precocious -- but I had rather you SAW the real infantine efforts. . (verses at six years old, -- and drawings still earlier) -- than this ambiguous, feverish --. Why not wait?" (*Correspondence* 11.317).

In contrast to *Pauline*, Browning's next poem, *Paracelsus* (1835), was reviewed with respect in a few periodicals and, though it did not pay for its publication, it was taken up by enough readers to insure Browning a place at the same dinner table with Wordsworth. On another occasion, Elizabeth Barrett's barrister brother George attended a dinner party, he claimed, "just to see the author of 'Paracelsus' dance the polka" (*Correspondence* 1.318).

In *Paracelsus*, Browning solved the most awkward and obvious generic problems of *Pauline* by writing a "diagrammatic" closet drama, already established by the Romantic poets as a form which could carry the weight of philosophical inquiry and make complex ideas accessible (Harper 66). The poem is based on the life of the historical Paracelsus, a medieval doctor and magician who, in Browning's version, dedicated his life (though not, like Faustus, his soul) to scientific knowledge. The hero has moments of outrageous glory. His university lecture hall is packed to the rafters. Rumors spread that he can raise the dead. He warms his hands at a bonfire of his rivals' books. And although he soon realizes that single-minded pursuit of nature's secrets has rendered him incapable of human connection, and therefore of spiritual wholeness, not until the end of his life does Paracelsus also understand that the knowledge to which he aspires lies, like the stars, forever beyond his grasp, distanced by his own human limitations, the limitations imposed by history, and by his own inability to reach out to others. The secondary characters - his friends Festus and Michal and a rival poet Aprile - clarify the main character's sometimes obscure thought, voice the reader's potential horror or amazement at Paracelsus's soaring ego, and suggest by contrast his dangerous emotional and intellectual isolation.[21]

The character of Paracelsus adds a new dimension to Browning's ongoing exploration of poetic identity. Even more than *Pauline*, *Paracelsus* problematizes the "subjective" or prophetic stance of an intellect such as Shelley's: the subjective poet, writes Browning in the 1852 essay,

> digs where he stands, -- preferring to seek [the primal elements of humanity] in his own soul as the nearest reflex of that absolute Mind, according to the intuitions of which he desires to perceive and speak [. . .] . He is rather a seer [. . .] than a fashioner, and what he produces will be less a work than an effluence. (1002)

Sometimes Paracelsus is a poet, but always he is a magus - or a seer - aspiring to the condition of disembodied intellect. He wants to know all, to know it all at once, to attain an unmediated knowledge of god. If *Pauline* suggests that poetry can fragment individual consciousness by separating it from the rest of humanity, in *Paracelsus*, Browning suggests the more refined theory that not only Romantic poetry, but any kind of single-minded intellectual or creative endeavor, attenuates the relationship between individuals and their human surroundings and has the potential for isolating them. The descriptions of the "objective" poet such as Shakespeare and, even more, the "subjective" poet such as Shelley are also, in fact, ambivalent: in the essay on Shelley, Browning writes that even though his insights are powerful, the subjective poet works "Not with the combination of humanity in action, but with the primal elements of

---

[21] In his analysis of dynamics among characters in *Paracelsus* in *The Dialectical Temper: The Rhetorical Art of Robert Browning* (14-16), Shaw invokes James' term *ficelles* to describe Festus and Michal, suggesting that these characters function only as a pretext for Paracelsus to speak.

humanity [. . .]" (1002). The statement implies that, even though the romantic poet is motivated by love, in searching for truth within his own nature, he risks solipsism and isolation. Elizabeth Barrett had suggested the same thing in "The Poet's Vow," as had Tennyson in "The Palace of Art." Only with his dying breath does Paracelsus acknowledge that self-absorption has blinded him to the power of the moment, the beauty of the other, and the connection between love and hate: "All this I knew not, and I failed" (885).

It was difficult for Browning to be satisfied with such a mechanically structured work as *Paracelsus*. Although he had expressed himself more clearly than before, he still had not devised a form which demonstrated his theme. Browning's most profound contribution to Victorian culture would be his articulation of the indeterminacy of truth and the limits of words. In his next poem, *Sordello* (1840), he tried, not only to narrate the human failure to connect through the imperfect instrument of language, but to demonstrate it. Sordello himself thinks that poetic language "scarce allowed a tithe/ To reach the light" (II.572-73). The multiple frames and broken lines of the narrative represent attempts to embody this insight.

Sordello was actually begun before the completion of *Paracelsus* and revised or rewritten several times before publication. Browning based his poem on the life of a troubadour who is fictionalized as Dante's guide in *Purgatory*, and he read more about Sordello in Danielo Bartoli's *De' Simboli Trasportati al Morale*. In retelling the story, Browning returned to two themes which he had already begun to develop in *Pauline* and *Paracelsus*: isolation from friends and peers and the difficulties of emotional or aesthetic affiliation.

In Browning's poem, Sordello is the missing heir of Taurello Salinguerra, head of the Ghibellines, or the Imperial party. The aim of the Ghibellines was to centralize power, thereby further enslaving the peasantry. However, believing he is an orphan, and isolated from his peers, Sordello grows up committed to poetry and to the Guelf or Papal cause, which seems to him better to represent the interests of the Italian people. Sordello's double political and aesthetic commitment results from a loneliness which allows him to empathize with suffering, but for young Sordello, principles are literally a substitute for love and communication, and, as such, they prove to be an inadequate guide for living. When he leaves his childhood home, a castle near Mantua, Sordello comes into the city to attend a Court of Love. Although his poetry is an instant success because he has so thoroughly mastered the literary forms, yet Sordello is unable to understand the subjective poetry of his bested rival, Eglamor. Meanwhile, Eglamor is so devastated by Sordello's technical brilliance that he dies.[22] After the competition, Sordello becomes acquainted with the politically powerful, including Palma, an eligible and astute young woman who may be able to restore peace through a shrewd marriage. However, finding that his own ideas about poetry are not shared by his audience, Sordello retreats to the castle of his childhood, where he stays for a year. At the end of that time, he is summoned back to public life by the beautiful Palma, who reveals that she has fallen in love with him. Soon, Sordello discovers that his father is Taurello, and that Palma is also allied with Taurello and the Ghibellins. Sordello becomes confused about which side in the struggle has the interests of the people at heart, but he realizes that getting to the root of this problem is impossible - as is getting to the root of the conflicts within poetic practice. When in turn Taurello discovers his son's identity, Taurello makes him the head of the family and inserts Sordello inevitably into the political struggle. Finally, Sordello dies, confused and once again alone. Sordello's father has not fathered him; Eglamor, the elder poet he displaces, has not taught him; the woman who claims to love Sordello cannot be extricated from political alliances which make love suspect.

Like the protagonist himself, the reader is left to wonder what Sordello should have done, how he might have made the right political choices, how he might have served the people through his art, how he might have found love, why he died. According to Bakhtin, the poet ordinarily achieves "unity and singularity" by "destroying all traces of social heteroglossia and diversity of language" (*Discourse in the Novel* 296, 298). In lyric poetry, especially, the poet's word is his alone, and, even when it is ambiguous, the poet controls the ambiguity. In contrast, Browning's poem demonstrates indeterminacy. His goal in *Sordello* is to involve the audience in making the meaning of the poem: the protagonist, for example, is put before the reader:

---

[22] A common theme in Browning criticism and biography is the plot of *Sordello* (and other poems) as an "exorcism" of Shelley, and the dismissal of Shelley at the beginning of the poem as a clear signal that Browning was conscious of engaging in a very different poetic enterprise:

> stay -- thou spirit, come not near
> Now -- not this time desert thy cloudy place
> To scare me, thus employed, with that pure face! (I.60-62)

But the system of references to Romantic poetry undermines the narrative logic which most readers need in order to make sense of the story. See, for instance, Altick, Miller, Ryals, and Bloom.

By making speak, myself kept out of view,
The very man as he was wont to do,
And leaving you to say the rest for him. (1.15-17)

In this passage, which is representative of the narrative approach throughout, Browning radically departs from the norm in poetic language, giving "primacy [. . .] to the response, as the activating principle: [this primacy] prepares the ground for an active and engaged understanding" (*Discourse in the Novel* 282). Built upon what Bakhtin calls "the interindividual word," Browning's discourse in *Sordello* constitutes a community - of reader, writer, and literary history - within the text.

Browning's intention to disrupt the normal unity of poetic discourse is signaled in a subtle way even by his choice of subjects: the historical Sordello was an Italian poet who wrote not in his own vernacular, but in Old Occitan, the language of the troubadours. The work of a poet like Sordello was literally alien to his place. Additionally, only the most attentive reader can be sure at all times who is actually speaking: there are many minor speaking characters in *Sordello*, and the narrator of the poem has been likened by Daniel Stempel to the impresario of a Victorian diorama, whose point of view continually shifts from near his subject to above and beyond it ("Browning's *Sordello*: The Art of the Makers-See"). This narrator is himself sometimes interrupted by Browning *in propria vox* - and yet, "Browning" is here, in Tucker's term a "fashioned self" ("Browning as Escape Artist" 10). About half-way through the poem, at the end of Book III, Browning reveals himself behind the scenes, as he sits on the steps by the lagune in Venice, watching the women of the street and musing on the nature of poetry. He tells us that if Eglamor's songs were complete because he was at one with his music, then Sordello's songs were "true" because "the singer's proper life was 'neath/ The life his song exhibits [. . .]./ his lay was but an episode/ In the bard's life" (3.622, 625-30). The best poets, he continues, "Impart the gift of seeing" to their hearers (3.868). Browning suggests that he is himself such a poet, "ply[ing] the pulleys" (3.933) behind the characters in his history, expecting the audience to join in "our business" (3.975), creating the meaning of the performance.[23] By the time he wrote *Sordello*, Browning had consciously rejected for himself the role of prophet or priest for that of "Maker-see," and he had fully embraced, not a language "illuminated," as Bakhtin says,

---

[23] Riede's article, "Genre and Poetic Authority in *Pippa Passes*," pursues the metaphor of the puppeteer within an analysis of Browning's reader-writer dynamic in *Sordello*.

"by one unitary and indisputable discourse," but a layered, heterophonic language which he would continue to refine in the decades to come.

Sordello probably comes closest of any of Browning's works, including *The Ring and the Book* (1868-69), to the state of the polyvocal novel as it developed in the middle of the nineteenth century and continued to develop into the twentieth. Broaching a theme which has been further developed in more recent Browning criticism, J. W. Harper called the poem "perhaps the subtlest and most complex psychological novel in English poetry" ("'Eternity our Due'" 66). *Pauline* may be read as a parody of the self-absorbed romantic poet whose audience (Pauline) deconstructs his discourse. *Paracelsus* is about a brilliant but self-absorbed intellectual who fails because he does not allow communication. Technically, *Sordello* represents a tremendous advance beyond Browning's earlier efforts; it is so intricate that Isobel Armstrong writes,

> the poem is not a story or a linear narrative at all [. . .]. It is and is about the act and process of mediation itself. It lives out its epistemology, experiencing the contradictions of the unstable process of discerning, becoming what you behold, which is continually falling into onesideness. (*Language as Living Form* 143)

Browning's childhood and youth, when he was surrounded by affection but isolated from the intellectual rapport and creative community he needed, gave him special insight into the possibility of literature as dialogue, as an indeterminate art form in which the meaning lies between or among different perspectives. *The Ring and the Book* is, of course, the best known work in which this principle is obvious, but the dialogic impulse in fact motivates almost all of Browning's work. In *Sordello*, Browning consciously crafted a language in which meaning is constructed in a dialogue with the reader. The story is full of gaps which must be filled by the reader through, perhaps, what Vygotsky terms "zones of proximal development."[24] But Browning's contemporaries, taught by the Romantic poets to look for unity, dismissed these dialogic works as obscure: the experience of rejection must have been painful in the extreme for the young poet. At the end of the century, Swinburne would astonish friends by committing the whole poem to memory at the age of nineteen. In *Victorian Revolutionaries*, Morse Peckham calls *Sordello* one of Browning's four

---

[24] Just how conscious Browning was of trying to force readers to learn by exerting themselves is suggested in Hair's discussion in the first chapter of *Robert Browning's Language* of Browning's debt to Johnson's dictionary, Locke's language theory, and contemporary Congregationalist thinking about language.

greatest works. Ryals has devoted several volumes to an argument for recuperating Browning's lesser-known poetry, including *Sordello*. Tucker, in *Browning's Beginnings* and elsewhere, argues that Browning's early works were prototypical in their deliberate resistance to closure. Similarly, in *Robert Browning's Language*, Hair reads these works as prototypical experiments with language to which he would return in the "parleyings"of the 1880s.

Still, even after a hegemonic Modernism which enabled readers to appreciate these aspects of Browning's early works, critics have not agreed about how successful they are. In one of the most attentive readings of the poem, "Browning's *Sordello* and the Parables of Modernist Poetics" (52), Christine Froula argues that *Sordello* failed on its own terms as an attempt to communicate the importance of language to Browning's contemporaries. Even Elizabeth Barrett called it "a noble picture with its face to the wall just now -- or at least, in the shadow" (*Correspondence* 11.67). In spite of the pain it must have caused him, the reception of the poem redefined for Browning the perennial problem of how to integrate himself into poetic tradition and communicate with readers in the present.[25]

After *Sordello*, Browning continued to experiment with dogged persistence. *Bells and Pomegranates* - with its obscure but catchy title - was a varied series of works published between 1842 and 1845 in eight pamphlets, printed in small type in double columns, meant to appeal to the tastes and pocketbooks of more casual readers than he had envisioned for his first three works. By the end of this series, Elizabeth Barrett had become Browning's mentor, and his desire for a wider readership was answered by her wish to help him find it.

The series begins with *Pippa Passes* (1841), another generic experiment which, like *Paracelsus*, includes clear signals to readers about who is speaking, and where, and when. Although Browning's reputation for obscurity and uncomfortable depth largely deprived him of the readership

---

[25] Without denying the importance of an educated readership, Erickson has suggested a line of inquiry which provocatively places Browning's work, as well that of Wordsworth, Carlyle, and Austen, within an economic context. Erickson argues in *The Economy of Literary Form: English Literature and the Industrialization of Publishing, 1800-1850* (1996) that cheaper publication costs enabled readers to buy longer, less condensed and demanding works than poetry; consequently, poetry declined in popularity during the first part of the nineteenth century as readers became less willing to pore over details, although critics and poets did not yet understood the reasons for this market trend. If Erickson is correct, Browning's misdiagnosis of his failure to reach many readers contributed to his difficulties.

he sought for *Bells and Pomegranates*, *Pippa* is in fact a brilliant appeal to both casual readers and the more serious readers Browning had intended to reach with his longer poems. It was, and still is, read as a poem about innocence so pure that it remains untouched even in close proximity to evil because:

> God's in his heaven --
> All's right with the world!

But Browning's earlier themes are still present, as powerful and as ambiguous as ever. Like Sordello, the young singer on her yearly holiday from the silk mills is a friendless but gifted orphan. Like him, she reaches her auditors with her song, but if she changes them at all, it is for the worse. Hearing the girl sing, corrupt priests still continue to conspire; cruel young men persist in a brutal practical joke on a companion; and a young assassin rushes headlong into his crime. In a letter to Mitford, Elizabeth Barrett noted in particular Part I, in which the lovers Ottima and Sebald, when they hear Pippa beneath the window, realize that hatred has begun to replace erotic attraction after they have conspired to kill Ottima's husband: "But if you see no genius in that magnificent scene of pure passion in Pippa Passes [. . .] we differ again & widely" (*Correspondence* 10.33). To Browning himself, she wrote that *Pippa Passes* displayed the vast range of his poetry and his ability to harmonize the grotesque aspects of the world with its beauty, and she claimed to wish she had written it herself (10.79, 91). The form resembles that of Guiseppe Parini's eighteenth-century satire *Il Giorno*, which follows the typical day of a typical gallant. In a carnivalesque reversal, Browning recast the story as the typical day of a typical child laborer in a silk mill. Formally closer to his other plays than *Paracelsus*, *Pippa Passes* was nevertheless not intended for the stage. In one sense, it is a genre unto itself. In another sense, the poem is one of Browning's most representative early works, for in it, he brings about a synthesis between the explicitly dramatic pieces written for the stage and the dramatic lyrics and romances which would be central to his future work. In *Pippa Passes*, perhaps more than any other early poem, Browning created "action in character."

Bells and Pomegranates also includes plays, some intended for the theatre (*The Return of the Druses, A Blot in the 'Scutcheon*) and some for readers only (*Colombe's Birthday, Luria,* and *A Soul's Tragedy*). In addition, Browning sent two children's poems to Macready's bedridden son, one of which, "The Pied Piper," was published almost immediately in *Dramatic Lyrics* (1842). At the same time, he began to experiment with pure sound in lyrics such as the "Cavalier Tunes," which appeared in the same volume (the third number of *Bells and Pomegranates*).

But the dramatic monologue is more central in Browning's work and dominates several numbers of *Bells and Pomegranates* as well. These poems are relatively short and accessible to readers unwilling to sort through the confused and conflicting narrative layers of a poem such as *Sordello*. By 1836, when he published "Porphyria's Lover" and "Johannes Agricola in Meditation" in Fox's journal *The Monthly Repository*, Browning had already discovered and begun to refine this form. In these shorter works, Browning writes from the idiosyncratic perspectives of lunatics, isolates, and eccentrics. In addition to the extreme and original Antinomian, Johannes Agricola, and the lonely madman who has loved Porphyria literally to death (these two poems were paired in 1842 under the title "Madhouse Cells"), the new characters include a blithering monk consumed by jealousy of his brother's sincere piety, an Old Regime courtesan who poisons her rival with a delicate pastille, and a senile bishop who, in his death-bed ravings, confuses the peachy flesh of a long-dead mistress with the striated marble he has hoarded for his own tomb. There are crazy misogynists, lovers stymied by doubt, and idealistic revolutionaries. All are isolated within the lonely prisons of their own consciousness. Within the frame of the monologue, Browning could distance and dramatize the self-centered or obsessive personality, and objectively render complex psychological phenomena. Even in these early poems, Browning exploited the irony of the form, in which a speaker explains himself or herself to a silent auditor at a moment of crisis, revealing under pressure more than he or she intends - or even knows. The dramatic monologue focuses attention on suggestive details rather than general ideals; in this form, Browning was able to exercise his ability to notice and describe, to draw with words as his father drew with pencil and watercolors. Finally, the dramatic form of the monologue was more suited to Browning's personality, for, like many of his characters, he was divided by conflicting impulses. Browning wanted to communicate and at the same time to protect himself against misunderstanding.

Even within the time frame represented by these poems, Mermin detects a growing technical and psychological complexity: in the earlier poems, the speakers address vague, absent, or purely imaginary audiences. In the later ones, especially those written in 1845 and after, the audiences are present and responsive (*The Audience in the Poem*). To use Bakhtin's terminology, "The Bishop Orders His Tomb at Saint Praxed's Church," for example, which appeared in 1845, is thus more dialogic than the earlier "Madhouse Cells." This development represents the trend in Browning's poetry toward literary dialogue. In other words, Browning gradually learned to exploit and control the ironic potential of juxtapositions among languages, dialects, genres, and individual perceptions.

After his association with Elizabeth Barrett began in 1845, he became more conscious that, paradoxically, the complex trope of literary dialogue in his poetic language so alienated his readers that it endangered the possibility of a living conversation with them. And he began to work from this premise. Although Barrett's struggle was similar, she herself was struggling not so much with language as with form. Her temporary solution was a kind of artistic amputation - of emotion from some of her poems and logic from others. This strategy worked for her readers, if not for her. She was also older, more experienced, and more generously acknowledged for her efforts. Several Browning critics have suggested that the poet decided that he was an "objective poet" and then sought out a "subjective poet" in the hope that dialogue with her would enable him to be more successful.[26] In 1846, Browning wrote to his future wife, in a letter which is frequently quoted,

> I have lost, of late, interest in dramatic writing, as you know -- and, perhaps, occasion -- And, dearest, I mean to take your advice and be quiet awhile and let my mind get used to its medium of sight, seeing all things, as it does, thro' you: and then, let all I have done be the prelude and the real work begin -- (*Correspondence* 12.70)

Whether this statement should be read primarily as a moment in a courtship, as Karlin suggests in his study of the courtship correspondence, or whether it is simply a statement about Browning's intentions, the reception of his poems and plays had by this time convinced him that his

---

[26] Ryals also suggests that Barrett Browning exacerbated the tension between subjectivity and objectivity within Browning's work, mostly because Browning identified her as a purely subjective poet. In his article, "Projection and the Female Other: Romanticism, Browning, and the Victorian Dramatic Monologue," U. C. Knoepflmacher puts it this way: "Both in her poetry as well as in her own person, Elizabeth Barrett had tried to maintain that Keatsian 'central self' she has Aurora Leigh adopt. Barrett thus furnished Browning with a further link to the Romantic idealization of a female complement who might restore an incomplete male self" (141). However, this idea of the subjective-objective continuum had been used and overused ever since Coleridge brought the terms into the vocabulary of every poet and critic. While they undoubtedly express an important tension in Browning's work and provide him with a convenient way to discuss Shelley within English literary history, these terms were probably not as freighted with meaning for him as they had been for poets of the previous generation.

"real work" was not the interior monologue he had attempted in *Pauline*, nor the long multi-layered historical narrative of *Sordello*, nor the drama, in which interiority is perceived from outside, not even just the *études* in abnormal psychology. When his friendship with Barrett began, he was poised to enlarge the dialogue in poetry and in life. She would be the conversational double poor Chatterton never found.

Chapter 2

A Broken Poem
1844-1846

In his 1912 biography, G. K. Chesterton wrote that Browning "adored Shelley, and also Carlyle who sneered at him. He delighted in Mill, and also in Ruskin who rebelled against Mill. He excused Napoleon III and also Landor who hurled curses against Napoleon. He admired all the cycle of great men who all contemned each other" (56). As a poet, Browning certainly saw himself as a social isolate, but the other side of his remarkable personality was a capacity for affection and tolerance which permitted him to cherish people with whom he disagreed. Although Browning's capacity for contraries is responsible for the rich complexity of his poetry, it sometimes brought him to a dead stop. The composition of *Saul* was such an impasse.

In the three years before his correspondence with Barrett began, Browning's social life seemed more complete than it had ever been before. Although their collaborative literary projects languished, the Dowsons, Young, Arnould, and Dommett, the "Colloquial," as they now called themselves, still met for frequent evenings of talk in Camberwell. Browning's friendships with Thomas Carlyle and with his father's old school friend John Kenyon were strengthening. Shelley's friend Leigh Hunt also became a friend of Browning. Through Fox and Eliza Flower, Browning met the poet and adventurer R. H. Horne, a supporter of Tennyson and the "spasmodic" school of poets in fashion during the thirties and forties. In *A New Spirit of the Age*, compiled with the collaboration of Elizabeth Barrett, Horne lavishly praised Browning's work.

After the poor reception of *Sordello*, Browning was piecing his career back together again. More than ever, his friends were also his literary associates, and much of his published work between 1842 and 1845 was written at their request or suggestion.[1] For Thomas Hood, who founded and

---

[1] For more complete accounts of Browning's literary friendships, see Maynard, *Browning's Youth*, Chapters 5, 7-8, and also Irvine and Honan, *The Book, the Ring, and the Poet*, Chapters 7-9.

briefly edited *Hood's Magazine*, Browning wrote several poems which were re-published in 1845 in *Dramatic Lyrics and Romances*. In 1842, he contributed the Chatterton essay anonymously to *The Foreign Quarterly*, edited by his friend John Forster. The *Bells and Pomegranates* series continued with poems and plays - *Dramatic Lyrics* in 1842, *The Return of the Druses* and *A Blot on the 'Scutcheon* in 1843, *Colombe's Birthday* in 1844.

Late in 1844, when he returned from a tour of Rome, Pisa, Florence, and Naples, Browning discovered his name again in print - this time in an unexpected place, the copy of Elizabeth Barrett's new *Poems*, which Kenyon had just presented to Sarianna. Since Barrett was his cousin, Kenyon no doubt felt some pride of ownership in the volume. In "Lady Geraldine's Courtship," a modern ballad narrating the love affair between a poet and a great lady, the courtship is conducted by proxy, through the two characters' habit of reading aloud to each other. Bertram the poet selects from the literary monuments of Western culture,

> Or at times a modern volume, Wordsworth's solemn-thoughted idyl,
> Howitt's ballad-verse, or Tennyson's enchanted reverie, --
> Or from Browning some 'Pomegranate,' which, if cut deep down the middle,
> Shows a heart within blood-tinctured, of a veined humanity.

Inspired by the flattering reference, Browning wrote to Elizabeth Barrett on January 10, 1845. What he found in his correspondent, if not his own rare capacity for extremes, was a spirit which accepted and understood this quality. Barrett commented on the wholeness of Browning's poetry in her second letter to him:

> You have in your vision two worlds -- or to use the language of the schools of the day, you are both subjective & objective in the habits of your mind -- You can deal with both abstract thought, & with human passion in the most passionate sense. Thus, you have an immense grasp in Art; & no one at all accustomed to consider the usual forms of it, could help regarding with reverence & gladness the gradual expansion of your powers. Then you are "masculine" to the height -- and I, as a woman, have studied some of your gestures of language & intonation wistfully, as a thing beyond me far! & the more admirable for being beyond. (*Correspondence* 10.26)

Barrett's response must have come as an enormous relief, for she seemed to understand the reach of his work. He began to send his manuscript poems to her almost immediately, for "corrections," he said. At his request, Barrett undertook a meticulous reading of his poems and plays, and a review of proofs for *Dramatic Romances and Lyrics*, the *Bells and Pomegranates* number to appear in November.

Despite their continual protests to the contrary throughout the ensuing correspondence, it is clear that Browning and Barrett were attracted to each other first and primarily through their poetry. Their courtship was profoundly verbal, and their correspondence adds to the impression given by their poetry, that each understood language itself as both an abstract system and an extension of the physical body. It is not coincidental that each was also multilingual, for, as Yopie Prins argues in her brilliant dissertation, "Translating Greek tragedy: Elizabeth Barrett and Robert Browning," translation became the two poets' private metaphor for intersubjective space, belonging to neither and both, in which disinterested communication could occur. Furthermore, their conversations about language and translation helped them to articulate their sense that language was an imperfect medium of exchange - not ever quite clear enough for lovers.

The attraction between Barrett and Browning was not based simply on the complementarity or differences in the way they wrote, although this complementarity was essential to their relationship and their future development as poets. There are also considerable parallels in the ways Barrett and Browning deploy poetic language, experimenting with complex groupings of varied meters, stretching metrical feet often beyond immediate recognition, cobbling together odd slant rhymes or eye rhymes, playing sense against sound, resorting to colloquial diction, and in general undermining the poetic diction which they inherited. Each also felt that the other represented some opposing quality, but they respected each other's craft and commitment. Again, it is helpful to return to Chesterton, one of the few early critics to treat the two Brownings with an even hand. Chesterton comments that what distinguishes the two poets is like "the difference between two primary colors, not between dark and light shades of the same color" (58). It is not surprising that at first Browning appeared ready to lapse back into the childish habit of choosing an older woman for a mentor, but his relationship with Elizabeth Barrett soon developed into something more profound than his earlier friendships with Fanny Haworth and the Flower sisters. Barrett was more emotionally engaged with Browning's work - and far more exacting in her criticisms of his poems.

Within months after their correspondence began, Barrett had annotated, in her fine, spidery script, a number of shorter poems which would appear shortly thereafter in *Dramatic Lyrics and Romances*, including "Pictor Ignotus," "The Confessional," "Garden Fancies" (the paired poems "The Flower's Name" and "Sibrandus Schafnaburgensis"), "The Boy and the

Angel," "The Bishop Orders His Tomb at Saint Praxed's Church,"[2] and "The Laboratory." "The Flight of the Duchess" elicited four pages of notes, and when she was asked for her opinions about the plays, Barrett responded by writing at least ten pages of commentary on *Luria* and five on *A Soul's Tragedy*. These responses, which range from enthusiastic praise to considered advice, are in addition to extensive commentary on these and other poems by Browning in her letters to him.[3]

One of Barrett's favorite poems at this time appears to have been "How They Brought the Good News from Ghent to Aix," which she loved for its pure physicality:

> You hear the very 'trampling & breathing' of the horses all through -- and the sentiment is left in its right place through all the physical force-display. Then the difficult management of the three horses, of the three individualities, . . & Roland carrying the interest with him triumphantly! I know you must have been fond of this poem: & nobody can forget it who has looked at it once. (*Correspondence* 11.387)

"Trampling," "breathing," "physical force" - the erotic attraction evident in Barrett's description sounds out fully only in the sonnets she was secretly writing at the same time. When Roland (one of the horses) lies dying from exhaustion in the last stanza, his rider "pour[s] down his throat our last measure of wine" (58). Her comments resonate with a passage in the Chatterton essay, which suggests that literary and erotic energy are closely related: "the very notion of obtaining a free way for impulses that can find vent in no other channel [. . .] is implied in all literary production" (116). In a letter that summer, Barrett mentions the poem again, remarking that "that touch of natural feeling at the end [. . .] prove[s] that it was not in brutal carelessness that the poor horse was driven through all that suffering" (*Correspondence* 11.167).

The exchange of letters, the pages of notes on Browning's poetry, and no doubt the regular visits included much discussion of writing in general and writers in particular. Unlike Bertram and Lady Geraldine, Barrett and

---

[2] In "Wanted, Dead or Alive: Browning's Historicism," an analysis of "The Bishop Orders His Tomb," Tucker examines an episode in Elizabeth Barrett Browning's reading of Browning's poems in the summer of 1845. He notes that her reading was accurate (in contrast to Ruskin's rather narrow requirements for Browning's work) and worded with particular tact, to enable the poet to make changes, while preserving the subtleties.

[3] From Barrett's manuscript notes on Browning's poems, which are in the Wellesley Browning collection, I derive the number of pages she devoted to each poem. The notes are printed in Appendix IV of *Correspondence* 11.

Browning found themselves in an occasional disagreement. For Barrett could be critical as well as complimentary, as she is, for instance, in her four pages of notes about "England in Italy" (In 1849, retitled "The Englishman in Italy"). The two poets argued on paper about the lines describing a religious procession:

> And then will the flaxen-wigged Image
>   Be carried in pomp
> Through the plain, while in gallant procession
>   The priests meant to stomp. (269-72)

Barrett emphatically objected to the word choice and the rhyme:

> 'The priests mean to stomp.' But is this word 'stamp', & is it to rhyme to 'pomp'.
> I object to **that** rhyme -- I!!⁴

Over her comment, Browning again wrote "stomp," and he retained his own word in every edition. He usually made changes where Barrett suggested, though rarely as she suggested. In this poem, however, he clung stubbornly to sounds which Barrett evidently found jarring.

"Influence" is usually one-sided. Even "mutual influence" implies a willingness of each to capitulate, or to incorporate without necessarily assimilating, something from the other. In this sense, Barrett and Browning did not influence each other at all, although eventually they shared a fund of imagery and ideas and, more important, they created together a dialogic space in which new ideas and meanings could emerge and find their way back into both bodies of poetry. From the beginning, as the exchanges about Browning's poetry suggest, the whole correspondence between the two poets reveals an erotic energy which ebbs and flows, surfaces and subsides, as the two poets argue with and encourage each other. There are frequent forays of humor and wit in the letters, but the feelings and concerns are never trivial or simple. Indeed, Browning proposed marriage - even before meeting Barrett - and she threatened to drop the correspondence if he broached the subject again. Throughout their courtship, Barrett entertained common sense fears about real obstacles to the intimate relationship which Browning urged upon her. Her father inexplicably rejected the notion of marriage for any of his children, but her health was an even more serious concern. Barrett's deepest fear was the possibility that grief and guilt about her brother's death, and her consequent

----

⁴ The manuscript notes show that EBB boldfaced the word "that."

entombment in the dark room on Wimpole Street, had robbed her of the vitality that Robert Browning deserved in a partner. He respected her grief, but urged her to overcome it.[5]

Barrett often spoke of herself as disembodied; at thirty-nine years, she was already a myth, known to her reading public as an invisible spiritual presence in their midst. But her comments on Browning's poetry continually reveal a belief that one aspect of poetry must be the physical effect of the language through which the emotion is conveyed. In spite of her appreciation for Browning's poetry, Barrett was concerned about its lack of commercial appeal:

> You perplex your readers often by casting yourself on their intelligence in these things -- and although it is true that readers in general are stupid & cant understand. . . & they dont catch your point of sight at first unless you think it worth while to push them by the shoulders & force them into the right place" (*Correspondence* 11.110 Barrett's ellipse).

(Perhaps she worried about the damage that misunderstanding readers could inflict on the poet himself: it is significant that the next topic in this letter is an inquiry about Browning's migraine.) Furthermore, Barrett felt that Browning's poetry could not fulfill its social function of teaching if it were not read. In a sense, he replaced Bro as "Mentor" to her boundless intellectual energy - but in addition to Browning's pedagogical role in her life, Barrett held fast to the conviction that the poet's role in society is to instruct. Thus, her suggestions for the poems in *Dramatic Romances and Lyrics* were made not only for the sake of the poet himself, but to place Browning's ideas and personality in a clearer light for the reading public.

Especially revealing of Barrett's presence in Browning's poetry is the exchange of ideas about *Saul*, a poem which Browning began writing in April 1845 and showed Barrett the next month. In its conception, *Saul* was a more mature poem than he had ever written before, a more serious and conscious attempt to solve problems with genre and literary affiliation than Browning had ever made before, and, I believe, a more conscious examination of the gender norms which structured both his life and his poetry.

When Browning suspended work on *Saul* in 1845, he was unable to solve the compositional problems attendant upon his emerging insights about himself and his work, but he knew that he had untangled several

---

[5] Karlin's *The Courtship of Robert Browning* and *Elizabeth Barrett* is the most detailed account of the courtship as it is revealed through the correspondence.

loops of the knot. The completion of *Saul*, which stretched out over the next nine years, attests to Browning's persistent struggle to write a new integrative poetry, both subjective and objective, built on dramatic principles, appealing to the public, accessible to his friends, and adhering to the Victorian desideratum that poetry serve the social and spiritual needs of its readers. The poem is one of Browning's few explicitly religious works. It also contains some of the most erotic language in Browning's *oeuvre* - unexpectedly, for it is the story of David, the young poet and future giant-killer, when he sings for King Saul in an effort to heal his broken spirit.

Significantly, *Saul* is the only poem for which Barrett was petitioned for substantive rather than merely editorial help (Sullivan, "Some Interchange of Grace" 59). When he first mentioned the poem to her, in fact, Browning couched his request in collaborative terms. "The Flight of the Duchess" (a long poem of rescue and romance) is destined for *Bells and Pomegranates*, he explains: "So is a certain 'Saul' I should like to show you one day. . . I should not be sorry if, in justice, you knew all I have really done, -- written in the portfolio there, -- tho' that would be far enough from this me, that writes to you now. I should like to write something in concert with you -- How I would try!" (*Correspondence* 10.201). Barrett's written response to this poem, five pages of commentary, was even more attentive than usual, and, although he did not make all the alterations Barrett suggested for his poems, Browning did make no fewer than fourteen changes in the hundred lines of the *Saul* fragment. As usual, she commented frequently about the meter, but she was more interested in pointing out the beauty and power of particular lines or phrases. More important, Barrett seems to have understood the writing of *Saul* as part of the process through which Browning was finding himself as a poet: in her note on the poem, she writes, "Full of power & beauty it is, -- in the conception, very striking -- (*Correspondence* 11. 390). In a letter written about the same time, she reminds him, "And do you remember of the said poem, that it is there only as a first part, & that the next parts must certainly follow & complete what will be a great lyrical work [. . .]" (*Correspondence* 11.235). In the meantime, she encouraged him to publish the first nine sections in 1845 as a fragment, suggesting in several letters the need to "confess" the poem as a fragment -- "Because as a poem of yours it stands there & wants unity, & people cant be expected to understand the difference between incompleteness & defect, unless you make a sign" (*Correspondence* 11.145).

Browning's uncharacteristic decision to publish an unfinished poem has inspired numerous theories, some of which implicate Elizabeth Barrett. Miller interpreted the publication history of *Saul* as a chronicle of the

Brownings' "affinity and disparity" *(Robert Browning: A Portrait* 190). DeVane argued that, although Browning's religious doubts blocked his ability to develop the Christian iconography embedded in the David story, Barrett Browning's religious views eventually provided him with enough post-marital religious certainty to develop the poem's Christian potential ("The Virgin and the Dragon," 1967). More recently, although he does not credit Barrett with Browning's religious "conversion," Hair asserts that the halting start and the Christian content of Section IX, in particular, "demand" the conclusion Browning added in 1854, in which David's love for Saul prefigures the Christian myth *(Browning's Experiments with Genre*, 1972). Then, argues Hair, Browning was ready to accede to the demand partly because of his association with Elizabeth Barrett Browning. Similarly, although he does not credit Barrett with exorbitant influence, Shaw interprets the poem as part of Browning's religious development, arguing that "Browning's dilemma in 'Saul' is part of a larger question: how can religion be made to include the believer's self-activity without jeopardizing Christian doctrines of dependence on God?" (212-13). The answer, according to Shaw in *The Lucid Veil*, is Browning's understanding God as "a verb implying a process of development" (217) - thus, Shaw seems to suggest, David glimpses the possibility of the future Incarnation, which will exceed the limits of his own capacity for love.[6]

That the relationship between these two poets affected their poetry, there can be no doubt, but there is every reason to doubt that either simply adopted a belief from the other. Explanations which emphasize collaboration or mutual influence are more helpful. Sullivan suggests that when Barrett Browning finally revealed sonnets she had written in 1845-1846, the thematic link she had made in these poems between love and art inspired Browning to finish the poem ("Some Interchange of Grace" 61). In 1845, she argues, Browning was able to imagine David's art as a balance between an objective, loving poetry and a subjective, prophetic poetry. However, he could not predict the effect of that poetry on the suffering Saul until years later, after he had witnessed the effect of his own love on Elizabeth Barrett and heard her version of their courtship. Karlin offers another biographical argument about the poem's puzzling history. In his analysis of the 1845-46 correspondence, Karlin argues that if Browning did

---

[6] The controversy over *Saul* derives from its transitional place within his poetic development. Roma King argues that Browning got into such a generic tangle that he could not find his way out and that, even when finished, the poem is unsuccessful. Thomas J. Collins argues that the poem was a crucial step in Browning's development and that it was ultimately a success *(Robert Browning's Moral-Aesthetic Theory 1833-1855)*.

not actually write *Saul* for a critical moment in the courtship, he did find it useful to submit it to Barrett at a critical moment, when their relationship was delicately balanced (*The Courtship of Robert Browning and Elizabeth Barrett*, 99).

Whether or not *Saul* was intended as a covert love letter, through the text of the poem, Browning revisits his perennial theme of love and rescue. One of the enabling myths, throughout Browning's poetry and his life, was the story of Andromeda, rescued from the snaky-haired Medusa by the hero Perseus, riding Pegasus, the winged horse who came to be associated with poetry. Although the course of love never does run smooth in Browning's poems which retell this myth, love is the impetus for and result of the rescue. Adrienne Auslander Munich argues that in his later poetry, Browning continues a process of thinking about gender which he began in *Pauline*, *Paracelsus*, and *Sordello* - a process which was represented for him by an engraving of Caravaggio's painting "Perseus and Andromeda," which hung above his desk in his parents' Camberwell home. Munich suggests that Browning found in the engraving a circular pattern which is repeated in a number of his poems. This pattern "collapses the polarities" between male and female, monstrosity and creativity. By the time he began writing *Saul*, Browning had already reworked the Andromeda myth several times. The dearest wish of the narrator in *Pauline* is to rescue the reputation of Shelley; the protagonist of *Sordello* is a would-be savior of the downtrodden; in "Count Gismond" (1842), a more ironic treatment of the story, a young woman is rescued from death at the hands of men who have accused her (perhaps accurately) of adultery.

But while Browning was writing the poem, life was imitating art. Barrett was trapped in a third-story room by circumstances which made her story an instant myth: depression and respiratory illness, a grim and forbidding father, even a magical attendant animal, Flush. Browning's own social whirl failed to compensate for a lifelong existential loneliness which made him reluctant to reveal the intimate details of his mind and heart. The two poets were rescuing each other: it is not surprising that the dynamic of rescue also informs *Saul*, and that the polarities of gender are again collapsed in this poem. With his music, a young, feminized David, with "gracious gold hair" (12) and blue lilies twined around his harp, tries to rescue the spiritually damaged Saul, who is described in both Christ-like and phallic terms - the type and the anti-type of Christ.[7]

---

[7] In *Robert Browning's Language*, Hair claims that this detail is part of a large and intricate web of typological references throughout the poem (160).

He stood as erect as that tent-prop,
   Both arms stretched out wide
On the great cross-support in the centre,
   That goes to each side;
He relaxed not a muscle, but hung there
   As, caught in his pangs
And waiting his change, the king-serpent
   All heavily hangs,
Far away from his kind, in the Pine,
   Till deliverance come
With the Spring-time, -- so agonized Saul,
   Drear and black, blind and dumb. (53-64)[8]

But no biographical approach to *Saul* is sufficient in itself for explaining the anomaly of Browning's unusual decision to publish a fragment, for the emotional tensions Browning was experiencing when he wrote it intersected with perennial creative problems for which he had not yet found solutions. Browning's pursuit of Elizabeth Barrett also suggests that the erotic tensions in his life were imbricated with the stresses he was experiencing in writing poetry. *Saul* was published as a fragment, not just because Barrett advised it, but because Browning understood that he had reached an impasse.

The Biblical David is a puzzling and complex character, ideally suited to Browning's complex project. Because his works stand literally at the center of the Canon, David must have been in some ways a far more terrifying model than Shelley. Browning was not the first to take the risk: he was preceded by Thomas Wyatt in *Seven Penitential Psalms* (1549) and Christopher Smart in "A Song to David" (1763).[9] But David the man was not flawless: he was not only the beautiful and talented boy who slew Goliath and sang to the king, he was also a ruthless politician who often placed his own desires above God's law. He loved the king's son Jonathan, he married Jonathan's sister Michal, and he arranged the death of his lover Bathsheba's first husband. David was a great poet and a great warrior. He

---

[8] Although from other poems I will usually quote from the more readily available (Pettigrew and Collins edition), I will rely on the Oxford edition (Vol. IV, Ed. Ian Jack, Rowena Fowler, and Margaret Smith) for the 1845 version of *Saul*. When the poem was finished and republished in 1855, the lines were not printed as short verse, as they were in the *Bells and Pomegranates* version.

[9] In the 1995 Oxford edition (*Volume V: Men and Women*), Ian Jack and Robert Inglesfield also identify John Brown's *A Dissertation on. . . Poetry and Music, To which is prefixed, The Cure of Saul. A Sacred Ode* [1791] and Johan Gottfried Herder's *Vom Geist der ebräischen Poesie* as sources (358n).

evades easy categorization as a moral being and, as a lover of women and men, evades the gender polarities of Browning's own time.

Browning's 1845 fragment ends at almost the same point as its source, I Samuel xvi, with David still ministering to Saul in his tent. The indeterminate ending of the Biblical source is surely one reason Browning found his poem hard to complete. But Smart's pyrotechnical "A Song to David," Browning's second source and inspiration, ends differently. Smart's last reference to David himself is in Stanza LXXXIII:

> More precious that diviner part
> Of David, even the Lord's own heart,
>   Great, beautiful, and new:
> In all things where it was intent,
> In all extremes, in each event,
>   Proof -- answering true to true.

This allusion to the Christ who will descend through David's line, and to the divine replication of David's great heart in Christ, is followed by three more stanzas, a montage of images and ideas relating to God, to human pain and achievement, to nature, and to art. Smart's gloss to these eighteen lines is only tangentially related to their substance: "That the best poet which ever lived was thought worthy of the highest honor which possibly can be conceived, as *the Saviour of the World was ascribed to his house, and called his son in the body*" (Smart's italics). Smart's brilliant, eccentric celebration of David's life and poetry both inspired and intimidated Browning. Forty years after writing "Saul," he describes, in "Parleying with Christopher Smart," the moment of discovering "the miracle" of Smart's poetry, which "Broke on me as I took my sober way" (12-13) and speaks with wonder and awe of Smart's inspired madness, the source of all his poetry.

During the composition of "Saul," Browning was also reading the tragedy *Saul*, written in 1782 by Vittorio Alfieri, whose sonnets also provided Elizabeth Barrett with models of another kind. Browning wrote an ambivalent tribute to Alfieri in a letter to Barrett in April of 1845, just when he was probably writing the poem (153):

> Alfieri, with even grey eyes, and a life of travel, writes you some fifteen tragedies as coulourless as sallad grown under a garden glass with matting over it -- as free, that is, from local colouring, touches of the soil they are said to spring from, -- think of "Saulle," and his Greek attempts! (X. 184)

Equivocal though this comment about Alfieri may be, Browning ended his fragment with a device lifted from Act III, Scene IV of the tragedy. In the Argument, Alfieri characterizes this scene from the play as, "a succession of lyrical poems of varying metres, adapted to the different themes he commemorates" (108). Likewise, Browning's fragment ends with a set of ten distinct lyrical poems. In Alfieri's version, David's poetic power is so strong that he is able not only to heal Saul again with song, but also to drive him back again to madness. Such a perfidious depiction of his hero must have interested Browning immensely, although he chose not to follow Alfieri's lead in this instance.

Browning's models were not only literary. They may have even included Robert Schumann's *Davidsbündlertäne*, a collection of dances for piano (Erickson, *Robert Browning: His Poetry and His Audiences* 130). Certainly from childhood trips to the Dulwich Picture Gallery, Browning had known Poussin's *The Triumph of David*, and he had long been acquainted through Giorgio Vasari's *Lives of the Artists* with the powerful images of David in Italian art.[10] Browning's acquaintance with Renaissance art had deepened during his visits to Italy. One Renaissance representation of David is Donatello's statue, characterized by Vasari as "so natural in its vivacity and delicacy that other artists find it impossible to believe that the work was not moulded around a living body" (152). The fluid beauty Vasari finds in Donatello's David reflects one side of his complex character. In contrast to the Donatello David, Vasari emphasizes the harmony, strength, and symbolic significance of Michelangelo's. Vasari suggests that David's pose and his weapons indicate Michelangelo's message: that

> just as David had defended his people and governed them with justice, so, too, those who governed [Florence] should courageously defend it and govern it with justice. [. . .] the contours of [the statue's] legs are extremely beautiful, along with the splendid articulations and grace of its flanks; a sweeter and more graceful pose has never been seen that could equal it, nor have feet, hands, or a head ever been produced, which so well match all the other parts of the body in skill of workmanship or design. To be sure, anyone who sees this statue need not be concerned with seeing any other piece of sculpture done in our times or in any other period by any other artist. (427-28)

These statues and Vasari's hyperbolic descriptions of them presented models perhaps as powerful as Smart's. And even though Bernini's work was disregarded in the nineteenth century, most serious visitors to Italy

---

[10] *The Lives of the Artists* by Vasari, a Florentine Renaissance painter and gossip, was one of Browning's favorite childhood books, and would be an important source for the poems in *Men and Women* (1855).

would have been acquainted with his Baroque David as well. Unlike the two Renaissance statues, Bernini's is vigorous, angry, and active. Like Browning's own verbal portraits, Bernini's David is caught at the defining moment of his life, his arms drawn back in preparation for slinging the stone at the giant. Unlike the other two Davids, this one is not self-contained: instead, he is defined by "the implied presence of Goliath" (Janson 408).

With the sculptural interpretations of his character, Browning was faced, then, with several visual images of David: Donatello's - life-sized, graceful, feminine, bedecked with flowers; Michelangelo's - masculine, powerful, unadorned except by his weapons, with massive hands and feet; and Bernini's, active and fluid, embedded in time. These images of the poet are not synthesized in Browning's poem, but are allowed to co-exist.

If the characters in the poem are complicated, the plot of the 1845 *Saul* seems simple enough: David is called to heal the king with his music; he tries, without obvious success. However, the simplicity of the plot masks the general complexity of the poem. Retelling the story of I Samuel xvi, 14-23, David first describes his arrival at the Israelite camp on the eve of battle with the Philistines and his immediate empathetic bond with the agonized king. Then David lists the decalogue of songs he has performed, from "the tune all our sheep knew," coming into the fold "as star follows star" to "the chorus intoned/ As the Levites go up to the altar." At its conclusion, the 1845 version of the poem opens out into David's thirty-line summary of the king's epic life, in which Saul is placed within concentric circles of parents, siblings, friends, and the Israelite people. Finally, David describes Saul's career as a pivotal moment in history and Saul as a special creature.

The anapestic couplets of David's narrative and songs, reminiscent of the metrical design in Alfieri's rendering of David's lyrics, serve a multiple function. The speed suggests the youthful fire of David's music and the spiritual energy he tries to infuse into the demoralized Saul. For Hair, the effect of the regular, long, fifteen-syllable lines is that "music and words become one" (*Robert Browning's Language* 159). In the 1845 version, the sensation of speed is even more pronounced than in the 1855 printing because, as a space-saving measure, in *Dramatic Lyrics and Romances*, the poem was printed in alternating lines of dimeter and trimeter. What Alfieri did through the dramatic framework of the tragedy, Browning had to accomplish in other ways: the metrical consistency of Browning's poem suppresses the generic complexity - the fact that the poem contains narrative, lyric, and epic passages - and the enjambed lines also suppress the sense of order which would ordinarily result from reading a poem written entirely in couplets. Instead, the verse form often mimics the effect of the unrhymed symmetrical units, separated by the caesura, which are characteristic in Hebrew verse.[11] The last lines of Section IX, for instance, contain a complementary symmetry typical of *Proverbs* and many of David's *Psalms*:

> "Oh, all, all the world offers singly,
> > On one head combine,
> On one head the joy and the pride,
> > Even rage like the throe
> That opes the rock, helps its glad labour
> > And lets the gold go --
> And ambition that sees a sun lead it,
> > Oh, all of these -- all
> Combine to unite in one creature
> > -- Saul! (181-90)

"Gifts, which the world offers singly" to those less heroic than Saul are balanced by the complementary idea of the combined gifts offered to Saul, and "Joy" is balanced by "pride." (In the completed version, Browning heightened this effect with "Beauty and strength," which are traits of body and soul balanced by the emotions of "love and rage.") "Rock" is balanced by "gold." The only break in the anapestic bass line occurs at the end of the fragment, in a striking monosyllable: David reminds Saul that beauty, strength, love, rage, deeds, ambition, and fame -

> "Oh, all of these -- all
> Combine to unite in one creature
> > -- Saul!

When he wrote the first nine parts of "Saul," Browning apparently intended a synthesis of subjective and objective poetry by blending genres as he did in *Pippa Passes*. The blend here is less obvious, however, because of the metrical consistency. The language of David's songs is objective: it describes the exterior world and projects outward toward Saul in a healing gesture. At the same time, the songs are placed within a subjective, metapoetic frame in which David also describes his intentions and the nature of his own poetic gifts. One important feature of the 1845 fragment is the lack of reconciliation among the poem's various generic strands and its two voices. In Bakhtin's terms, such stylistic layering is a feature of the

---

[11] On the basis of the structure and rhetoric of the poem, J. H. McClatchy argues in "Browning's 'Saul' as a Davidic Psalm" that it is, generically, a psalm. This article also contains a useful summary of the criticism of *Saul* before 1976.

novel, the Victorian dominant. This layering persists in the completed version; whether he knew it or not, Browning was moving toward that dominant in this poem.

So, too, Browning faced the difficulty of reconciling the various sources of his imagery, which is drawn from conflicting representations of David which Browning had inherited from his predecessors. *Saul* represents a qualitative development from Browning's earlier poetry, in which he invoked the gendered imagery of Andromeda on the rock and Perseus wielding his sword. But here, Saul contains homoerotic imagery so powerful and transparent that its relevance to the Brownings' courtship has been difficult to assess.[12] This imagery in "Saul" in fact allows Browning to explore human intimacy outside the normal confines of gender polarization.

The homoerotic tradition in Western art is a divided stream. The Biblical story of David and Jonathan, Saul's son, turns on an equal affective relationship between men. Classical literature also contains this theme as well as the tradition of the strong man-beautiful boy relationship which functions, not by gender alignment, but by the construction of artificial gender differences between man and boy. The depictions of David in Western art and Vasari's descriptions of them, which were influenced by the classical erotic tradition rediscovered during the Renaissance, are similarly contradictory. So, even setting aside the sexual frustration in Browning's relationship with Elizabeth Barrett at that time, it is not

---

[12] Twentieth-century readers have generally been more aware of homoerotic references in "Andrea del Sarto" than in *Saul* (probably because Andrea del Sarto, unlike David, is not at all heroic -- and this is as much a reflection of unconscious homophobia, perhaps, as it is a reflection of the two poems). Two articles on this poem, which Browning wrote just about the time he completed *Saul* (probably in late 1853 or early 1854), argue Browning's interest in and familiarity with homoerotic tradition. Both Mario L. D'Avanzo's "King Francis, Lucrezia, and the Figurative Language of 'Andrea del Sarto'" and Elizabeth Bieman's "An Eros Manque: Browning's 'Andrea del Sarto'" analyze the homosexual/ heterosexual contrasts in the poem; Bieman, in addition, relates Browning's imagery to the Renaissance paradigm which represents homosexuality as gold and heterosexualty as silver. Sussman observes in *Victorian Masculinities* that the "phallic virility" (109) which David praises in Saul (including the "lordly male sapphires" of his turban and the king's still but "erect" body) made Section VIII an icon in the homoerotic culture of the late nineteenth century (209 n26). (Barrett was quite taken, too, with the sapphires.) According to Sussman, of Browning's mid-career poems, "'Saul' most clearly brings to the surface the homoeroticism implicit in the centrality of the male-male bonds within a masculine poetic" (108). It would seem that *Saul* elicits either "queer"or "straight" readings.

surprising that Browning's characterization is equivocal - androgynous at one moment, thoroughly male the next, like the role of the male Victorian poet.

The erotic subtext begins in the very first lines:

> Said Abner, "At last thou art come!
>   "Ere I tell, ere thou speak, --
> "Kiss my cheek, wish me well!" Then I wished it,
>   And did kiss his cheek. (1-4)

Abner has hopes for David's success in healing the king because David is an Apollonian youth; blue lilies, reminiscent of the flowers on the cap of Donatello's David, twine around his harp and hair. (Fascinated as he was by such negative emotions as jealousy, Browning must have been interested in the part jealousy plays in Alfieri's play, in which Abner later, and predictably, becomes jealous of the beautiful and eloquent boy.) David is like the sunbeam which "burst[s] though the tent-roof" and outlines the figure of Saul. In high contrast, the king is "more black than the blackness" against the filtered light. Saul suffers intensely; nevertheless, he stands, in phallic isolation, "erect as that tent-prop, both arms stretched out wide [. . .].

> So he bent not a muscle but hung there
>   As, caught in his pangs
> And waiting his change the king-serpent
>   All heavily hangs (57-60)

David is tender, Saul hard; David light, Saul dark. Barrett also sensed the erotic subtext, apparently. Her response to these lines is similar to her note about "Ghent to Aix": "The 'All heavily hangs' as applied to the King-serpent, you quite feel in your own muscles" (*Correspondence* 11. 389).

But the language of the poem transcends gender stereotypes: David is not only tender, but strong, Saul not only hard, but weak. Browning's Saul is sick because he is separated even from God, and because he has subscribed to the masculine mystique to a point of sterility and silence. Saul suffers because he has been unbending and isolated, and his suffering forces him to come to terms, through David, with the fierce, active role he has willingly accepted.[13] Thus, paradoxically, Saul also fits into

---

[13] In "The Masculine Mode," Peter Schwenger examines a common masculine archetype of unreflective silence that coincides with Browning's characterization of Saul. Schwenger adds that "when masculinity is intensely pursued this is often done at the risk of self-annihilation" (110-11).

Browning's personal schema as Andromeda, the maiden who must be rescued. (In some ways, the Saul-David dynamic parallels the relationship between Shelley and the narrator of *Pauline*, for whom Shelley is the object of desire and a figure in the narrator's rescue fantasy.) The young poet David is placed, less paradoxically, in the position of Perseus, the savior who exercises masculine power in the service of the weak. In this respect, the poem echoes Vasari's analysis of Michelangelo's masculine and powerful David, who protects his people and rules them with justice, and perhaps borrows from Bernini's David as well. Both David and Saul, then, fit with complex precision within Browning's Perseus-Andromeda archetypal schema.

Since *Saul* is about a man who loves another man passionately, the homoerotic imagery persists throughout, but as the poem unfolds, Browning's language also, simultaneously, becomes heteroerotically charged. Even more than in *Pauline* and *Paracelsus*, in *Saul*, Browning scrambles gender construction. After greeting Abner, David offers a prayer and begins to cross the boundaries Saul has erected between the world and himself. Barrett was especially impressed by the ending of stanza three, which suggests David's eventual success with the image of a stray sunbeam, which suddenly illuminates the sick king: "I have told you how very fine I do think all this showing of Saul by the sunbeam -- & how the more you come to see him, the finer it is" (*Correspondence* 11. 389). David describes Saul's psychic defenses as if they were analogous to a woman's bruised body, and he speaks of his progress through the king's enclosures in a language of sexual aggression. Approaching the exterior tent, David says,

> I pulled up the spear that obstructed
>   And under I stooped;
> Hands and knees on the slippery grass-patch --
>   All withered and gone --
> That extends to the second enclosure,
>   I groped my way on,
> Till I felt where the foldskirts fly open:
>   Then once more I prayed,
> And opened the foldskirts and entered,
>   And was not afraid (31-40)

Then, as David sings to the unresponsive Saul, he also watches for the music to take effect, for Saul to open to its healing influence. Barrett commented that in these lines, "The entrance of David into the tent is very visible & characteristic -- & you see his youthfulness in the activity of it --

and the repetition of the word 'foldskirts' has an Hebraic effect" (*Correspondence* 11.389).

At the end of the Biblical account, "Saul was refreshed, and was well, and the evil spirit departed from him" (I Samuel 16: 23). However, Browning's 1845 version ends with a panegyric to Saul rather than a narrative denouement. The erotic imagery continues. After nine songs, Saul groans, there is a breathless pause, and the shimmering jewels on Saul's turban shudder, though the body hangs still motionless, silent, dark, and erect. David answers the tremor with another song, twenty-five lines celebrating Saul's life, in images reminiscent of the visceral language admired by Elizabeth Barrett in "Ghent to Aix":

> The rending their boughs from the palm-trees, --
>   The cool silver shock
> Of a plunge in a pool's living water, (139-41)

the lion hunt, the powdery dates, locusts steeped in wine, his father's white locks, his mother's thin hands, the "seething grape-bundles," "the spirit so true" of men's friendship - all of these gifts contribute to Saul's future and that of his people. And here, like the figure of Saul hanging from the center pole of his tent, the poem is suspended.

Browning's dramatic monologues of the late 1830s suggest that he had been interested in sexual indeterminacy as a literary theme for some years before he began writing *Saul*. And in 1837, he planned a play about Narses, a eunuch general of sixth-century Byzantium who reconquered Italy from the Goths; as a eunuch, Narses would have been a marginal figure, not only sexually, but socially and politically as well. (Apparently, Browning dropped the idea to write *Strafford*, a tragedy about the Commonwealth period, because his friends Bulwer and Forster were engaged in projects on the same historical subject matter. In his article on *Strafford*, Latané argues that this material offered all three writers a better vehicle for exploring political conflict.)

Browning's descriptions of the intimacy between Saul and David seem equivocal because, as Christopher Craft has pointed out, it was no less difficult for the Victorians than it is for readers of the late twentieth century to imagine that sexual attraction between members of the same gender may be a "reasonable and natural articulation of a desire whose excursiveness is simply indifferent to the distinctions of gender, that desire may not be gendered intrinsically as the body is, and that desire seeks its objects according to a complicated set of conventions that are culturally and institutionally determined" (223). Certainly, this was not Browning's only difficulty, however. As biographical critics have suggested, the poem's overdetermined sexual language probably reflects Browning's internal tensions, and especially the sexual tension between him and Elizabeth Barrett. Tentative, intense, and strained as that relationship was before the flight to Italy, Browning's feelings for Barrett were more safely expressed in homoerotic than in heteroerotic language: how better to disguise and displace heterosexual desire? How better to communicate it?

But that construction of the poem is ungenerous and incomplete: it would deny that Browning knew anything about the homosexual tradition he invokes, or that he was capable of critical distance from the gender norms of his own day. Moreover, although the woman with whom Browning was in love was from one perspective an entrapped Andromeda waiting for rescue, she was anything but conventionally feminine, and Browning did not wish her to be. For at that moment Browning himself was in need of rescue from a society which placed contradictory demands on its artists - to serve as a powerful masculine moral force from a feminized and privatized position at its margins. In the early years of his relationship with Elizabeth Barrett, Browning may have chosen to enact the rescue myth which motivated his poetry, but one of the greatest ironies of literary history is that his relationship with her was far from the conventional heterosexual romance it came to epitomize.

For Browning, *Saul* accomplished two psychic essentials. Through the doubleness of David - conventionally feminine beauty and spiritual power - the poem allowed Browning to work out the possibility that femininity was an essential aspect of poetic power. In addition, through the homoerotic imagery, Browning undermines the prevailing gender hierarchy (men on top): Elizabeth Barrett was not a "normal" woman, and Browning did not wish to dominate her. The prospect of an erotic connection with her was a curtained vista into undiscovered country. He would accept what he found there with an open mind and an open heart.

All personal matters aside, the project itself was daunting. In a new, unwieldy, heterologic poetic form which combined lyric and dramatic, Hebrew and Greek, Renaissance and modern poetic material, Browning was attempting to work out several philosophical and prosodic problems through the stark figure of Saul and the complex and self-contradictory character of David. Partly because writing the poem was difficult, it provided a strategy for negotiating the conflicts brought about by the untenable identification of the artist with both gender extremes. In 1845, when Elizabeth Barrett urged Browning to publish the fragment, he acknowledged that he had taken the poem as far as his own personal and poetic development allowed.

When Browning resumed work on Saul in 1853,[14] he ended the poem much as Christopher Smart had ended "A Song to David," transforming David's gift of poetry into one of prophesy, and Old-Testament history into theodicy. Looked at stylistically and narratively, the finished *Saul* appears seamless, but a discernable generic rift separates the nine sections Browning published in 1845 from the ten sections he composed during the fall or winter of 1852-53, spent first in Paris, then Florence. If the earlier sections connect to Hebrew and Greek traditions, the last ten sections are distinctly Christian. The solution Browning eventually found to break Saul's lethargy and move the poem forward, suggests Ryals, "was to go beyond the Psalms [. . .] to the Prophets" (*Becoming Browning* 223). Thus the completed *Saul* is not only one of Browning's few poems about Christianity, a retelling of Christian myth, but a unique experiment in historical narrative, in which David's vision of the future recreates a Christian past.[15] David foresees and, in himself, prefigures Christ. He recalls in the penultimate section the erotic and filial love he has felt for Saul in the early part of the poem and reforms it into Christian love:

> "As thy Love is discovered almighty, almighty be proved
> "Thy power, that exists with and for it, of being Beloved!
> "He who did most, shall bear most; the strongest shall stand the most weak.
> "'Tis weakness in strength, that I cry for! my flesh, that I seek
> "In the Godhead! I seek and I find it. O Saul, it shall be
> "A Face like my face that receives thee; a Man like to me,
> "Thou shalt love and be loved by, for ever: a Hand like this hand
> "Shall throw open the gates of new life to thee! See the Christ stand!'
> (305-12)[16]

David's epiphany occurs in section XVI, which consists of one line, a fragmented exclamation:

> Then the truth came upon me. No harp more -- no song more! Outbroke --
> (237)

---

[14] On the basis of thematic similarities between the latter sections of *Saul* and "An Epistle Containing the Strange Medical Experience of Karshish, the Arab Physician" Pettigrew dates the completion of *Saul* in 1853.

[15] In *The Lucid Veil*, Shaw notes the parallel between David's intuition of the Incarnation and the Higher Criticism, which theorized the God concept as the result of human need. Shaw also notes the typological similarities between David and Christ (212).

[16] The text of the completed *Saul* is from the Oxford edition, Volume V, ed. Ian Jack and Robert Inglesfield (1995).

During Saul's dark night of the soul, David, too, grapples with the meaning of the experience in Saul's tent, an experience which parallels the process by which Browning reached his conclusion, reconciling strength and weakness, the masculine and the feminine, the human and the divine.

The resolution of these tensions, erotic and imaginative, depended on Browning's unique, professional, emotional and erotic dialogue with another poet, who could write to him of "the tone & spirit of these lyrics . . broken as you have left them. Where is the wrong in this? For the right & beauty, they are more obvious -- & I cannot tell you how the poem holds me & will not let me go untill it blesses me" (*Correspondence* 11.48-49). Browning was able to postpone the completion of *Saul* because, with Barrett's support, he was learning to be more patient with his own internal creative processes, to value more highly his own creative processes, and to hope for better communication with other readers as well. In May 1846, almost a year and a half after his first letter to her, Barrett told him,

> you have the superabundant mental life & individuality which admits of shifting a personality & speaking the truth still. That is the highest faculty, the strongest & rarest, which exercises itself in Art [. . .] . Several times you have hinted to me that I made you care less for the drama, & it has puzzled me to fancy how it could be, when I understand myself so clearly both the difficulty & the glory of dramatic art. Yet I am conscious of wishing you to take the other crown besides, -- & after having made your own creatures speak in clear human voices, to speak yourself out of that personality which God made, & with the voice which He tuned into such power & sweetness of speech. I do not think that, with all that music in you, only your own personality should be dumb, not that having thought so much & deeply on life & its ends, you should not teach what you have learnt, in the directest & most impressive way, the mask thrown off however moist with the breath. (*Correspondence* 12.358)

Finally, Browning was becoming a more "Victorian" poet -- less involved in his own private passions, and more connected with the world, with its streams of religious feeling and the great movements of its history. A new passion fully emerges in the poems which were to become *Men and Women* and, even earlier, in 1850, gives rise to the strange and ebullient energy of *Christmas-Eve and Easter-Day*.

In the completed *Saul*, Browning speaks about individual emotional experience as one thread woven into an intricate social fabric, stretched through history. He speaks, not straightforwardly, for that was not Browning's way, but as one who knows his own mind. And in *Saul*, he begins to speak as one who understands the relationships between religion and eros, tradition and the individual poet, artist and audience.

Chapter 3

Double Voices
1844-1846

On January 4, 1846, almost exactly a year after Browning wrote to Elizabeth Barrett for the first time, she looked back at their relationship as an exercise in doubleness, in which she saw herself constantly trying to reconcile the Robert Browning she knew in the flesh with the man she had known earlier through the writing:

> You never guessed perhaps. . what I look back to at this moment in the physiology of our intercourse, . . . the curious double feeling I had about you. . you personally, & you as the writer of these letters, . . & the crisis of the feeling, when I was positively vexed & jealous of myself for not succeeding better in making a unity of the two. I could not! -- And moreover I could not help but that the writer of the letters seemed nearer to me, long. . long. . & in spite of the postmark. . than did the personal visitor who confounded me, & left me constantly under such an impression of its being all dream-work on his side, that I have stamped my feet on this floor with impatience to think of having to wait so many hours before the "candid" closing letter c^d come with its confession of an illusion. (*Correspondence* 11.280, EBB's ellipses)

Doubtless, Browning would have appreciated Barrett's own duplicity, had he known what occupied most of her attention at the time: she was, in fact, writing about their relationship, and Robert Browning was both a subject and audience in the sonnets she was writing. The years between 1842 and 1846 were among the most productive in Elizabeth Barrett's life. In May 1845, after the poets' first meeting, she had secretly begun the poems that came to be known as *Sonnets from the Portuguese*. That summer, not only was she reading Browning's plays and editing the poems for *Dramatic Romances and Lyrics*, she was also hard at work on her own writing.

Although she had been worn down by sorrow and ill health during her early and middle thirties, by the time Browning came into her life, Barrett had already begun to enjoy it more. Her health was still poor, but it had stabilized. She was beginning to appreciate, if not physical, at least financial health - indeed, she was the only one among her siblings to be independent.[1] She could buy her own books, pay her own maid, and support the opium habit which improved the quality of her sleep and allayed the pain in her lungs. After numerous moves, terrifying illnesses, and profound grief, Barrett was ensconced once and for all, she thought, with the rest of the Barrett family in Wimpole Street.

By 1844, she was eagerly aware of the city's cultural life, often vicariously through her active and sociable brothers and sisters, almost daily through the newspapers and magazines she was able to read as soon as they were published, and gradually through the numerous important literary friendships which she made and sustained through her correspondence. Barrett was not entirely deprived of flesh-and-blood company either, since she made occasional wheelchair excursions to Regents Park and entertained occasional visitors. One was the independent minister George Barrett Hunter, whose attentions were welcome until he became possessive and overbearing. (When Browning began to visit, Hunter became so hostile that she likened him to Chiappino, the tortured protagonist of Browning's 1846 play, *A Soul's Tragedy*.) Another visitor was her cousin John Kenyon; he called frequently, bearing books and news of Browning, whose poetry she had admired since reading *Pippa Passes* and *Dramatic Lyrics*. When she was in London, Mitford called to see Elizabeth and Flush. The art critic Anna Jameson besieged Barrett until she was allowed to visit, and Barrett came to admire her vitality. The painter Benjamin Haydon not only filled his letters with sketches, he sent around his unfinished portrait of Wordsworth when Barrett expressed regret that she could not go out to see it

After her diminished output in the early 1840s, Barrett began to assemble the poems which would be published in 1844 to widespread, and mostly positive, critical response. The collection included sonnets, ballads, the centerpiece of the collection, *A Drama of Exile*, and, of course, the fateful "Lady Geraldine's Courtship." Although Barrett had invested her highest hopes in the title poem, a revision of the story of the fall in which Eve's experience takes center stage, the public much preferred "Lady Geraldine's Courtship," which she had dashed off in a few days, with some annoyance, to fill a second volume which her publisher Moxon demanded

---

[1] In 1838, Barrett started receiving the income from several thousand pounds left to her by her uncle, Samuel Moulton-Barrett, and from his share in a trading vessel; from her paternal grandmother, she had already inherited 4000 pounds. Forster's biography *The Life and Loves of a Poet: Elizabeth Barrett Browning* includes information about Barrett's financial status, as well as a detailed reconstruction of Barrett's London life before Browning.

at the last minute. Much of 1844 was given over to completing these poems, arranging them, and reading the reviews with eager pleasure.

During her London years, Barrett also undertook other projects.[2] In 1845, she returned to the *Prometheus*, a translation of which she had published twelve years before, to her subsequent regret. In the "Advertisement" to the *Poems* of 1850, she called it "a sin of my youth."[3] "Now I may sleep at nights, & Aeschylus's ghost not draw the curtains. . . 'all in his winding sheet'," she wrote to Mitford (*Correspondence* 10.67, Barrett's ellipsis). That same year, Kenyon's friend Anne Thompson planned to publish an album illustrated with a set of engravings from carved gems illustrating Apuleius's *Metamorphoses*. She asked Barrett to contribute a series of translations explaining the images on the gems. Barrett was amused by the whiff of her own pedantry in these pieces, not to mention the album itself, writing to Kenyon, "After all I said & you said the other day, about Apuleius, & about what could'nt, should'nt, & mus'nt be done in the matter, I ended by trying the unlawful art of translating this prose into verse, &, one after another, have done all the subjects of the Poniatowsky gems. . . except two. . ." (*Correspondence* 10.171).[4] She was writing criticism as well. In 1842, at the request of Charles Dilke, editor of *The Athenaeum*, she contributed four essays on the Greek Christian poets. This project, on admittedly second- and third-rate figures, appealed to her scholarly bent and inspired a somewhat spiteful wit.[5] In 1843, Barrett published "The Book of the Poets," a review article on the history of English poetry and drama in which, according to Mary Thale, Barrett (not T. S. Eliot) first argued for the importance of the metaphysical poets. To Horne's *A New Spirit of the Age*, in which Browning received such lavish praise, she contributed ideas, editorial assistance, essays on Carlyle and

---

[2] For a listing of Barrett's periodical pieces, see "Contributions to Periodicals, Newspapers, Gift Books, and Anthologies" in Warner Barnes' descriptive bibliography of Barrett Browning's works.

[3] Alice Meynell, one of Barrett Browning's most sympathetic editors, chose the earlier translation of *Prometheus*, however, as the copy text for her selection of Barrett Browning's poems in 1896 because she felt that the translation had real strengths which had been overlooked, and because she feared the earlier edition might well be lost entirely.

[4] Thompson never published the project on the Poniatowsky gems, and Barrett's translations remained unpublished until *Last Poems*, compiled by Browning in the months after Barrett Browning's death.

[5] For instance, after presenting in detail the numerous flaws of Gregory Nazianzen's poetry (A. C. E. 329-89), Barrett adds, "The poem on Celibacy, which state is commended by Gregory as becometh a bishop, has occasionally graphic touches, but is dull enough generally to suit the fairest spinster's view of that melancholy subject" (*Some Account of the Greek Christian Poets* 605-06).

Moncton Milnes (anonymously), and additional passages in the articles on Landor, Hunt, Wordsworth, and Tennyson (Forster 379-80 n 3; *Correspondence* 8.341-67). Barrett was not pleased to be linked in the same work with the popular and somewhat infamous Caroline Norton, who wrote sentimental poetry and later (after the Brownings had moved to Italy) a powerful feminist analysis of English divorce and custody laws. And she may well have been even less pleased that Horne took full credit for her work.[6] Nevertheless, she was conscious of a debt to him.

The collaboration with Horne was one of Barrett's most important working relationships during this period, and not only because he supported her forays into literary criticism. He began to replace the ponderous and depressive Boyd in Barrett's mental life. In addition to contributing her verses of "The Knight's Tale" to Horne's modernized Chaucer, Barrett started collaborating with Horne on a drama, and, although it was never finished, she learned from the experience. Probably more important than the publishing opportunities were Horne's devotion to her, his recognition of her gifts, and his generous and interesting correspondence, which was another link with the outside world. His sojourn in England during the late 1830s and 1840s was a temporary pause between periods of adventure - in his youth as a participant in the Mexican war of independence (on the Mexican side) and later as a government official in Australia. Horne also taught gymnastics and swimming, and was an experienced sailor. In a letter to Mitford in July, 1843, Barrett exclaims that "He seems to me to talk in all tongues, from Spanish to Syriac -- is a director in a South American mine company, -- writes reviews in divers quarterleys, -- & commissioner-reports for government, -- & dissertations upon the folios of Albertus Magnus, -- & Orions [Horne's new epic poem] in the interstices of it all!" (*Correspondence* 7.194). Changing his given middle name of "Henry" to the more exotic "Hengist" certainly reflected the spirit of adventure which ruled Horne's life. He appealed to Barrett's own youthful desire for adventure, which had begun at least by the age of nine, when she persuaded her parents to take her with them on a second honeymoon to Paris.

A few months after her exclamations on the talents of the fabulous Horne, she again wrote to Mitford, the recipient of so much gossip and literary opinion, so many daydreams:

---

[6] In "Elizabeth Barrett Browning and the Art of Collaboration," Sullivan gives an account of Barrett's collaboration with Horne, suggesting that Horne's failure to give credit where it was due made Barrett wary of joint authorship, even with Browning. In addition, Sullivan notes that Mitford, Barrett Browning's favorite correspondent at this time, also printed at least one of the poet's works in a gift book without crediting her. Sullivan does identify a collaborative pattern in the Brownings' poetic exchange, however.

If I were strong & free as you, you w.^d hear of me keeping witch-sabbath on the Brocken, with a tame will o'the wisp running beside me. I should be running myself all over the world --. I should be at Paris. . (there is a chivalry in the French which I like) . . I should be in Italy --. I should be longest in Germany -- I should be in the Alps & Pyrenees --. I might be peradventure in the eternal mist of Niagara. Seriously & certainly I should very much like to spend the next three years in the midst of new lands & strange souls -- I should very much like it ---- but far, far is the dream of it! ---- (*Correspondence* 7.281)

Elizabeth Barrett's life was a paradoxical mixture of desire and containment, precariously balanced, which enabled her to write poetry. She could imagine no other way to be the poet she wished to be, but Horne had provided her with a dress rehearsal for a more significant relationship which would suggest an alternative.

Robert Browning's entrance into Barrett's life strengthened her desire for freedom and adventure, but it threatened the equilibrium which she had struggled to achieve. It took time for her to understand that she might learn to write poetry under other circumstances, but Browning's struggles as a poet, which she witnessed at close range, made him a trustworthy teacher and confidant. As she reconsidered her carefully balanced life, and articulated her fear that bookishness made for mediocre poetry, details from Browning's poetry started to resonate in hers. Phrases from their letters and poems are picked up, exchanged, and transmuted through their dialogue.[7] In her sonnet sequence, Barrett demonstrates her ambivalence, but also the direct, immediate influence of positive lived experience. Browning's presence in her life was thus crucial, but in 1844 and 1845, it did not amount to an influence so much as an enabling.

Barrett's half of the courtship correspondence makes little mention of her own work, aside from translations. After several months of constant

---

[7] In "'Some Interchange of Grace': 'Saul' and *Sonnets from the Portuguese*," Sullivan documents the collaboration between the Brownings by showing that Barrett picked up phrases from Browning's letters and his poems, then elaborated and transformed them in the sonnets. When Browning returned to *Saul* six or seven years later after its initial publication, phrases from the *Sonnets* found their way into the completed poem. According to Sullivan, these parallels are simply the most easily documented evidence of constant, and perhaps almost inadvertent, collaboration between the two poets. She concludes that "The evidence of mutual influence in this one limited period of their careers may have implications for the larger works that each produced later; at the very least, such evidence gives added meaning to Browning's often minimized claim in the 'Lyric Love' section of Book I, *The Ring and the Book*, that Elizabeth's influence was pervasive and essential" (66). Sullivan also notes that even the convoluted phrasing of these particular lines in *The Ring and the Book* suggests a mutual exchange.

discussion of his poems during the spring and summer of 1845, it occurred to Browning that, despite Barrett's earlier request for editorial reciprocity, he had seen none of her recent work except her new *Prometheus Bound*, upon which he made almost eight pages of notes.[8] He admired the work, concluding his remarks:

> And so it is all magnificently rendered. The above attempts at notification ere all the merest stoppings for a moment where I did not know my old path through the text again [. . .] . If the work were mine, I should be happy and proud, and let it alone [. . .] . This is not the opportunity I waited for to say my humble say on your works. Aeschlyus is here, and I would find you alone. As it is, take my true praise and congratulations.
> (qtd. Sotheby, Wilkinson, Hodge 32)

Indeed, in a letter postmarked August 8, Browning almost scolds, as he promises to deliver "a few more hundred lines" of his own poetry for her scrutiny,

> but, "my poet," if I would, as is true, sacrifice all my works to do your fingers, even, good -- what would I not offer up to prevent you staying. . perhaps to correct my very verses [. . .] perhaps read and answer my very letters[. . .] staying the production of more Berthas and Caterinas and Geraldines, more great and beautiful poems of which I shall be -- how proud! Do not be punctual in paying tithes of thyme, mint, anise and cummin, and leaving unpaid the real weighty dues of the Law, -- nor affect a scrupulous acknowledgment of "what you owe me" in petty manners, while you leave me to settle such a charge, as accessory to the hiding the Talent, as best I can! I have thought of this again and again [. . .] . for, observe, you have not done. . yes, the Prometheus, no doubt. . but with that exception, have you written much lately [. . .] .
> (*Correspondence 11*.16)

Barrett responded that same day to Browning's expression of concern: "I do confess that the novelty of living more in the outer life for the last few months than I have done for years before, makes me idle and inclined to be idle [. . .] . " Still, she continues, she has done

> some work [. . .] nothing worth speaking of & not a part of the romance-poem which is to be some day if I live for it. .lyrics for the most part, which lie written illegibly in pure Egyptian -- oh, there is time enough, and too much perhaps! & so let me be idle a little now, & enjoy your poems while I can --
> (*Correspondence 11*.19)

---

[8] Browning's notes on the *Prometheus*, now lost, are listed in the catalog of materials from the Browning estate sold in 1913 by Sotheby's (item # 142, *The Browning Collections*).

Those "pure Egyptian" lyrics, which became *Sonnets from the Portuguese*, occupied Barrett until the eve of her momentous departure to the Continent with Browning in September the following year.

Barrett's *Sonnets from the Portuguese* is one of the few sonnet sequences in English by a woman. The sonnets of Barrett's near contemporaries Charlotte Smith, Letitia Landon, and Felicia Hemens, like the other "women's poetry" which Barrett subtly critiqued in her ballads, equate love with grief; Barrett disapproved of this model.[9] Three hundred years before *Sonnets from the Portuguese*, Louise Labé had written a sonnet sequence lamenting the death of her best friend and, later, the loss of her lover. But Labé's work was apparently not available to Barrett, either in French or in translation; nor were the sonnets of Sor Juana de la Cruz, whose publication history has made it impossible to determine whether any of her numerous sonnets were written within the context of a sequence.[10] In the absence of foremothers in the sonnet tradition, Barrett wove into her work threads from the poetry of Sappho and Aphra Behn, and the fiction of George Sand. And so for the first time, a sonnet sequence in English narrates the development of female desire, extending and dramatically departing from the amatory tradition of Western poetry, taking the genre onto novel ground. No wonder she joked that her new poems were written in "pure Egyptian." In the August 8 letter to Browning, in the same breath with her covert reference to the sonnets, Barrett openly mentions her plan for the "romance-poem" which was to become *Aurora Leigh*: within the context of her new relationship with the world and with Robert Browning, she was working out the related demands of the novel-poem and the sonnet sequence. Both genres had unrealized narrative potential and seemed particularly suited for expressing women's experiences. Until her relationship with Browning, she had not found the right material for a sonnet sequence. That relationship not only provided the material, but the inspiration for Barrett's first attempt at generic experimentation, a lyric sequence with plot, setting, and the psychologically complex characters which typify the Victorian novel.[11]

---

[9] See Stephenson's *Elizabeth Barrett Browning and the Poetry of Love* for a more complete exposition of the argument that Elizabeth Barrett Browning wished to distinguish her work from that of other women poets.

[10] In his monumental biography of Sor Juana, Octavio Paz includes a publication history of her works.

[11] In "Notes for a History of Victorian Poetic Genres", Fleishman suggests that a new form--the lyric sequence -- was needed "to convey the stages of personal experience -- especially during periods of alienation or recovery from it" (368). He lists Barrett Browning's sonnet sequence as the earliest example of this new genre; however, his

It is difficult to see beyond the greeting-card mode in which the *Sonnets from the Portuguese* are usually presented, difficult to believe that these poems are more carefully crafted and less autobiographical than they seem, difficult to read them as new and revolutionary. There have been more than one hundred and seventy separate reprints of the sonnets, in various degrees of fancy - beribboned, gilded, illuminated with flowers, populated with fairies, and sentimentalized for the last century by Edmund Gosse's long-accepted fabrication: that a year after eloping to Italy with Robert, Elizabeth shyly thrust them into his back pocket as he gazed out into the Florentine morning. The famous 1893 forgeries by Thomas J. Wise, which were presented to the world as a private printing of the sonnets before their appearance in the *Poems* of 1850, gave new life to the legend, which refuses to die even now, years after being disproved.[12]

Contrary to this fictional image, the poems were the result of scholarly depth and intellectualized feeling as well as passion. Between 1838 and 1842, Barrett had studied the sonnet tradition from its beginning to her own century, a painstaking investigation which resulted in twenty-eight separate sonnets which first appeared in the 1844 *Poems*. The fact that she never published her translations of sonnets by Petrarch, Dante, and Zappi suggests that she made them to learn more about sonnet form and perhaps more about the language in which the sonnets were written.[13] In general, the individual sonnet is one of the most structured and bounded of literary genres, focusing exclusively upon the perspective of the speaker, and often on the speaker's desperate attempt to gain emotional control. Although the sonnet is an inherently dramatic form, the climax and narrative movement signify and develop within the speaker/ poet's solitary consciousness and control. Significantly, sonnets respond well to formalist criticism because,

---

assertion that lyric sequences "show little interest in tracing interpersonal relationships," I think, describes the genre too narrowly.

[12] *Elizabeth Barrett Browning at the Mercy of Her Publishers*, by Colin Franklin, is a lavishly illustrated publication history of *Sonnets from the Portuguese*. Franklin includes an account of the connection between Gosse's story and the forgeries of Wise. One need only look at the pictures to see that EBB's work could scarcely have avoided the sentimentalizing of her own century and ours. Lootens begins her reception study of Barrett Browning with an account of responses to *Sonnets from the Portuguese* as a series of "standing jokes and ritual readings." According to Lootens, the sonnets pop up everywhere from an Arby's roast beef slogan to Ruth M. Adams' assertion (in the 1974 Cambridge edition of Barrett Browning's poetry) that Barrett Browning's slight reputation would rest entirely on them (116-17).

[13] These translations remain unpublished, but they are available in both Phillip David Sharp's Ph. D. dissertation, "Poetry in Process: Elizabeth Barrett Browning and the Sonnets Notebook" and his MA thesis, "Elizabeth Barrett Browning and the Wimpole Street Notebook." The translations from Petrarch which follow are from Sharp's transcriptions.

to quote Bakhtin's assessment of structured lyric verse in general, they are composed according to "*an unmediated involvement between every aspect of the accentual system of the whole*" and because the prosodic elements "further the unity and hermetic quality of the surface of poetic style, and of the unitary language that this style posits" (*Discourse in the Novel* 298, Bakhtin's emphasis).

Similarly, the traditional sonnet sequence is a self-centered, monologic mode; to borrow Jessica Benjamin's description of phallocentric desire, the sonnet sequence usually expresses "the one-sided individuality of subject meeting object, a complementarity that idealizes one side and devalues the other" (98). Mermin argues that Barrett's primary agenda with *Sonnets from the Portuguese* was "to take her place in the tradition, not to prove herself an outsider" (*Elizabeth Barrett Browning* 144). But Barrett's gendered position as an outsider almost made it necessary for her to change the conventions. Before Barrett, there was little deviation from Petrarch's pattern in the sonnet sequence: the love-lorn poet is first blinded and imprisoned by the beauty of a lady (or, in bisexual Shakespeare's case, a fascinating woman and a beautiful man), he courts her, she proves cold or distant, he struggles with his consuming passion, and he finally accepts (or not) the hopelessness of his predicament. The poet is always a man; the lover and the beloved never share an equal passion. According to Marjorie Stone, Barrett's revision of the sonnet tradition was so compelling for Christina Rossetti that Rossetti (grudgingly, sometimes) followed her lead in a number of departures from Dante and Petrarch. Although Rossetti resists Barrett Browning's "movement from divine to human love" (47), she follows the elder poet in articulating female subjectivity, "breaking [the]centuries-old convention of the lady's silence," "subvert[ing] the dynamics of the dominant male gaze," "avoid[ing] an inventory of the beloved's appearance," omitting the convention of the first meeting, rejecting the inequality between the lover and the lady, creating a web of allusions to the tradition being subverted, and invoking "heroic feminine figures of the classical and Biblical past" ("*Monna Innominata* and *Sonnets from the Portuguese*: Sonnet Traditions and Spiritual Trajectories" 64-66). Stone also notes the central importance for both Barrett and Rossetti - even in their titles - of translation as a figure of speech, suggesting that, for all their sense of entitlement to the tradition of the fathers, feeling and insight must still be presented under a veil (62-63).

Most of the individual sonnets Barrett published in 1844 are formally unadventurous and predictably unitary; like those of Landon, Smith, and Hemens, Barrett's early sonnets, with a few exceptions such as the sonnets to George Sand, concern abstract virtues, details of nature, and minor human failings. But in the forty-four Petrarchan sonnets that make up *Sonnets from the Portuguese*, two subjects emerge, and the dramatic voice of the poet sounds in the intensely imagined presence of another.[14] In Bakhtin's terminology, Barrett's sonnet sequence is more dialogic than most lyric poetry, including her own earlier efforts.[15] Barrett's sequence embodies an intersubjective "mode of thought that suspend[s] and reconcile[s]" the "opposition[. .] between self and other," which Benjamin finds characteristic of female desire (98). Near the beginning of the sequence, Sonnet VI establishes a visceral closeness between the two subjects of the sequence: the speaker says that whatever separates her from the beloved

> leaves thy heart in mine
> With pulses that beat double. . . .
> And when I sue
> God for myself, He hears that name of thine,
> And sees within my eyes the tears of two. (9-10, 12-14)

The speaker of Barrett's sonnets is not the only center and source of creative activity, as in traditional sonnet sequences, but one participant in a dialogue that can take place only between two autonomous, creative minds. Unlike the sonnets which were her models, Barrett's love sonnets do not project a unitary universe, and do not respond well to formalist criticism.

At Browning's suggestion, in *Poems* of 1850, Barrett Browning adopted the title by which we know these sonnets because it recalled one of his favorites, the "Catarina" of her own early dramatic monologue "Catarina to Camoens" (published for the first time in the 1844 collection). As Browning no doubt realized, the title also suggested that the poems were translations and encouraged readers to separate the speaker from the poet herself.[16] In other words, Browning helped to frame the sequence as a fiction, or a veil, but in doing so, he was by no means distorting Barrett's conception of the poems. Loy Martin suggests that Barrett "found in the

---

[14] Mermin's book-length study of Barrett Browning's work explicates the doubleness of the poems in depth.

[15] Allison Chapman notes that "The octaves[. . .] frequently break into the sestets by the use of a caesura break in line nine [. . .] . This adaptation of the conventional structure, which occurs in twenty-one of the forty-four sonnets of the sequence, puts into question the stability of the Petrarchan form and the secure relation between the two parts of the sonnet [. . .]" (311).

[16] I owe to Patsy Boyer the insight that Barrett Browning's title also invokes the powerful, anonymous *Love Letters from the Portuguese*, putatively a seventeenth-century French fraud. The "writer" of the *Love Letters* is a young Portuguese girl abandoned by her foreign lover, a soldier.

English sonnet sequence an enclosing fiction for the day-to-day vacillations of her feelings for Robert Browning" and in so doing transformed the sonnet sequence into a series of dramatic monologues (169). However we define the poems, they were indubitably a technical development in the poetry of Barrett Browning, and they introduced into English poetry a new, fully conscious mode of expressing female desire - unstable, iconoclastic, ambivalent, and intersubjective. The rugged diction and the violations of formal conventions, which recall Donne and anticipate Hopkins, indicate a conscious creative response to the emotional upheaval which inspired them. Indeed, the presence of an auditor is as pronounced in most of these sonnets as it is in the dramatic monologue. And that auditor, of course, is a fictionalized Robert Browning.

The *Sonnets from the Portuguese* are most accurately read as a fictionalized rendering of an intimate dialogue, originating in Elizabeth Barrett's life. Writing to Browning in 1845 about *Pippa Passes*, Barrett reflects on the possibility that:

> far beyond any work of <u>re</u>flection [. . .] appears that gathering of light on light upon particular points, as you go (in composition) step by step, til you get intimately near to things, & see them in a fulness and clearness, & an intense trust in the truth of them which you have not in any sunshine of noon (called <u>real</u>!) but which you have <u>then</u> . . & struggle to communicate [. . .].
> (*Correspondence* 10.266)

In emphasizing the insights that Browning finds in intimate acquaintance with his fictional characters - with the details of their lives, with the moments of their historical existence - Barrett of course avoids saying that her own poetic material is her relationship with Robert Browning himself. It is not surprising that she describes the composition process as the cultivation of intimacy and closeness, through which understanding comes more clearly than through sunshine and open space. Benjamin suggests that "the intersubjective mode of desire" - the theme of the sonnets and the letter - takes shape in "spatial rather than symbolic representation, and that this mode does have something to do with female experience" (94-95).

In *Elizabeth Barrett Browning: The Origins of a New Poetry*, Mermin frequently notes the unexpected literalness of Barrett's transforming poetic, her habit, that is, of reconverting dead metaphors into literal statements. (Such reconversions of metaphor occur in religious language, in which the soul is characterized as female, or the suppliant as a child, or in amatory discourse when the speaker places the lover at a higher level.) The disconcerting impact of *Sonnets from the Portuguese* derives not only from these literalizations identified by Mermin, but also from the reverse process, when Barrett turns into metaphor language which in other contexts would be literal. In particular, Barrett turns the metaphorical geometries of the traditional sonnet sequence into literal ones. Her sonnets develop a pattern of potential and then actual emotional closeness, much like the closeness she describes in the letter. This geometry contrasts with the separation which informs traditional sonnet sequences. For instance, Petrarch's Sonnet 61, according to Barrett's own translation, describes the moment when he "first survey[ed]/ Two beauteous eyes which took me prisoner." This moment occurred long ago and far away, and since then, the speaker has blessed "the many breaths I did respire/ In calling round the world my lady's name" (Sharp 8). He has no hope of closeness. In contrast, Barrett's sonnets show imprisonment as all too visceral, and breath as all too short: "a year ago," she writes in Sonnet XX, she "heard the silence sink" and

> link by link,
> Went counting all my chains as if that so
> They never could fall off at any blow.   (2, 4-7)

Again in contrast to Petrarch, in Barrett's poems, intimacy is blessedly possible: now, she says, she "feel[s] thee thrill the day or night/ With personal act or speech" (10-11). If the speaker in Petrarch's poem experiences an enhancement of subjectivity and autonomy because of his "imprisonment" to the power of Laura's eyes, the speaker in Barrett's poem finds full subjectivity and autonomy only after the loneliness and silence of her life have been interrupted by the exchange of "personal act or speech."

Another aspect of this new geometry is that Barrett typically moves the sonnet sequence out of a cosmic or natural setting and into the literal domestic interior of the novel. Although this geometry is evident throughout the sequence, the linked Sonnets XXI ("Say over again, and yet once over again") and XXII ("When our two souls stand up erect and strong") offer particularly clear examples. Both poems develop around a contrast between exterior space, which threatens and separates, and interior space, the place of intimacy and the source of creativity. In XXI, "hill or plain,/ Valley and wood" stand for the speaker's open and vulnerable frame of mind when she finds herself doubting the beloved's constancy. Nature, which here seems to stand for ordinary human existence, must be awakened in the spring by the cuckoo. (The sonnet is not, ostensibly, about jealousy, but the symbolic resonance of the cuckoo is difficult to overlook.) In contrast, her own emotional life depends upon being able to function within a closed space: the speaker must be reached in her literal darkness by "the silver iterance" of her lover's reassurance; and even the continual reassurance of his words is finally inadequate unless he remembers "To love me also in silence, with thy soul" (14). Echoing the language in which Browning describes Saul, the first line of Sonnet XXII repeats the last word of Sonnet XXI in a striking cosmic image:

> When our two souls stand up erect and strong,
> Face to face, silent, drawing nigh and nigher,
> Until the lengthening wings break into fire
> At either curved point, -- what bitter wrong
> Can the earth do to us that we should not long
> Be here contented?   (1-6)

These opening lines falsely anticipate a conclusion in which the lovers are translated into the upper realms. Instead, the speaker finally rejects the cosmic power and beauty of the opening lines. The idea of the sonnet's initial statement is reversed in an unexpected and unorthodox fashion, not at the beginning of the sestet, but with an abrupt monosyllable in line 6, which wraps the idea of the octet into the sestet:

>   Think. In mounting higher,
> The angels would press on us, and aspire
> To drop some golden orb of perfect song
> Into our deep, dear silence. Let us stay
> Rather on earth, Beloved, -- where the unfit
> Contrarious moods of men recoil away
> And isolate pure spirits, and permit
> A place to stand and love in for a day.
> With darkness and the death-hour rounding it.   (6-14)

The enjambment postpones metrical closure until line 13, adding to the poem's bottom heaviness. The weight of the last eight lines demonstrates the idea that the lower, enclosed, earthly realm is the proper setting for the speaker's human, yet spiritual, love.

Sonnets XXI and XXII typify the ways in which Barrett reverses the cosmic but alienated geometry of the traditional sonnet sequence. The distance between Laura and her worshipper - and between the poet and his own better self - described in Petrarch's Sonnet XI - is typical. The poet describes Laura in terms which became conventional (again in Barrett's translation):

> The eyes I spake such ardent praises on,
> The arms, the little hands, the feet and face

> That twixt myself and me did thrust their grace
> And forced me in the world to dwell alone --,

The poet then describes the beloved as an angel on earth:

> The angel smile's sun-lightening, which apace
> Made paradise where earth showed no such place [. . .].   (1-6)

In contrast, the speaker in Barrett's sonnets does not bring heaven to earth through the lover, but eschews heaven altogether. She is more at home in an interior space, circumscribed by "darkness and the death hour," but also intimate and spiritually powerful.

The plot of *Sonnets from the Portuguese* is as unconventional as the spatial dynamics. With a rare exception, such as the *Amoretti*, with which Spenser introduced his *Epithalamion*, sonnet sequences chronicle the poet/speaker's hopeless love for an unreachable object. In contrast, Barrett narrates a requited passion, starting with her own shocked recognition and fearful rejection of love, followed by intense self scrutiny, then by analysis of the relationship as an equal exchange, joy and acceptance of her lover's passion, more doubts, adjustments to the prospect of absolute sharing, and, finally, commitment to love and the lover, her "unexpected angel." The unrequited passion of the traditional English sonnet sequence typically inspires a guilty internal struggle when the speaker realizes that his desire for the lady deflects his attention from sacred or moral values. Typically, this struggle is mitigated only when the speaker succeeds in making his earthly desire an emblem of divine love, but even then, the speaker's shame continues to haunt him. Her reading of this tradition was part of the foundation upon which Barrett rewrote the sonnet sequence. The lover's Augustinian guilt, which she rejected, is, in fact, the subject of Petrarch's Sonnet 1:[17]

> Hearers [?], in broken rhyme, of echoes old,
> Of those weak sighs wherewith I fed mine heart
> In my first youthful error, when in part
> I was another man than ye behold:
> My weepings and my singings manifold,
> The balance of my vain desire and smart,
> Give me to hope from those who know Love's dart,
> Some pity, . . though their pardon they withhold.
> But not I can descern how very long
> I was the people's proverb, ~~and~~ I wear

---

[17] Petrarch wrote Sonnet I last, as a disclaimer, but it is of course read first, as an explanation.

A blush before mine own soul, thus to seem!
And shame is all the fruit of that vain song,
And late contrition [?], and the knowledge clear
That what the world calls sweetest is a dream.
(Sharp, "Wimpole Street Notebook" 6)

Barrett's deviation from the typical sonnet sequence plot includes a reversal of the earthly-celestial dynamic which drives it: for Barrett, divine love and angelic joy become an emblem for an earthly love which contains the divine - not the other way around. The religious images of Barrett's earlier poetry, which are relatively thin and weak, become more profound and more vital within the erotic framework of the sonnets.

Barrett's reversal of earthly and heavenly priorities appears as early in the sequence as Sonnet II, a poem of struggle to accept God's apparent prohibition against love. The sonnet's last five lines contrast God's authority to the strength of the lovers' feeling: "Men could not part us with their worldly jars [. . .]. And, heaven being rolled between us at the end,/ We should but vow the faster for the stars." Sonnet XX compares the speaker's past failure to guess her lover's existence to the spiritual blindness of atheists, "Who cannot guess God's presence out of sight" (14). In XXX the speaker compares complicated emotions about her beloved to those the acolyte experiences as he falls on his face "Amid the chanted joy and thankful rite." In all these poems, as in *Saul*, religious imagery expresses erotic emotion.

The further Barrett progresses in the sequence, the more daring her religious imagery becomes. Sonnet XXVII is a turning point; here, the speaker finally conquers doubts about her beloved, who with godlike power "has lifted me/ From this drear flat of earth where I was thrown [. . .].

> My own, my own,
> Who camest to me when the world was gone,
> And I who looked for only God, found <u>thee!</u>   (1-2, 6-8, Barrett's italics)

By itself, the lived experience of being in love would not have enabled Barrett, whose evangelically rooted faith encompassed even the literal truth of angels, to skirt so narrowly around sacrilege. But what Martin calls the "enclosing fiction" of the traditional sonnet sequence allowed her to take both literary risks and the personal, even spiritual, risk of transforming the language of faith into the language of love (169). *Sonnets from the Portuguese* offers no better example of the way Barrett veered off from tradition than this Sonnet XVII: instead of shame and guilt, the speaker experiences a rush of spiritual power and insists upon the legitimacy of erotic love:

> I find thee; I am safe, and strong, and glad.
> As one who stands in dewless asphodel
> Looks backward on the tedious time he had
> In the upper life, -- so I, with bosom-swell,
> Make witness, here, between the good and bad,
> That Love, as strong as Death, retrieves as well.   (9-13)

Switching from Christian to pagan imagery, Sonnet XXXVII merges the erotic with the religious even more openly. The speaker has built a "graven image" of the beloved for herself; perhaps it is a mental image, perhaps simply the line of poetry in which she describes him. Whatever the form of the image, the poet regrets that it has been constructed of sand, "fit to shift and break." With a happy irony which calls attention to her poetic prowess as she laments the lack of it, the speaker compares her efforts to those of "a shipwrecked Pagan, safe in port," who,

> His guardian sea-god to commemorate,
> Should set a sculptured porpoise, gills a-snort
> And vibrant tail, within the temple-gate. (11-14)

Nowhere in the poet's work is there a more joyful celebration of phallic beauty or female erotic openness.[18]

The erotic potential suggested in this poem is made literal in the next, Sonnet XXXVIII, in some ways the climax of the sequence. Again, the religious merges with the erotic, as progressively more intimate kisses suggest parallels among erotic seduction, religious conversion, religious commitment, and the imaginative act. The beloved's first kiss, on the fingers of the hand which writes the sonnets, has made them grow "more clean and white" (3). The second, which "sought the forehead, and half missed" was "the chrism of love, which love's own crown,/ With sanctifying sweetness, did precede" (8, 10-11).

> The third upon my lips was folded down
> In perfect, purple state; since when, indeed,
> I have been proud and said, "My love, my own."   (12-14)

---

[18] Sharon Smulders sees Barrett's shipwreck trope in this sonnet as a revision of similar language in Sidney's *Astrophel and Stella*, Sonnet 85, and a nod to Spenser's *Amoretti*, as well, where the metaphor of the shipwreck occurs in no fewer than five poems.

In this declaration of pride, the erotic religious dynamic of the sonnet tradition is reversed: instead of finding in worldly love a guilty inspiration for religious faith and divine love, Barrett finds in her religious experience a way to understand, accept, and finally explain desire.

So much for the Neo-Platonic ladder of courtly love. In creating this new pattern, Barrett rewrites masculinist literary conventions describing female behavior: the woman who speaks in these poems is not cold or remote. Furthermore, she subverts the spiritual values which she is supposed to represent, and she rebels against the values which have informed the Petrarchan tradition. In terms of the language of the sonnet, this is indeed "pure Egyptian."

The nature of Barrett's experiment is most clearly revealed in terms of relationships - speaker and auditor, lover and beloved, poet and poet - and in the internal struggle between the voice of desire and the carefully constructed, detached female persona Barrett holds over from her earlier poetry. Mermin points out that Barrett's voice is "doubled" by her consciousness of the gendered genres in which she worked. Barrett's consciousness of female identity, while she is exercising the masculine privilege of authorship, ironizes almost everything she writes, even the popular early ballads she wrote for the sentimental gift annuals.

The sonnet sequence, however, is Barrett's first work in which such doubling is open rather than suppressed, central rather than peripheral. The consciousness behind *Sonnets from the Portuguese* is aware of the psychic split which seemed to trap the writer behind the mask of a female Alexander Pope, inside the heroic couplets of "Essay on Woman": now this split is no longer an obstacle to, but the material for, poetry. And the material is perfectly suited to the split form of the sonnet itself.

A critical aspect of this transformation is the fact that the object of the poems, Robert Browning, is also a poetic subject. Because she thus shared the role of central authoritative intelligence with the beloved, the speaker of Barrett's sonnets cannot claim, and she does not need to claim, the creative force which usually endows the sonneteer's beloved with fame or immortality. Instead, she seems painfully aware that the beloved himself writes with subjective and expressive power equal or superior to her own. In Sonnet III, she asks him what, since his art is made for brilliant public display,

> hast *thou* to do
> With looking from the lattice-lights at me,
> A poor, tired, wandering singer, singing through
> The dark, and leaning on a cypress tree?
> (9-12, Barrett's italics).

In Sonnet IV, the beloved is a "gracious singer of high poems," whose music "drop[s]. . . In folds of golden fulness at my door" (2, 7-8). This time, he must look up at the window, to hear her "cricket," which "chirps against thy mandolin" (11). The language in which Barrett describes Browning's situation contrasts with the general tenor of the poet/speaker's own life, lived outside the brilliance of public life, so that her "singing" takes place in the dark and in the gloomy shade of the cypress tree.

The dialogue between the two poets, then, is fraught by unresolved and unresolvable tensions. Especially in the first half of *Sonnets from the Portuguese*, the speaker continually refers to herself and her lover as different, competing poets. Later, their voices merge and double; in Sonnet XXXII, the speaker at first fears that she is "an out-of tune/ Worn viol, a good singer would be wroth/ To spoil his song with," but then realizes that

> perfect strains may float
> 'Neath master-hands from instruments defaced, --
> And great souls, at one stroke, may do and doat.
>   (7-9, 12-14)

Perhaps because both the speaker and the beloved are poets, however, perfect love is paradoxically expressed not by music but by silence. In Sonnet XLI, the speaker thanks everyone "Who paused a little near the prison-wall/To hear my music,"

> But thou, who, in my voice's sink and fall
> When the sob took it, thy divinest Art's
> Own instrument didst drop down at thy foot
> To hearken what I said between my tears, . . .
> Instruct me how to thank thee!   (2-4, 7-ll, Barrett's ellipsis)

From the beloved's autonomous consciousness, words may come to the speaker/ poet herself. But it also seems that even the words the beloved teaches her will be ultimately equivocal, and that only time for dialogue - and the completion of the sonnet sequence itself - will enable her to speak fully.

Every aspect of the sequence declares the speaker herself a dynamic character, first grief-stricken, guilty, and remote, but finally capable of joy, as she moves "intimately near" to her material. The speaker sees herself as the inhabitant of literary, then symbolic, and finally literal spaces, and as the sequence progresses, her character merges with the spaces she inhabits. Throughout the sequence, exterior space threatens and separates; however, by the end of *Sonnets from the Portuguese*, the outside is brought literally inside. In the first sonnet, in a reference to Theocratus' Idyl 30, the speaker situates herself within the language of literature; like the dear dead years in the lament for Adonis, the speaker's own dead years reappear when Love, a new force in her life, violently pulls her "backward by the hair," to relive and reinterpret the past. But gradually the speaker divests herself of allusive and symbolic language, replacing it with the more literal language of her own unique position within and against masculinist literary tradition.

A progression from exterior and symbolic nature - the traditional language of the sonnet - to interior and literal nature can be traced in the imagery of Sonnet XXIX ("I think of thee! -- my thoughts do twine and bud") and Sonnet LVIV, the last ("Beloved, thou hast brought me many flowers"). Two-thirds of the way through the sequence, Sonnet XXIX punctuates a moment of retrograde motion as the speaker vacillates between acceptance and avoidance. Developing around an image cluster which is almost a cliché, the strong tree and the clinging vine, the poem represents a last late link between Barrett's sequence and the gendered cultural tradition which it revisits. Like Milton's description of Eve, whose seductive hair

> in wanton ringlets waved
> As the vine curls her tendrils, which implied
> Subjection, but required with gentle sway   (*Paradise Lost* IV. 306-08)

the speaker describes her own thoughts, which

> twine and bud
> About thee, as wild vines, about a tree,
> Put out broad leaves, and soon there's nought to see
> Except the straggling green which hides the wood.   (1-4)

Unlike Milton's vegetative imagery, the goal of Barrett's encroaching vine is not the expected emotional support but borrowed cerebral vitality. And unlike Eve, the speaker rejects the easy gender dynamic represented by the feminine vine drawing strength from the phallic tree:

> Yet, O my palm-tree, be it understood
> I will not have my thoughts instead of thee
> Who art dearer, better! Rather, instantly
> Renew thy presence; as a strong tree should,
> Rustle thy boughs and set thy trunk all bare,
> And let these bands of greenery which insphere thee
> Drop heavily down, -- burst, shattered, everywhere!   (6-10)

The retroactive starting point of the poem is the one-sided female dependence celebrated in the traditional sonnet sequence; finally, however, the poem celebrates the destruction of the dependent role. Seeing the tree, with its boughs and phallic trunk, and rejecting dependence on the tree, become a "deep joy" for the speaker. The subjective thoughts which have encircled the tree give way to something deeper: "I do not think of thee -- I am too near thee" (12, 14). The speaker in Barrett's poem is willing to imagine temporary pain for the sake of liberating the tree from the clinging vine. Within the context of the other sonnets, it is clear that only by being torn away from her masculine support can the speaker liberate herself from dependence.

It is interesting that Barrett later repeats the image of palm tree and constricting vine in Book I of *Aurora Leigh*, to reject the idea that her poet heroine has ever participated in the role of the dependent vine (with dependent children). In fact, the fecundity of variations on the imagery of vine and tree in Barrett's poetry exemplifies the way in which she took poetic conventions, subverted them, and rewrote them for her own purposes.

During the 1840s, Robert Browning's work, especially in the dramatic monologue, was moving toward a dialogism which represented what Bakhtin refers to as "someone else's semantic position" (*Problems of Dostoevsky's Poetics* 184). Barrett's dialogism developed differently: the speaker in *Sonnets from the Portuguese* monologically excludes the independent, uninterpreted, uninterrupted voice of the other person, but, on the other hand, the speaker dialogically (and endlessly) analyzes her own construction of the beloved, dissecting the ambiguity of the words in which she encloses her own meaning, inspecting the gender stereotypes she herself borrows from the sonnet sequence, and deconstructing the ideology of the genre in which she has chosen to work. The semantic center of the sonnets engages in a particular kind of dialogue which is unusual in lyric poetry, but, according to Bakhtin, always possible

> toward one's own utterance, toward its separate parts and toward an individual word within it, if we detach ourselves from them, speak with an inner reservation, if we observe a certain distance from them, as if limiting our own authorship or dividing it in two. (*Dostoevsky* 204, 184)

The gap between composition and disclosure, the secrecy, and the jokes confirm the hesitation and doubt apparent within the sonnets themselves. Together and separately, the sonnets seem in some way part of an "unfinished, still-evolving [. . .] reality" ("Epic and Novel" 7), and Barrett herself seems to have understood the dialogic potential of the sonnet and the sonnet sequence better than her predecessors.

The last sonnet, XLIV, written in September, 1846, just before the poet was uprooted from her old life and transplanted into a new one with Robert Browning, concludes *Sonnets from the Portuguese*, but does not provide closure. Sonnet XXIX, in which the tree and the vine form the metaphorical core, suggests Barrett's fear that Browning would be overwhelmed by her own habits of dependence, Browning's stubborn insistence on her poetic superiority, and the external circumstances of their relationship. The last sonnet also resonates with a fear that Browning's urge to rescue would entrap her in a role of clinging dependence. But Barrett was resolved to avoid such a future, and her final word in *Sonnets from the Portuguese* points toward a positive transformation of the clinging vine. This last poem is no more comfortable than Sonnet XXIX, but it describes an equal rather than a one-sided relationship. For the flowers the beloved has again and again brought into her darkened room, in the final sonnet, LXIV, the speaker offers these poems: "Take back these thoughts" which, like the beloved's flowers, have been plucked from the "heart's ground." Imperfect as they are, still,

> here's eglantine,
> Here's ivy! -- take them, as I used to do
> Thy flowers [. . .]. (10-12)

In giving back these "flowers," that is, her poems, she has obeyed Browning's injunction against "paying tithes of thyme, mint, anise and cummin, and leaving unpaid the real weighty dues of the Law." The clinging vine of uncertain species has changed to eglantine and ivy - symbols of love and eternal life. Nature has been brought inside and described in the language of intimacy rather than distance. The poem and the sequence end with an image that is both spiritual and visceral:

> Instruct thine eyes to keep their colors true,
> And tell thy soul their roots are left in mine.

But even with the assurance of love and intimacy, and even in the flowers, appear traces of violence, competitiveness, and indeterminacy: in the shadow image of these lines, the roots of a torn-up flower remain embedded in alien flesh, and the flowers given as prizes in medieval courts of love make a final appearance.

Browning did not know about these poems until three years after they were finished. Plunged into emotional turmoil by Pen's birth and his mother's death, he began to recover when, with faultless timing, his wife brought out the sonnets she had written about their relationship.

To the last word, these poems defy their popular characterization as a simple emotional outpouring. The sentimentality imposed upon the poems by publishers has suppressed Barrett's dialogue with two "alien discourses": first, with the sonnet tradition, which made her an outsider, and second, with the poetry and letters of her lover Robert Browning. Barrett did not write the sonnets only for Browning: she wrote them, first, for herself. The fact that he could inspire such poems enabled Barrett to trust that her vocation could continue with him in Italy, and that Browning's world would enrich her poetry, not stifle it.

In this moment, the inspiration he provided was necessary for her creative development.

And in these poems, she was inspired to begin the process of creating a new voice and experimenting with new forms: *Sonnets from the Portuguese* represents a quantum leap in Barrett's development, the first in a series of radical experiments which she would undertake during the next decade - experiments in which her voice takes on new resonances, new layers of meaning, and new relationships with literary tradition - in other words, becomes more dialogic. The poems she began to write when she met Robert Browning suggest that dialogue in literary language is, in fact, a metaphor for dialogue in life. That dialogue within *Sonnets from the Portuguese* opened the way to an emotional and aesthetic reality in which the separate pieces - life and art, scholarship and aesthetics, tradition and the contemporary - began to merge and enrich each other

Chapter 4

Browning Beside Himself
1847-1851

The summer of 1846, the last the couple would spend in England, was given over mostly to worries. Still, in addition to the sonnets, Barrett managed to write "A Woman's Shortcomings" and "A Man's Requirements," cynical commentaries on love affairs gone wrong, which appeared in *Blackwood's Magazine* a few weeks after she left for Italy with Browning. The timing must have seemed inexplicable to readers who did not understand that her feminism was as much a matter of principle as personal experience. As for Browning, in April, his last two plays, *Luria* and *A Soul's Tragedy*, were published together, as the thirteenth and last number of *Bells and Pomegranates*, to generally favorable reviews. Some of the poems which eventually found their way into *Men and Women* may have been drafted during this time. Certainly, the poems about dueling, "Before" and "After," reflect the couple's quarrels on the subject. And internal evidence in "Evelyn Hope" and "The Last Ride Together" suggests that, like Barrett, Browning may have been meditating on frustrated or one-sided love.[1] But the energy each put into writing shrinks in significance when compared to the intense effort of deciding how to transform their courtship into a marriage. The secrecy surrounding their connection was stressful, but Elizabeth felt it was necessary: her father still controlled every aspect of his adult children's lives and showed no signs of relaxing his prohibition against marriage for any of them. But she dreaded a break with him so much that sometimes, up until the last few days in his house, she seemed willing to postpone a decision indefinitely. Browning, whose ties to his own family were just as close, if not as vexed, found himself in the uncomfortable position of applying pressure to his lover, with the knowledge that after their marriage, life would change inevitably and fundamentally for them and everyone else they cared for. The delay gave

---

[1] Jack and Inglesfield show in Vol. V of the Oxford edition that DeVane's dating of these and other poems ("A Toccata of Galuppi's," "Instans Tyrannus," "Love in a Life," and "Misconceptions") in the *Handbook* is speculative. Still, there is some textual evidence that these eight poems were at least drafted during the summer of 1846.

Browning nightmares and headaches, but it was the dread of her physical decline if she spent another winter in London that made him frantic.

Finally, matters reached a crisis when Barrett *père* announced in early September that the family would move to temporary quarters in the country so that the town house could be cleaned and refurbished. The window of opportunity would soon be closed; Elizabeth would have to endure another English winter; Robert would be forced to witness an illness which might well be her last. Both saw a sojourn in Italy as Elizabeth's salvation.

On September 12, 1846, the couple married secretly in Marylebone Church and returned to their respective parents' homes. Hastily, they consulted train and boat schedules - almost miscalculating disastrously. They left London on September 19 for Paris, taking few possessions, and accompanied by Flush and Barrett's loyal maid Elizabeth Wilson, who had been informed of her mistress's plans only the day before the wedding. Barrett's sisters had suspected her intentions, but she had kept them in the dark so that they would not have to choose between lying to their father and betraying her. Browning had borrowed money for immediate expenses from his parents, but told few others. For the most part, the letters each left behind for friends and family bore tidings which came as a shock. Private and public reactions - heartfelt congratulations from their closest friends, recriminations from the Barrett men, predictable jokes from literary acquaintances[2] - added yet another layer of experience which would have to be examined and understood in the months and years to come.

After a rough crossing and a night coach to Paris, the Brownings landed, almost literally, on the doorstep of Anna Jameson, who was in transit there with her niece Gerardine. Jameson reported her own shock - and the couple's weary disarray - in a letter to Lady Noel Byron, and she took charge of them for the next few weeks. They were tired, but giddy. Despite her exhaustion, Elizabeth insisted on going with Jameson, Robert, and the admiring Gerardine to restaurants, and even to the Louvre. A week after the Brownings arrived in Paris, the party embarked on what must have seemed to Elizabeth a grueling progress by train, river-boat, and ship to Italy, where Jameson intended to undertake research for her next book. Along the way, the Brownings were especially pleased to be passing through Vaucluse, the home of Petrarch's Laura, and to see the scenery along the Italian Riviera. Jameson and Gerardine left the couple in Pisa, where they took a short lease on an apartment.

Elizabeth's complaints about the staid social and cultural life of the town show just how much and how deliberately she had changed her outlook.

---

[2] Wordsworth, for instance, is reported to have hoped aloud that the two poets might understand each other, since no one else did.

With Robert, she eagerly looked forward to exploring more of the country when their lease ended. For three years after their flight, the Brownings led a peripatetic existence, taking in the sights and sounds of Italy, searching for a permanent home, adjusting to their life together. After leaving Pisa, they took apartments in Rome and, later, in two different locations in Florence. They were devoted to city sightseeing and made numerous short trips to the more picturesque villages. During this time, the Brownings found themselves part of an expanding social circle which included Italian neighbors and notables and various English and American expatriates.

Their lives were both enriched and disrupted by familial forces as well. Elizabeth experienced two miscarriages - and then, in 1849, the birth of a son, Robert Wiedemann Browning, who would come to be known as Pen. A few days later, Robert received letters from his sister informing him first of his mother's serious illness, and then of her death. Later, he discovered that Sarianna had concealed his mother's sudden death by writing first of her serious illness and later, after he would have had time to prepare himself, of her death. As for Elizabeth, although she felt undiminished support from her sisters, she received from her brothers only grudging, belated forgiveness and from her father none at all. He refused to answer her letters and turned over the management of her finances to John Kenyon. The Brownings were moved to discover that Kenyon's friendship and family feeling strengthened as their needs increased: in fact, he established an allowance to supplement Elizabeth's income and, in 1856, left generous bequests to both poets.

During the first three years after their dramatic departure to Italy, the Brownings together had experienced such domestic upheaval, and such emotional extremes of love, joy, and terrible grief that neither wrote much poetry. Browning's vocation had depended on the security and routine of his parents' home, Barrett's on the silence and inertia of her sickroom. And though both poets hoped to create a new environment in which they would write even better poetry, the choice they made to dislodge themselves from lives ordered around scholarship and writing involved them in one of the greatest achievements of their life together - seizing freedom at the risk of art.

The Brownings did produce some work, however. In 1846, Barrett Browning finished a long dramatic monologue, "The Runaway Slave at Pilgrim's Point," and dispatched it to the organizers of the National Anti-Slavery Bazaar in Boston, despite her conviction that the poem would be too fierce for them (it wasn't). In 1847, after witnessing the beginnings of the Risorgimento from the balcony of Casa Guidi, the house in Florence

1   *Casa Guidi*, artist unknown, *The Tuscan Republics* (1893) by Bella Duffy

where they finally settled, she composed the first part of *Casa Guidi Windows*. During the same time, in 1847-48, Browning wrote an uncharacteristically autobiographical short poem, "The Guardian Angel," after seeing in Fano a sentimental painting on the subject by Guercino, whose work he had encountered in the Dulwich Gallery when he was a child. But both poets at first found it more congenial to take stock of themselves and their poetry by editing and re-organizing their previous work. From Browning came a two-volume edition in 1849 with his new publisher, Chapman & Hall; Barrett's two-volume edition, which included the sonnets, appeared in 1850, under the same imprint. Each was devoted during this time to helping the other with the sheer labor of preparing the volumes for publication.

In the winter of 1849-1850, Browning's lassitude was finally broken, and in *Christmas-Eve and Easter-Day*, the conflicting voices of his youth began to order themselves into patterns, resolving from ambivalence into the productive ambiguity of his mature work.

Shelley was on Browning's mind again because he had been asked to write the introduction for a published collection of recently "discovered" letters by Shelley. The letters turned out to be fraudulent, but the exercise proved to be the inspiration for one of only two critical essays from Browning's pen, and it provides invaluable insights into the way he understood Romantic poetry and his own work in relation to it. Now he could do in prose what he had not been able to do in the poetry he wrote during the 1830s: he could explain the inward-turning, egocentric drive of Romantic poetry as an effort to understand human consciousness, through the inner life of the poet himself. And (especially since the details of Shelley's marriage to Harriet Westbrook were not yet generally known) he could rationalize Shelley's faults as well. His wife's opium addiction had taught Browning that Shelley's acquaintance with laudanum resulted from physical illness, that addiction resulted from the power of the chemical rather than weakness of will, and that Shelley's delusions issued from terrible health, not terrible morals.

The excess of passion, the material expedients, the poetic infelicities - these were perpetrated by a boy who died just as his adolescence ended, in Browning's view. Even Shelley's atheism, Browning explained:

> Nor will men persist in confounding, any more than God confounds, with genuine infidelity and an atheism of the heart, those passionate, impatient struggles of a boy towards distant truth and love, made in the dark, and ended by one sweep of the natural seas before the full moral sunrise could shine out of him. (1007)

In the essay on Shelley, written in late 1851, Browning looked back at his predecessor as an older brother interprets the mistakes of a younger: at last, without ambivalence, he saw in Shelley a younger self. Finally, Browning ended the struggle with Shelley which drove his first published poem, *Pauline*. It is not coincidental that, in *Christmas-Eve and Easter-Day*, written just the year before, Browning for the first time was able to deal directly with his own subjective experience in poetry. But instead of doing so in the forms used so successfully by the Romantic poets - the sonnet, the short lyric, and the greater Romantic lyric - Browning resorted to the less personal forms of classical and medieval literature.

In part, both the inspiration to speak in his own voice and the scholarly framework of this personal speech emerged from Browning's dialogue with his wife, in person, in the letters, and in her poetry. In saying this, however, I do not subscribe to the usual argument that Browning wrote *Christmas-Eve and Easter-Day* at her behest. It would be logical to assume that the first major poetry written by the married poets would exhibit clear lines of influence, one on the other. In fact, a critical industry has developed around this supposition, and in the criticism devoted to this issue, Barrett Browning is sometimes depicted as the culprit responsible for Browning's supposed failures and inadequacies. An unusually detailed, but otherwise typical, response to *Christmas-Eve and Easter-Day* (that is, before the critical rehabilitation of Barrett Browning's work by feminist critics) is DeVane's. In a 1947 article, suggestively entitled "The Virgin and the Dragon," he maintains that *Christmas-Eve and Easter-Day*, among other poems of Browning's middle period, failed partly because of Barrett Browning's influence. At his wife's urging and against the grain of his own poetic temperament, goes the elliptical argument, he undertook the work to express his own religious beliefs. Consequently, the work was flawed:

> Being an obedient husband, he tried his best to be the kind of poet his wife wanted him to be. And so, in 1850, he published the first volume since his marriage, *Christmas-Eve and Easter-Day*, in which he spoke in the first person upon the problems of religious faith and doubt in contemporary terms. In spite of many splendid passages the result was not significant for its day, and is even less so for ours. *Christmas-Eve and Easter-Day* must be reckoned a failure also on commercial grounds, for it sold only two hundred copies. (187)

DeVane's claim about the commercial failure is inaccurate: in fact, two hundred copies were sold in the first two weeks after publication (*Poems* [Pettigrew] 1102). But more important, this *argumentum ad feminam* denies the moral power of both poets and also apparently relieves its maker of the responsibility for close attention.[3]

---

[3] Influence studies of the Brownings thus take place in a problematic context. As Karlin has pointed out, "Two myths about Browning's marriage are current. The first, and still the dominant and popular one, is the myth of an ideal union [. . .]. Inevitably [. . .] a counter-myth has grown up about the Brownings' marriage" (Woolford and Karlin 134, 138). This view is articulated most fully in Miller's 1952 biography, of an unequal marriage, based on psychological need, which quickly grew stale as the two poets' different values, tastes, and intellectual gifts inevitably surfaced. Similarly, Armstrong ends her article on the Brownings in *History of Literature in the English Language* with a suggestion that marriage to a second-rate poet forced the power and eccentricity out of Browning's work (a view Armstrong relaxed somewhat when she revised this essay for *New History of Literature* several years later). Even Erickson, who argues that Browning gained psychological and artistic support from the relationship, writes that "the influence of Elizabeth's poetry does

To grasp the complexities of Barrett Browning's presence in *Christmas-Eve and Easter-Day*, it is helpful to go back to an often-quoted letter of May, 1846, in which she did, in fact, urge Browning to speak more directly in some of his poetry because she felt he had much to teach. (DeVane presumed that this letter was responsible, five years after it was written, for Browning's decision to write the paired religious poems *Christmas-Eve and Easter-Day*.) Here is what Barrett says:

> But you,. . you have the superabundant mental life & individuality which admits of shifting personality & speaking the truth still. That is the highest faculty, the strongest & rarest, which exercises itself in Art, -- we are all agreed there is none so great faculty as the dramatic. Several times you have hinted to me that I made you care less for the drama, & it has puzzled me to fancy how it could be, when I understand myself so clearly both the difficulty & the glory of dramatic art. Yet I am conscious of wishing you to take the other crown besides, -- & after having made your own creatures speak in clear human voices, to speak yourself out of that personality which God made, & with the voice which He tuned into such power & sweetness of speech. I do not think, with all that music in you, only your own personality should be dumb, nor that having thought so much & deeply on life & its ends, you should not teach what you have learnt [. . .] . And it is not, I believe, by the dramatic medium, that poets teach most impressively. (*Correspondence* 12.358)

A careful reading of this letter suggests that Barrett Browning's words inevitably affected Browning's conceptions about his work, but she did not press him. In documents such as this, the mutual exchange between the Brownings is easy to see, but it is difficult to assess. Certainly, their effect upon each other is of a different order than Barrett Browning's indebtedness to Pope and Wollstonecraft, or Browning's to Shelley.

---

not seem in retrospect to have had a salutary effect upon Robert's work" until later in their marriage (*Robert Browning: His Poetry and His Audiences* 120); the supposed artistic failure of Browning's 1850 religious poems is Erickson's case in point.

Feminist "defenders" of EBB are sometimes inclined to find Browning at fault. For example Nina Auerbach, who argues in her 1986 essay "Robert Browning's Last Word" that, while highly respected biographies by Ryals and by Irvine and Honan err in implying that Browning's marriage "entailed the sacrifice of his deepest convictions and of the irony native to his poetic voice," recent feminist scholarship has ignored Browning's fictionalizing gestures and their possibly deleterious effect on his wife's reception (92). The dragon of partisanship is far from dead. Recently, I saw its ugly head reared again, in a catalog blurb for a selection of Barrett Browning's poems published by Paul & Co.: "She was in a sense the conscience of her husband," the advertiser confidently proclaims, "and his work suffered a steep decline after her death" (5).

The Brownings' shared field of reference, on the other hand, is perfectly visible under the right light. Eventually, both poets were heavily invested in Italian culture and contemporary issues such as the status of women and European politics, which were in a parlous state during the entire period of their marriage and beyond. Not only is this web of contemporary allusion evident in the poetry written by both, learning and scholarship inform their work in similar ways. Their correspondence is peppered with allusions to western cultural tradition, both obscure and canonical. In 1841, Browning wrote a letter to Jameson consisting entirely of a wry "explication" of a painting, probably by William Etty, of Cupid and Psyche. The letter begins with a citation of Apuleius's *Metamorphoses*, chapter and verse, and ends, "N. B. No attempt at fun in what goes before -- but strict rendering, as far as I remember -- having read the story this morning" (*Correspondence* 5.2). Five years later, Browning read Barrett's new translation of Aeschylus's *Prometheus* as well as her translations from the *Metamorphoses* and perhaps her monologue on Aeschylus, as well.[4] These exercises were a frequent topic in the correspondence. Referring to an episode from one of them in a letter dated 26 March 1846, Browning writes to her, "As if you had to write the meeting of Hector and Andromache, not the parting! By the way, dearest, what enchanted poetry all your translations for Miss Thompson are [. . .]" (*Correspondence* 12.183). Barrett's own references to these stories in letters to Browning were as wry as his earlier letter about Cupid and Psyche. Their deep, shared knowledge of literary history was a significant bond between the Brownings - as least as significant as the "influence" about which critics have speculated so diligently.[5]

---

[4] The letters contain incomplete information on the separate poem Barrett was writing about Aeschylus. A recent article by Margaret Reynolds and Barbara Rosenbaum argues, I think conclusively, that she wrote "Aeschylus' Soliloquy" about the same time she was doing the translation. Despite persuasive evidence offered by Martha Hale Shackford in 1947, say Reynolds and Rosenbaum, G. D. Hobson's and DeVane's objections were enough to keep the question open -- and the question of authorship tilted to Robert Browning -- because the only surviving copy of the poem (it was thought) is in his hand. DeVane's reasoning echoes his argument, given above, about Barrett Browning's influence on *Christmas-Eve and Easter-Day*: being a good husband, Browning wrote "Aeschylus' Soliloquy, but suppressed it because his wife's poetic version of Aeschylus' creative process (now lost), was weaker, and he didn't want to call attention to his own superior gifts (Reynolds and Rosenbaum 331). A rough draft of the poem in Barrett's hand was discovered in the Huntington Library in 1982, but the significance of the find not fully considered until the publication, fifty years' after Shackford's claim, of Reynolds' and Rosenbaum's work in 1997. Now, the only thing proved by the draft in Browning's hand is that he was at times very much involved in his wife's work -- something we already knew, not only from letters, but from abundant manuscript evidence.

[5] Browning included all ten of the unpublished translations from Apuleius in his wife's *Last Poems* (1862). The volume also included previously unpublished translations from

In particular, the references in their correspondence to Apuleius are germane, for *The Metamorphoses* is one of the best known examples of the Menippea, the genre of *Christmas-Eve and Easter-Day*. These paired poems are meditations on the nature of religious faith in an age of doubt - a work about religious questions rather than answers, about the psychology of religion rather than theology. The work first appeared in bookshops on Easter Monday, April 1, 1850, and, as the publisher hoped, had a seasonal appeal. But sales fell off rapidly after the first two weeks. Although some reviewers responded favorably, others accused the work of the same flaws they had found in *Sordello* more than ten years before - "obscurity of hazy thought and indistinct expression" (Litzinger and Smalley 139), flippancy, or even coarseness.[6] Unlike most of the poetry Browning wrote during his years in Italy, *Christmas-Eve and Easter-Day* has continued to annoy and befuddle twentieth-century readers at least as much as it did our Victorian counterparts. Despite the fact that the work is as interesting and challenging as some of Browning's better known poems and more important than many of them as a point of reference in his poetic development, it has had few readers since shortly after its publication.[7]

Christmas-Eve and Easter-Day does present difficulties of several kinds. Syntactically, these two poems are dense and contorted, the narratives are hard to follow, and the narrators seem almost at times to assault the reader. If Browning's contemporaries were nonplussed at *Sordello*, many of them found their objections amplified when they picked up the religious poems of 1850. Their suspicions were perhaps heightened by the fact that *Christmas-Eve and Easter-Day* seemed less clear than Clough's pessimistic and ironic religious poetry, published in 1849 and

---

Theocritus, Nonnus, Hesiod, Euripides, Homer, and Anacreon. Another interesting appearance of Apuleius which Browning had no doubt encountered is in *Woman in the Nineteenth Century* by Margaret Fuller, the Brownings' American friend who was a favorite of Elizabeth's in part because she was deeply committed to the cause of the Risorgimento. In her book, Fuller cites episodes from *Metamorphoses* and borrows some of Apuleius's rhetorical devices; Fuller's prose style is as florid as that of her original. (Fuller and her family drowned in a shipwreck off Fire Island the year before Browning wrote *Christmas-Eve and Easter-Day*.)

[6] Gertrude Reese Hudson provides a helpful and thorough account of the contemporary reviews of *Christmas-Eve and Easter-Day* in Chapter XV of *Robert Browning's Literary Life*.

[7] The few recent critical treatments of *Christmas-Eve and Easter-Day* which have appeared are excellent, although not comprehensive. See Linda H. Peterson's "Rereading *Christmas-Eve*, Rereading Browning" and Ryals' two articles: "Browning's *Christmas-Eve* and Schleiermacher's *Die Weihnachtsfeier*: A German Source for an English Poem" and "Levity's Rainbow: Browning's 'Christmas-Eve'." Less has been said of "Easter-Day."

1850, and less musical, less serious, and less affirmative than *In Memoriam*, also published in 1850.

Indeed, *Christmas-Eve and Easter-Day* still has few readers partly because the work does not fulfill expectations of what religious poetry should be. Most readings of the poems assume that they are basically commentaries on controversies about varieties of religious expression (in "Christmas-Eve") and about the nature of religious faith (in "Easter-Day").[8] Barbara Babcock Abrahams' remarks on modern criticism of the novel apply as well to the kind of poetry Browning habitually wrote, and to *Christmas-Eve and Easter-Day* in particular: "Studies of the novel," she argues, "have tended to overemphasize the 'serious' at the expense of the 'ludic' and to view the former in isolation from the latter [. . .] . Our critical categories are profoundly linear, logical, and metonymic. As a result, novels in which non-logical [. . .] forms of communication persist, or are re-created [. . .] are viewed as deviations from the norm, aberrations [. . .]" (913, 915). Browning's paired religious poems can best be understood as examples of Menippean satire, a form which mixes the serious and the ludic and which, according to Babcock Abrahams, exercised a considerable influence on nineteenth-century literature (930). Indeed, *Christmas-Eve and Easter-Day* is, in generic terms, probably the most sophisticated religious poem of the Victorian period. Browning knew the Menippea, not only from his study of English literature, but from his ventures into the more obscure byways of classical and continental literature. *Christmas-Eve and Easter-Day*, "uneasy and abortive works," as Karlin has recently called them (Woolford and Karlin 145[9]), lack comfort and closure, not because Elizabeth Barrett Browning forced her will upon her husband, but because the genre in which Browning was writing - the Menippea - is fundamentally unsettling.

Although Menippean satire was identified by Quintillian in the first century as a separate genre, the term as we use it today is a construct of twentieth-century genre theory. Certainly there is no evidence that Browning saw *Christmas-Eve and Easter-Day* as belonging to the genre of *The Metamorphoses* of Apuleius; nevertheless, the generic conventions of this work and the other Menippea he had studied had an impact on his work.

---

[8] Dowden's classic *The Life of Robert Browning* and Collins's *Robert Browning's Moral-Aesthetic Theory*, for instance, include appreciative readings of the work as a statement of belief, though neither writer suggests that Browning's beliefs are in any way simple.

[9] In this co-authored study, *Robert Browning*, Karlin wrote the chapter on Browning's marriage, in which this phrase appears.

And, certainly, he was aware of the history of religious poetry. *Christmas-Eve and Easter-Day* is riddled with allusions, both modern and classical, well known and obscure, and Browning was doubtless aware that the visions he narrates are linked to English and classical literatures as well as biblical and theological traditions. In short, Browning would have claimed as his own the tradition of the Menippea, if not the genre.

"Christmas-Eve" is, specifically, a vision in which discursive elements are linked by a narrative of the speaker's out-of-body religious experience. And "Easter-Day" is a vision of the last day surrounded by a dialogue - the speaker is literally of two minds and argues with himself about the nature and the demands of faith. When in *Christmas-Eve and Easter-Day* Browning turned to the genre of vision literature, he was adopting one of the most popular forms in English poetry, imported by Chaucer and his contemporaries from France, imitated by the Romantic poets, and often parodied by the same poets who introduced and reintroduced the genre to the reading public. Menippean satire, from which vision literature derives, is a prose and verse, seriocomic form which originated in the third century BCE and which, according to Bakhtin's analysis in *Problems of Dostoevsky's Poetics*, "possesses great external plasticity," the ability to absorb other genres, and the ability to "penetrate as a component element into other large genres" (119). Most important for Browning is the narrative instability of the Menippea, that is, the narrator's tendency to undermine and satirize his own position in the text, to the extent that he ceases "to coincide with himself" (Bakhtin 117). In *Christmas-Eve and Easter-Day*, Browning found in the classical forms of the Menippea a way to speak about religious controversies as well as his own religious experience, without revealing himself directly, without claiming universal truth, without speaking subjectively. And although poets from the early Christian era through the Middle ages frequently associated satire with religious expression, this association was attenuated by the time Browning wrote his religious poems, and, consequently, Browning's poems made less sense to others than they did to him.

Of the two poems, "Christmas-Eve" is better known, probably because, at first reading, it seems to be a relatively straightforward critique of contemporary religious practice. During the course of a dream journey, the narrator scrutinizes not only the evangelical tradition with which he is personally familiar, but Roman ritual and Higher Criticism as well. Already antique by the time it entered English literature, the dream vision is honored as much in the parody as the observance; Browning's poem is no exception. Typically in the dream vision, the spiritual quest begins when the dreamer falls asleep by a babbling brook. In contrast, Browning's narrator is drenched by a thunderstorm, takes refuge in a fundamentalist chapel amid a stupendously unattractive congregation (sheep with their "special clover," he calls them [136]), and is put to sleep by a fire-and-brimstone preacher who somehow manages to be boring. Usually, the narrator's vision is propelled and interpreted by a benign and talkative supernatural guide - an angel or a big bird - who transports him to various locales to see things for himself. Browning's narrator is guided by a less benign giant winged figure - Christ or perhaps an angel - who peremptorily deposits him on doorsteps or in pews and sometimes (seven times, to be exact) leads him on such a merry chase, whisking through doorways and around corners, that the narrator is able to keep up only by snatching continually at the hem of the guide's "sweepy garment, vast and white" (438).

Together, the narrator and his guide attend a Christmas Eve mass at Saint Peter's basilica and a professor's Christmas Eve discourse on the Higher Criticism in "Göttingen, -- most likely" (794). In the first episode of his journey, in the grimy chapel, the narrator is repulsed by the "hot smell and the human noises" and "the preaching man's immense stupidity" (140, 144); in the second, he describes the crowded basilica as a bee-hive, devoid of rational thought; and, in a parallel description, he comments that the German lecture hall is a vacuum, with "no air [left] to poison" (911). One feature of Menippean satire is its abundance of grotesque, naturalistic detail; another, its attack on exhaustive erudition - with more of the same. Browning viewed with skepticism the attempts by exponents of the Higher Criticism to rationalize Christianity, and his dry imitation of its logic makes the point: the lecturer explains:

> How the ineptitude of the time,
> And the penman's prejudice, expanding
> Fact into fable fit for the clime,
> Had, by slow and sure degrees, translated it
> Into this myth, this Individuum, --
> Which, when reason had strained and abated it
> Of foreign matter, left, for residuum,
> A man!   (871-78)

He goes on at some length.

Such passages have left most readers with the impression that Browning's criticisms of evangelicalism, Roman Catholicism, and the Higher Criticism are the central focus of the poem. (In this reading, the narrator simply chooses evangelicalism in the end because it is what he knows, and because his own "doctrine of love" can fill in the defects of the creed.) And indeed, such a critique often constitutes an element of the Menippea (Frye 311). But *Christmas-Eve and Easter-Day* is much more complex: an understanding of the poem as a dream vision reveals Browning to be just as concerned with the quirky and grotesque in art and human nature and more interested in the process of questioning than the answers. (In so doing, however, Browning is following the pattern Shaw identifies in many of the poems - that is "deepen[ing] the indeterminacy and sense of mystery by turning monologues like 'My Last Duchess' and 'The Bishop Orders His Tomb' into puzzle poems or riddles' [*The Lucid Veil*, 181].")

Other Menippean elements in "Christmas-Eve" besides these doctrinal critiques suggest that Browning's true focus is elsewhere. In a dream vision, whether straightforward or parodic, the narrator's position is unstable because he is poised between positions of authority and passivity, between the role of one who reveals truth to the reader (someone who sees from a great height) and the role of passive channel for a visionary force (someone at the mercy of a supernatural humanoid or avian guide). And from the very first line of "Christmas-Eve," Browning dismantles his narrator's authority, not so much to deflate one doctrine or another, as to suggest that no totalizing discourse can be valid. Peterson suggests the dialogic nature of this poem when she comments that, whatever Browning may have believed about the superiority of the speaker's choice, he constructed the poem so that "we cannot recognize so easily the validity of [his] proclamations [. . .]. We are forced inevitably to interpret for ourselves and to decide, if we can, what Browning means" (377-78). If Browning's narrator identifies with any doctrinal position at all, it is Eve's: impatient with listening, he complains, "'Twas too provoking! [. . .]':

> So saying like Eve when she plucked the apple,
> "I wanted a taste, and now there's enough of it,"
> I flung out of the little chapel. (182-86)

The quest in "Christmas-Eve" ends as it begins, irreverently and no nearer to revealed truth. But the narrator has become more willing to accept the contingent nature of his own faith and the validity of doubt.

The poem's discursive and narrative instability is underscored by fractured meter and frequent hudibrastic rhymes (noted by early critics, including G. H. Lewes), which resonate with nothing else so much as Browning's own "Pied Piper," another poem in which a compelling supernatural figure leads his victims into a maze of unanswerable

questions.[10] In his own self-defense, the narrator of "Christmas-Eve" ends
by saying,

> if any blames me,
> Thinking that merely to touch in brevity
>   The topics I dwell on, were unlawful, --
> Or worse, that I trench, with undue levity,
>   On the bounds of the holy and the awful,
> I praise the heart, and pity the head of him,
> And refer myself to THEE, instead of him. (1343-49)

How close these lines sound to the chuckling moral tag of Browning's
children's poem:

> So, Willie, let me and you be wipers
> Of scores out with all men -- especially pipers!
> And, whether they pipe us free fróm rats or fróm mice,
> If we've promised them aught, let us keep our promise!
>   (300-304, Browning's accents)

In his discussion of Menippean satire, Frye points out that in nearly every
literary period, important works "have been neglected only because the
categories to which they belong are unrecognized" (312). Because
"Christmas-Eve" has not been understood within the traditions of vision
literature or satire, it has been assumed that the "I" of the poem - comic,
cerebral, oscillating between positions of authority and passivity - is Robert
Browning. But if the speaker is similar to the poet, the two do not coincide.
It would be more accurate to say that in this poem Browning fictionalizes
himself in order to explore the relativity and contingency of truth, and even
his own perspective. The narrator of "Christmas-Eve" may reflect
Browning's feelings and ideas, but the experiences he describes are clearly
fictional and hyperbolic.

"Easter-Day" is superficially similar to its companion poem, but the
narrative structure, the plot, and the verse form are heavier and more
complex. "Easter-Day" also bears an even more complex relationship to the
religious literature of the past than "Christmas-Eve." A dialogue between
doubt and belief, the poem belongs to the genre of the *logistoricus*, an older

---

[10] Several early reviewers of *Christmas-Eve and Easter-Day* noticed the prosodic
similarities to Samuel Butler's *Hudibras* (Hudson 270-89, *pass.*). In an intricate argument
based on Browning's own linguistic and religious study, Hair reads Browning's reaching for
hudibrastic rhymes in this poem as a way of increasing the difficulty for himself; "the more
difficult the search for a rhyme, the closer its finding brings us to the Word in which all
things chime" (*Robert Browning's Language* 168).

form than the dream vision. In the *logistoricus*, the out-of-body experience is combined with a philosophical dialogue about "ultimate questions" (Bakhtin, *Problems of Dostoevsky's Poetics* 115). Obviously, this genre is genetically related both to the post-Platonic dialogue and the medieval dream vision, both of which took up contemporary controversies. I also believe that, in "Easter-Day," Browning is more responsive to the religious controversies of his day than in any other poem. Certain other features which Bakhtin finds in Menippean satire seem especially central to this poem and, indeed, to an understanding of Browning's poetic development. First is "the creation of *extraordinary situations* for the provoking and testing of a philosophical idea" (l94, Bakhtin's emphasis). This element in Browning's poem indicates his concern with the validity and relevance of current thought and its relationship to inherited ideas. Another characteristic of the Menippea which seems especially important in "Easter-Day" is "the organic combination of philosophical dialogue, lofty symbol-systems, the adventure-fantastic, and slum naturalism" (118). A related feature is the convention of "fantastic sailings over ideological seas" or "travels though all the philosophical schools" (116); an aspect of such travels is the narrator's unusual visual perspective on the world - as we have already seen in "Christmas-Eve," from the tail of Christ's garment as he whisks through space. Finally, and most important for this discussion, is narrative instability: the narrator "ceases to coincide with himself" (117). In doubling his own voice, Browning's narrator works backwards toward an *"inner logic* [. . .] a linking up of all [the] elements of the piece," as Bakhtin says of Dostoevsky (119, Bakhtin's emphasis).

Though shorter than *Sordello*, "Easter-Day" makes even greater demands on the reader. The poem makes sense only if read with close attention to the intricate layering of three voices, no easier a task than in *Sordello*. The first voice, which continually poses the problem, "How very hard it is to be/ A Christian!" (1-2) is relentless and vexed; the second voice is more self-satisfied in its pragmatic approach to reconciling the demands of faith with the demands of the world. (The third voice pipes up later in the poem.) The use of dialogue was not uncommon in Victorian literature. Browning had doubtless encountered it numerous times, probably in Shelley's "The Two Spirits -- An Allegory" (published posthumously in 1840), Tennyson's "The Two Voices" (1842), and Fuller's *Woman in the Nineteenth Century* (1845), certainly in two short poems by Barrett Browning, "Man and Nature" (1838) and "Calls on the Heart" (1850). In 1842, Barrett Browning had also written about the post-Platonic dialogue as one of the rhetorical forms of the Greek Christian poets. Unlike the synthesis toward which most such dialogues tend, however, Browning's poem resists resolution: the two opposing points of view which dominate "Easter-Day" are never synthesized, although, at last, the first voice seizes the upper hand by reporting the insights received from a third voice, that of a visionary guide. In this way, the poem is typical of Browning's most difficult works, in which, as Hair points out, opposing positions are "blurred" (*Robert Browning's Language* 258). Thus, this poem remains more truly dialogic than most of the dialogues Browning might have taken as models.

If its narrative structure is complex, "Easter-Day" has a simple plot. The first voice challenges the second with the idea that religious faith is strong in proportion to the believer's struggles with doubt. The second voice, in turn, asserts that a Christian's duty is to live a good life, a more likely prospect if doubt can be avoided. (This conflict suggests the Gordian knot within evangelicalism, a creed which valorized faith over works, while its practitioners scrutinized works as the only real evidence of faith and election.) The first voice then counters this argument by narrating a vision he experienced three years before on the same village green where "our friend" (375), the cantankerous narrator of "Christmas-Eve," began his fantastic yuletide journey. The terrifying Easter vision began, he says, when he laughed complacently at the thought of his own certain salvation, and immediately thereafter saw a vision of judgement:

> Suddenly all the midnight round
> One fire. The dome of heaven had stood
> As made up of a multitude
> Of handbreadth cloudlets, one vast rack
> Of ripples infinite and black,
> From sky to sky. Sudden there went,
> Like horror and astonishment,
> A fierce vindicative scribble of red. (504-11)

The narrator then experiences alternating episodes of distorted visionary space and everyday time, during which he is tested by a spirit guide quite unlike the indifferent figure of "Christmas-Eve." The guide in "Easter-Day," a fierce avatar of Christ, teaches the narrator as well as judging him. Like Mephistopheles, though with a different motive, the guide tempts the speaker to content himself, first with earthly beauty, then with the attractions of art, and finally with the power of intellect. When, like the narrator of "Christmas-Eve," the visionary of "Easter-Day" concludes that the only true good is love, the guide stops sneering, rises into the air "with pity and approval" (953), and disappears. As the visionary narrator (the first voice) tells his unregenerate other self (the second voice), since his purpose on earth is to learn perfect love, he must "be crossed and thwarted as a man" (1022): he must experience confusion, sorrow, doubt, and love, the only possible consolation. The vision is over, and in the last lines of the poem, the narrator informs us - and his existential, unregenerate self,

> Easter-Day Breaks! But
> Christ rises! Mercy every way
> Is infinite, -- and who can say? (1038-40)

It is not in the nature of the Menippea to claim absolute truth, and it is impossible fully to choose between or synthesize the two opposing philosophical positions in "Easter-Day." The lofty symbols, the fantastic light show of Judgement Day, the looming figure of the Judge, the first narrator's weird visual perspective - all these details intensify internal divisions. Unlike the narrator of "Christmas-Eve," who is given a choice about the conduct of his spiritual life, the fragmented narrator of the second poem seems to be left only with arguments and rationalizations. And that is Browning's final word. Little wonder that his contemporaries did not wish to understand it. The "Easter-Day" narrator's dilemmas are even more fully consonant with those of the archetypal Menippean hero than the problems faced by the speaker in "Christmas-Eve."

The tradition with which Browning's 1850 poems resonate proved uniquely hospitable to his personal concerns, while at the same time it allowed for the distancing and ambiguity which is characteristic of his best known poetry. Together, "Christmas-Eve" and "Easter-Day" may represent Browning's examination of his own faith, but, as he inserts himself into the work, Browning fictionalizes and dramatizes himself. Most readers have brought to the poems an expectation that the Victorian religious poet must serve out helpings of faith or doubt; anything equivocal is insignificant, incomprehensible, or irritating. Jerome McGann's advice about reading the very different religious poetry of Christina Rossetti is surely useful in this regard to twenty-first century readers:

> we have to willingly suspend not only our disbelief in [his] convictions and ideas but also our belief in those expectations and presuppositions about religious poetry which we have inherited from those two dominant ideological lines -- Broad Church and High Church and Anglo-Catholic. (267)

Contrary to the expectations about religious poetry which McGann addresses, the truth status of Browning's narrators and their discourse remains ambiguous, and it is no more legitimate to speculate on the specifics of Browning's thought in these poems than in the dramatic monologues, for, as the poet himself warns in "Easter-Day,"

> Ah, that's a question in the dark --
> And the sole thing that I remark
> Upon the difficulty, this;
> We do not see it where it is,
> At the beginning of the race:
> As we proceed, it shifts its place,
> And where we looked for crowns to fall,
> We find the tug's to come, -- that's all. (21-28)

We can conclude, however, that Browning understood both his religious conflicts and his poetic practice as part of a dialogue with literary history. This aspect of the poem is the real link between his work in 1850 and Barrett Browning's, not exhortations on her part that her husband write non-dramatic poetry, and certainly not religious exhortations which helped him simplify his doubts.

Although it seems clear that Barrett Browning did not directly influence the form or content of *Christmas-Eve and Easter-Day*, inevitably, there are echoes of her work in Browning's poetry, as his poetry resonates in hers. Those echoes began when the two poets started writing letters to each other and became stronger over the next fifteen years. In *Christmas-Eve and Easter-Day*, for instance, the fantastic guides, who lead the narrators through mazes of religious impulses, seem to have migrated into Browning's poems from Menippean satire by way of the *Sonnets* and the religious poetry Barrett Browning wrote before their marriage - poetry which is populated by hostile, sympathetic, and indifferent angels. As John Schad remarks, the angels in Browning's poetry are generally "marked by a difficulty or undecidability that is, finally, monstrous; like biblical angels, they are neither male nor female, God nor man, light nor dark" (87).[11] It is also probable that Browning's familiarity with the Menippea was enhanced by Barrett's scholarship. Her translations, as well as the wit and obscure learning which inform her essays on the Greek Christian poets, resonate with the speech of Browning's narrators in *Christmas-Eve and Easter-Day*.

In her mature work, Barrett Browning consciously separated her

---

[11] Schad suggests in his deconstructive reading of several poems (especially those published after Barrett Browning's death) that Browning's angels, as well as other "supernatural" elements, can be read as a kind of haunting by EBB. Although Schad's argument is not hostile to EBB's influence, I think the similarity between her angels and Browning's evidences simply a shared vocabulary, not a haunting.

classical scholarship from her poetry, which dealt, with rare exceptions, almost exclusively with contemporary topics. Browning chose rather to look back at classical materials from a contemporary perspective, creating a rich and daunting mixture which contributed, in part, to the charges of obscurity leveled against him. The Brownings were original in different ways, and they constantly sought new forms appropriate for their work, but for both, history was crucial in their conceptions of literary production, and together, in the 1850s, they began to bring their poetry closer to the less structured and more vigorous Victorian dominant, the novel.

Without Elizabeth Barrett Browning's encouragement, Browning probably would not have felt the impulse to seek in the antique genres of the Menippea a way to write about personal spiritual conflicts, which were also among the most painful spiritual conflicts of his time. *Christmas-Eve and Easter-Day* is certainly more opaque than the poems Browning wrote immediately before and immediately after it, but it is also a continuation in the quest he began with *Saul*, to explore his own beliefs and integrate his own work within a religious literary tradition.

It is equally true that, without Browning's support, Barrett Browning would have been less confident as she transgressed the boundary into the male domain of political commentary in her own two-part poem, *Casa Guidi Windows*. The dialogic space between the two poets, which enabled Browning to experiment in his religious poems, also enabled her to return to the discursive mode which she had given up in her youth, once again to express directly her opinions about the history which shaped itself beneath the Brownings' balcony in Florence.

Chapter 5

Giotto's Tower
1847-1851

In 1847, for the first time since they had left London, the Brownings found a permanent home in Florence, although they did not at first realize it. In July, they rented an apartment in Casa Guidi, a converted palace across from the Pitti. The rooms in which the Brownings spent most of their time were huge and airy, with high vaulted ceilings and two tiny balconies. For Elizabeth, especially, these lodgings represented an ideal marriage of space and containment, freedom and safety: it was a perfect environment for the profound changes which would occur in her poetry. There, she wrote *Casa Guidi Windows*, the first poem in which she made full use of the psychic and artistic freedom which followed her marriage. It is not a perfect poem, but writing it enabled the poet to re-integrate the political once more into her poetry, from which it had been absent, at least overtly, since she wrote the unpublished "Essay on Woman."[1] And far more than in that remarkable piece of juvenilia, Barrett Browning was able in *Casa Guidi Windows* to articulate the connections between politics, poetry, and emotion. Robert Browning was the enabler of *Casa Guidi Windows*, and he is the audience within it.

Casa Guidi Windows, a two-part conversation poem of almost two thousand lines, was conceived and written in this house. The first part narrates the poet's reactions to the hopeful events in Italy in 1847-48. Sandra Gilbert suggests that, not only Casa Guidi, but all of Italy proved to be the nurturing space in which Barrett Browning found the freedom and confidence she needed, and that her own "personal politics" are "embedded in this story" of the Risorgimento (199).[2] In his work on *Ideologies of Epic*,

---

[1] In *Victorian Poets and the Politics of Culture*, Harrison traces Barrett Browning's political thought from the early poetry into her mature poetry; he finds that the difference between the important poems of her youth and her later works is that the later works are more politically overt, not that they are politically more aware. He detects a "radically feminist side" even in early monologues such as "The Virgin Mary to the Child Jesus" (93).

[2] Gilbert's article "From *Patria* to *Matria*: Elizabeth Barrett Browning's *Risorgimento*," suggests that in *Casa Guidi Windows* Barrett Browning works out

Graham argues that, in recasting or, as Bakhtin would have it, "novelizing" the life of a nation, Barrett Browning "feminizes and privatises the once-public, turning narratives of action into narratives of the drama of selfhood" (4).[3] I would argue that in *Casa Guidi Windows*, she accomplishes the opposite as well: she shows the relevance of the self in the life of a nation.

The history they saw unfolding around them seemed to the Brownings fortuitous, for on the first anniversary of their marriage, September 12, the Florentines celebrated the first in what they hoped would be a series of liberal reforms. The next day, Elizabeth described the scene in an exuberant, long letter to her sister Henrietta, which reads, in part:

> The fact was, that our Italians had resolved to keep our day for us on a most magnificent scale; an intention which we, on our parts, not only graciously appropriated, but permitted in return to perfect the glory by keeping at the same time the establishment of the civic guard & prospect of the liberty of Italy through union -- Ah, you should have seen our day! Forty thousand strangers were in Florence. . I mean, inhabitants of the different Tuscan states, deputations and companies of various kinds; and for above three hours the infinite procession filed under our windows with all their various flags & symbols, into the Piazza Pitti where the Duke & his family stood in tears at the window to receive the thanks of his people. Never in the world was a more affecting sight. . nor a grander, if you took in its full significance [. . .] . There was not an inch of wall, not alive, if the eye might judge -- Clouds of flowers & laurel leaves came fluttering down on the advancing procession -- and the clapping of hands, & the frenetic shouting, and the music which came in gushes, & then seemed to go out with too much joy, and the exulting faces, and the kisses given for very exultation between man & man, and the mixing of elegantly dressed women in all that crowd & turbulence with the sort of smile which proved how little cause there was for fear [. . .] . We went to a window in our palazzo which had a full view, and I had a throne of cushions piled up on a chair [. . .]. And then Robert & I waved our handkerchiefs till my wrist ached, I will answer for mine. At night there was an illumination, & we walked just to the Arno to have a sight of it [. . .]. And even *then*, the people were *embracing* for joy. It was a state of phrenzy or rapture, extending even to the children of two years old, several of whom I heard lisping . . *"Vivas,"* with their fat little arms clasping their mothers ['] necks. So wasn't our day kept well for us? (*Correspondence* 14.300-01)

---

aspects of female creativity and a feminist politic through an analysis of the politics governing a subject state.

[3] Graham's argument about the novelized epic is centered on *Aurora Leigh*, but it applies as well to *Casa Guidi Windows*, which I believe was, in part, a rehearsal for the later work.

Almost at once, Barrett Browning began to write *Casa Guidi Windows*. The resonance of this letter in vivid descriptive passages of the poem attests to the heat and immediacy of the experience. The celebration described at the beginning is colorful. Representatives of all regions in Tuscany, citizens of foreign lands, soldiers, dogs, children, and priests:

> Three hours did end
> While all these passed; and ever in the crowd,
> Rude men, unconscious of the tears that kept
> Their beards moist, shouted [. . .].
> Friends kissed each other's cheeks, and foes long vowed
> More warmly did it -- two-months' babies leapt
> Right upward in their mothers' arms [. . .]
> And peasant maidens, smoothly 'tired and tressed,
> Forgot to finger on their throats the slack
> Great pearl-strings; while old blind men would not rest. . .
> (522-24, 527-29, 532-34).[4]

Barrett Browning finished Part I in short order and submitted it to *Blackwood's* as "Meditation in Tuscany." The poem was rejected. In 1851, when the revolutionary tide seemed to have turned, she composed Part II, a shorter and more pessimistic work. It did not reverse or deny the relative optimism of Part I; nevertheless, the second poem was written in a qualitatively different revolutionary spirit. The double poem was published in 1851, with the earlier section intact as a testament to the revolutionary process in both public events and private life. Indeed, the work is an attempt to speak of public events from a domestic perspective; the framing title, repeated throughout as a refrain, tells us as much. And the perspective is limited. In Part I, the windows are a vantage point above the ecstatic political demonstration; in Part II, a limiting frame from which the poet has been unable to see into the future:

> From Casa Guidi windows I looked forth,
> And saw ten thousand eyes of Florentines
> Flash back the triumph of the Lombard north, --
> Saw fifty banners, freighted with the signs
> And exultations of the awakened earth,
> Float on above the multitude in lines,
> Straight to the Pitti. So, the vision went. (II. 28-34)[5]

---

[4] The text is Julia Markus's 1977 edition of *Casa Guidi Windows*. Her introduction and notes are essential reading.

[5] Lombardy, legally part of the Austrian Empire and completely under Austrian

Casa Guidi Windows has the flaws of raw experiment, but it is original, daring, and honest. As a point in her artistic development, this poem about Italy is perhaps Barrett Browning's most important work. Except for "The Runaway Slave at Pilgrim's Point," *Casa Guidi Windows* is the only major poem she completed between the sonnets, the last of which was written on the eve of her departure from London, and the publication of *Aurora Leigh* ten years later in 1856. *Casa Guidi Windows* appeared before the public at exactly the mid point between those two works, and generically it is also "between" them, combining the lyrical voice of the sonnets with the narrative and discursive elements of the later work. Because it represents the political energies of the Risorgimento, especially as these energies took shape in art, *Casa Guidi Windows* in some ways recalls the artistic prerogatives Barrett Browning claimed as a young girl - and gave up as soon as she began to understand that she could not completely avoid the compromises required of women poets.

But in this poem, she embraced once more the credo which she had announced in the preface to *Essay on Mind*, written more than twenty years before: "Poetry is the enthusiasm of the understanding; and, as Milton finely expresses it, there is 'a high reason in her fancies.'" In poetry, she writes, we find "the inspiritings to political feeling, the 'monumentum aere perennius' of buried nations," and she reminds her readers that even Gibbon considered Homer "the law-giver, the theologian, the historian, and the philosopher of the ancients" (28). *Casa Guidi Windows* shows her new willingness to tackle publicly the difficult social and political issues of her time and to risk radical experiments in search of new poetic forms, more responsive to contemporary life.

Casa Guidi Windows also attests to the new freedoms the poet experienced in her marriage to an unconventionally open and emotional man, and to their collaboration in establishing "a domestic economy of art" (Mermin). The dialogic nature of the Brownings' relationship, "the imaginative sympathies that may have provided the most abiding source of the Brownings' compatibility" (Alaya 14), is perhaps more evident in *Casa Guidi Windows* than in any other work by either poet - and not only because Browning is openly identified within the poem as the poet's

---

control, was the site of an unsuccessful rebellion in 1848. In November, blaming Pio Nono's retrenchment, a number of the Lombard Volunteers conspired to kill Pellegrino Rossi, the Pope's chief minister, as he entered the newly formed Council of Deputies in Rome. But earlier, in 1847, victory in Lombardy had seemed virtually assured because of the commitment of the Piedmontese government to the cause of its neighbor.

immediate audience. The circumstances surrounding the writing and publication of *Casa Guidi Windows* parallel those of Browning's recent *Christmas-Eve and Easter-Day*, which was written during the period between Barrett's composition of "Meditation in Tuscany" and her completion of Part II. In both of these two-part poems, the poets acknowledge uncertainty. *Christmas-Eve and Easter-Day* and *Casa Guidi Windows* are both anomalous within the poets' *oeuvres* - and both poems have been dismissed by critics as inept. Doubtless, Browning's example and his involvement in Barrett Browning's poetry at this point gave her a greater will to risk experimentation and to publish the results separately.

Barrett Browning's work also significantly echoes *Sordello*, Browning's massive poem on the relation of art and politics in Renaissance Italy. It had worried her since before she knew the poet himself. In letters written during April and May of 1845, she recommended *Sordello* to Thomas Westwood as a work of "true oracles," but oracles for which "Study is peculiarly necessary" (10.231, 153). Having mediated thus between poem and reader, half a year later, she pleaded the case of *Sordello* with Browning himself:

> I have been thinking much of your 'Sordello' since you spoke of it -- & even, I had thought much of it before you spoke of it yesterday, -- feeling that it might be thrown out into the light by your hand & greatly justify the additional effort. It is like a noble picture with its face to the wall just now -- or at least, in the shadow [. . .]. And such a work as it might become if you chose. . if you put your will to it.!! (*Correspondence* 11.67)

For Barrett, as for most of Browning's readers, *Sordello* was "misty" (*Correspondence* 12.4), and she continued to wish it more finely finished. Barrett Browning's poem is replete with overt and covert allusions to *Sordello*: in the self-conscious framing devices, the interrogation of the role of the poet in public life, the broader theme of culture as a political force, the system of imagery she found in Browning's poem. *Casa Guidi Windows* is mainly concerned, not with the details of Renaissance history which remained for Browning a lifelong fascination, but with current events, and it is not as dense or intricate as Browning's poem. Nevertheless, both poems explore the past in order to shed light on the present, and both interrogate so closely the poet's own internal processes that the external structure seems to break down. As it twists and turns through an argument about the place of the woman poet in a man's world of military force and Italian political intrigue, *Casa Guidi Windows* recalls Browning's struggles in *Sordello* to negotiate for the thinker and the poet a position of integrity amid the political and cultural chaos of late Renaissance Italy - and, by extension, in his own time. Both poems also contest, in different ways, the epic genres in which national struggles had been embodied in the past. *Casa Guidi Windows* is Barrett Browning's first attempt to write a radically dialogic work; it reveals as much about the development of her poetic consciousness as *Sordello* reveals about Browning's.

In terms of Bakhtin's analysis, *Sordello* can be read as a departure from epic into the territory of the novel, for its thematic center is "the hero's inadequacy to his fate or his situation," and his "wholeness [. . .] disintegrates" ("Epic and Novel" 37). In *Casa Guidi Windows*, on the other hand, there is no hero, only the hope that a hero will arise:

> This country-saving is a glorious thing,
> And if a common man achieved it? well.
> > Say, a rich man did? excellent. A king?
> That grows sublime. A priest? improbable. (I. 860-864)

The yearning for a hero was not simply Robert Browning's private hope, but a preoccupation of most who were interested in the fate of Italy throughout most of the nineteenth century. In her long essay on Florentine history and art, Mary McCarthy suggests that the restrained Florentine architecture, the city's wealth of public statuary, and even its street plan embody the desire for,

> an ideal republic made of *pietra dura*, *pietra forte*, rough bosses, and geometric marbles. This republic never existed as a political fact but only as a longing, a poignant nostalgia for good government that broke out in poems and histories, architecture, painting, and sculpture. That view of a pink towered city in the background of early Florentine fresco (it soon became a white Renaissance city with classic architecture and sculpture) is the same as Dante's vision and Machiavelli's, the vision of an ideal city washed in the pure light of reason, even though Dante and Machiavelli [. . .] looked to a Redeemer from above (an emperor or a prince) to come as a Messiah to save the actual city, just as Savonarola looked to Jesus and to a constitution [. . .] and the poor people of Florence looked to the angels. (*The Stones of Florence* 191-92)

By the 1860s, Italy's future was the most interesting subject in the English press and at English dinner parties. But because they witnessed so many events of the Risorgimento at close range - from the windows of Casa Guidi - and because Italy had replaced the home which they had lost in England through loving each other, the Brownings' political and intellectual energies were absorbed by the Risorgimento from the beginning of their lives together, and their opinions about these events were formed by the character of the city around them.

During her lifetime, Barrett Browning herself became an Italian national hero. The Italian nationalist poet Tommaseo spoke for public opinion in the memorial plaque affixed to Casa Guidi: "in the heart of a woman reconciled the learning of the scholar and the spirit of the poet," and in her verse, he continued, was forged "a golden ring between Italy and England" (qtd. Alaya 21). However, the poem was no better received at home than Browning's *Christmas-Eve and Easter-Day*, so, for once, Barrett Browning could understand her husband's frustrations with his readers first-hand. The reception of the poem with Anglophone readers did not improve until Barrett Browning's rehabilitation by feminist critics: from his Modernist vantage point almost fifty years later, Henry James wrote in his group biography of Victorian Anglo-American expatriates in Italy that, during this period in Italian history, "public events had hurried over the stage like the contending armies of Elizabethan plays" (*William Wetmore Story and His Friends* 53) - and he went on to pronounce a damning (and lingering) judgment of *Casa Guidi Windows* as a work clouded by histrionic passion aroused in Barrett Browning by these events.[6] In order to read this poem lucidly, however, and to understand both its flaws and its strengths, it is important to remember, as George Steiner has pointed out, that, our interpretations are shaped by the poetic values of our own time. For reading nineteenth-century literature, in particular, he observes, "We have for a time disqualified ourselves from reading comprehensively (a word that has in it the root for 'understanding')" (*After Babel* 15). And with any topical literature, "reading comprehensively" means not only attempting to set aside the poetic values of our own time, but reading within the appropriate historical context.

An accurate measurement of Barrett Browning's achievement depends in part upon a reading of the poem within its geographical and historical contexts, and upon a proper understanding of its genre.

---

[6] See also the negative assessment of the poem by Irvine and Honan. In the Preface to her edition of *Casa Guidi Windows* and her double biography of the Brownings, Markus has discussed the negative critical reception of the poem at length. In her view, one problem has been a misreading of the Preface, which can be taken to undermine the authority asserted in the text itself. Vivienne Rundle has addressed the problem of Barrett Browning's prefatory writings, finding that the poet pitched her "Advertisement" to *Casa Guidi Windows* deliberately to an audience who would value her sincerity; Rundle finds the tone "mock-defensive" (260-61). Also valuable in understanding the critical reception of *Casa Guidi Windows* is Alaya's "The Ring, the Rescue, and the Risorgimento: Reunifying the Brownings' Italy."

For centuries, Italy had been at the mercy of foreign powers; a viable plurality of conflicting governments during the Renaissance later became a staging ground for European intervention. Florence, for example, lost its democratic character entirely after the Siege of 1530, when the first archduke, a Spanish puppet, took over the city. This tyrant, Cosimo de Medici, was the first in a series of dictators who owed his primary allegiance to a foreign power. (Grand Duke Leopold, who ruled Florence during the Brownings' early years in the city, was the last.) After Spain, France and Austria interfered directly in Italy's internal affairs, and even Great Britain from time to time considered Italy to be within its sphere of influence. Since the end of the Napoleonic era, which had at least given all Italians a fleeting experience of unified and consistent government, and an orderly system of justice based on the Napoleonic Code, the middle classes and the intelligentsia had been absorbed by the prospect of reunification without the meddling of foreign governments. But popular uprisings in 1820 and 1821 had been quickly suppressed by Austria, which had extended direct or informal control over the entire peninsula. The secret, loosely organized revolutionary cells of the Carboneria emerged at this time, followed by the founding of Young Italy ten years later by the thoughtful and charismatic Mazzini. Neither Young Italy nor the Carboneria were successful in terms of armed struggle, but their existence shaped political thought in Italy for decades. During the 1830s the New Guelf movement arose, established upon the idea that the Pope could become the ideal ruler and spokesman for a federation of Italian states. And Florence became a center of revolutionary activity.

In 1846, the election of the new pope, Pio Nono, added momentum to the idea that Italy might be reunified through the influence of the Vatican. The Pope's unique position as a spiritual leader with considerable temporal power, this particular pope's liberal reputation, and his initial reforms (extended freedom of speech and freedom of the press, amnesty for political prisoners and exiles, the announcement that Rome would be ruled by an elected secular Council of Deputies) at first raised hopes for the Risorgimento. These hopes were strengthened for the Brownings by the response of Leopold, who shortly after the accession of Pio Nono granted the city the right to form a Civic Guard. But these halting steps toward democracy provoked another firestorm of suppression by the Austrians, who retaliated by occupying Ferrara. Events escalated in 1848, with revolution spreading to Palermo and Lombardy, constitutional charters established in Sardinia and Tuscany, Mazzini's unsuccessful invasion of Rome, the retrenchment of the Pope, the assassination of his chief minister, the intervention by Napoleon III to protect the Pope, the flight of the

Florentine archduke (and with it, the end of reform in Tuscany), and further repressive measures by the Austrians. By the end of 1848, the House of Savoy in Piedmont was the only pro-democracy government still standing, although revolutionary feeling throughout the peninsula was stronger than ever. In 1849, King Victor Emmanuel of Piedmont, with the indispensable aid of his crafty minister Cavour, began a series of domestic, diplomatic, and military moves which eventually resulted in liberal reforms at home, the engagement of Napoleon III on the side of pro-unification and democracy forces, and the expulsion of Austria from most of northern Italy by the end of 1860.

These changes represented a concerted effort by many different individuals, of many different political persuasions, and in the early 1850s, their ramifications were still not clear. Progress was stalled until the end of the decade, when Florence was temporarily made the capital, and it was not until 1866 that Venice became officially integrated into Italy. The period from 1847 to 1851, when Barrett Browning was composing *Casa Guidi Windows*, was a time of joy, confusion, betrayal, and success. Those who chose to speak publicly about the events of the Risorgimento necessarily took a "moral risk" because no tactic in the struggle was without compromise and duplicity (Alaya 9). The Pope and Napoleon III were inconsistent. The judgment of the charismatic Mazzinni was sometimes faulty, and that of Garibaldi perhaps moreso. Cavour was a duplicitous practitioner of *Realpolitik*.

Barrett Browning's response to this stage of the Risorgimento was conflicted and somewhat chaotic. Her perceptions were quick and penetrating, but they did not - and could not - coalesce into the unified account that has been expected of poetry since long before the Modernist theorists articulated that expectation as an unbreakable rule. Her rapid composition of Part I and her attempt to publish it in *Blackwoods* as soon as possible suggest that Barrett Browning thought of the work as a kind of reportage in poetry, the *métier* which best suited her. *Casa Guidi Windows* in fact does resemble in detail and narrative trajectory the dispatches of her American friend Margaret Fuller from Italy to the *New York Tribune* between 1847 and 1850. In fact, although Fuller was based primarily in Rome, some of her earliest articles for the *Tribune* describe the formation of a Civil Guard in Florence and Austrian rule in Tuscany and suggest the needs and reasons for revolution.

If the tendency to assess *Casa Guidi Windows* out of its political context has led to neglect and misreading, so has a misunderstanding of its genre. *Casa Guidi Windows* is a conversation poem, addressed to Browning in the same way Coleridge had addressed more than one conversation poem to his poetic collaborator and significant other, Wordsworth.[7] This genre, which is both lyrical and discursive, is ideally suited to informal discussion of serious matters. Although it is much longer than the conversation poems of Coleridge, in "Meditation in Tuscany," Barrett Browning follows his general practice. The Romantic conversation poem is structured as a weave of moments, past, present, and future, clearly grounded in a specific time and location. Typically, it consists of four sections, all approximately the same length, and mimics sonata form: the first is an exposition of one or two themes, the second a development or expansion of these themes, the third a recapitulation with modifications, and the fourth a coda, in which new material or new impressions may be added to the thematic ideas already developed in the work. In Romantic conversation poems, these divisions are not necessarily formally marked, as they are in musical works, but are nevertheless signaled as clear thematic shifts. A comparison of *Casa Guidi Windows* with one of Coleridge's conversation poems is instructive. In the first section of "France: An Ode," one of the most purely political meditations produced by a Romantic poet, the speaker indicates his point of view, from a cliff, in an open space, surrounded by the limited but increasing dawn light. In the second section, he recalls his earlier naive enthusiasm for the French Revolution; third, he considers his disillusion when the principles of the Revolution give way to the imperialist impulse; finally his hope revives, not through political analysis, but through the realization that liberty is less a material force than a spirit -

> The guide of homeless winds, and playmate of the waves!
> And there I felt thee! -- on that sea-cliff's verge,
>   Whose pines, scarce travelled by the breeze above,
> Had made one murmur with the distant surge! (98-101X)

The thematic development of Barrett Browning's "Meditation on Tuscany" parallels that of Coleridge's poem. The first section, through line 441, situates the poet herself in the present, seated at the window, and then in relation to the cultural and political history of Italy. In "France," the speaker's perspective is limited at first by the limited light, in Barrett Browning's poem, by the frame of the window. Both poems allow for the

---

[7] Although Wordsworth's *The Prelude* is, of course, also addressed to Coleridge, it remained unpublished until 1850. Therefore, it is unlikely that Barrett Browning knew about this (and other) parallels between Wordsworth's great poem and her own meditation on Italy when she was writing Part I. (However, she had undoubtedly read the work by the time she was composing *Aurora Leigh*, a poem much like Wordsworth's in its purpose, if not at the surface.)

broadening of perspective - Coleridge's, as the dawn breaks, Barrett Browning's, as the speaker witnesses more and more events from her window, and as she realizes that the uniqueness of her view actually allows for a feminine, contemporary understanding of the events in Italy - indeed, for her, this perspective is the missing piece of contemporary political discourse. The second section of "Meditation on Tuscany" opens out into a graphic description of what the poet sees from the window. The poetic power of this scene is in the rush of details about the masses of participants demonstrating for democratic reforms - the color, noise, motion, emotion of celebrants filling the streets of Florence. In the third part of Part I, Barrett Browning develops the most serious theme in the poem, the need for a leader who can direct these powerful energies into rebuilding Italy from its cultural foundations and usher the country into a strong future. Unlike Coleridge's coda, in which the speaker creates closure by changing the previous argument about freedom from political to philosophical terms, Barrett Browning's final section ends with uncertainty: it revisits the major theme of the first section - the interdependence between art and the body politic - and expresses strongly-worded, but more equivocal hopes for the future of both.

Part II, written about three years later, is less like a conversation poem in structure, but more like one in length - it is only about two-thirds as long as Part I. The second poem is less hopeful, less certain, and more fragmented than "Meditation in Tuscany." In fact, when Barrett Browning claims in her advertisement to present "no continuous narrative nor exposition of political philosophy," she is describing Part II, which she has just completed, rather than Part I (xli). She begins Part II just as she begins Part I, with a description of her perspective and an acknowledgment of its limitations, which are even more evident to her than before because, in light of the most recent events, it seems that her hopes for Italy's future have been too sanguine. In the next short section, Barrett Browning explains the failure of the 1847 initiatives and considers possible reasons these initiatives have failed. In the fourth section of the poem, the poet considers the indifference of other national states to the fate of Italy, which is, in many ways, ironically the source of their own cultural power. In the last hundred lines, the cultural riches of Italy, if not its people or its political leaders, do finally give the poet some hope that in years to come, the country will recover the meaning of its history and be reunified and reborn. But this hope is tentative: unlike Coleridge, who creates the impression of synthesis between hopes and fears by means of a rhetorical sleight of hand, Barrett Browning confesses the fragility that she perceives in Italy's future. In the end, her hopes for Italy are presented as a "dream of *matria* -- motherland and mother *langue* [. . . a] dream of identity, of making whole that which is severed and divided [. . .] " (Benstock 26).

If Elizabeth Barrett Browning had been able to write *Casa Guidi Windows* from a position of disinterested concern, and if her own identity as a poet had not been in the crucible of the Risorgimento, the poem would still have been fragmentary and inconclusive because of the writer's temporal and spatial proximity to events which confused even the most objective observers. But more than most of her contemporaries, Barrett Browning found that her passions were aroused by Italy's struggle against internal and external political forces, and that her private struggles were reflected in the public events which took place all around her.

Barrett Browning's early poetry, letters, and autobiographical records reveal a longstanding interest in ancient and contemporary Italy. In childhood, she was eager to learn Latin with her younger brother and his tutor, and she began to study Italian during her teens. From this study came her poem in Italian, the translations from Dante and Petrarch which taught her how to write her own sonnets at the margins of poetic tradition, and translations from contemporary Italian poetry. In Italy, as she knew, artists were considered necessary to the health of the culture and the state. One of the most powerful forces of the early Risorgimento was its literature, which included overtly political work - for example, Silvio Pellico's account of his experiences in Austrian prisons, *Le mie prigioni* (1832), which heightened anti-Austrian feeling, or Vincenzo Gioberti's huge, extremely nationalistic political treatise (1843), the inspiration for the New Guelfs - in addition to novels and poetry, particularly Alessandro Manzoni's *I Promessi sposi* (1827), as important for this movement as *Uncle Tom's Cabin* would be a few later for the abolitionist movement in the United States. As influential as Manzoni's work were the hortatory poems of Vittorio Alfieri, Vincenzo de Filicaja, and Giacomo Leopardi.

The role of the poet in England was perceived differently. The English Romantic poets who were Barrett Browning's poetic models were beset by the problem of negotiating between private experience and public concerns. Poets were expected to lead by teaching. Indeed, as Carlyle had pointed out with a jaundiced eye in "Characteristics," literature had come to be seen by many critics and ordinary readers as a substitution for the spiritual instruction once provided through organized religion. But already, a century or more before the rise of Modernism, the realm of poetry was understood as the realm of private experience, not public life. Since political and cultural problems in Italy were more acute than in England, however, the place of the artist in public life was less ambiguous. (Indeed, in the next century, Antonio Gramsci's theory of the power of cultural *egemonia* would be based on his experience of Italian literature as a political force.) This difference between the place of the poet in English culture and the position of the poet in Italian life would become one of the motivations for Barrett Browning's work. Barrett Browning had already resolved the conflict between public and private speech by giving up the discursive verse of her early years for ballads, translations, classical imitations, and lyrics. Her early penchant for direct social and cultural criticism had been subsumed in the indirect commentaries allowed by "women's" genres. Beyond poetry and fiction, women "were not supposed to speak in public, were not supposed to speak forth at all, and those that did, like Dickens's Mrs. Jellyby, were savagely *spoken about*, since if a woman spoke forth and entered the public sphere, she obviously had abandoned" the duties required by her family (Landow 39). But in Italy she was faced with a clearer choice: to comment on public affairs as a poet, or to be silent as a woman.

Unwilling and unable to choose, Barrett Browning found herself in the position of having to integrate both roles into one. In a sense the theoretical project of *Casa Guidi Windows* was imposed from outside: of necessity, the identity of the woman poet became the tenor and the vehicle of her commentary on public affairs.[8] And it is in this poem, more than any other, that we see the effect of Barrett Browning's yearning for literary "grandmothers": Wollstonecraft had written, against the conventions of her time, as a woman and a sage; Landon and Hemens had written overtly patriotic lyrics and narratives about political and military events. Barrett Browning was writing, for the first time in English literary history, in discursive poetry, a negative critique of her own country and an opinionated commentary on the political events in another. She had no precedents, and her anglophone readers were uncomprehending.

Barrett Browning's multiple intentions within the poem both enrich and undermine each other. She admits that *Casa Guidi Windows* is problematic when she writes in the "Advertisement" of the discrepancy between the two parts, the result of the unpredictable winds of history:

> If the discrepancy is painful to the reader, let him understand that to the writer it has been more so. But such discrepancies we are called upon to accept at

---

[8] In "Combating an Alien Tyranny: Elizabeth Barrett Browning's Evolution as a Feminist Poet," Byrd examines *Casa Guidi Windows* against the background of other political poetry by women. During the 1830s, Byrd argues, EBB began to participate in a female poetic tradition "in which authors take as their central subject matter and draw their metaphors from the lives of women" (31). *Casa Guidi Windows* is an extension of this trend.

every hour by the conditions of our nature, implying the interval between aspiration and performance, between faith and disillusion, between hope and fact. (xli)

The fragmentary nature of this poem is due to the rapid course of history between 1847 and 1851, the general disillusionment with the leaders of the Risorgimento, and the conflicting feelings about revolution experienced by most of the Victorian writers who contemplated it. Some of the intimacy and the unity of the conversation poem is lost because of the length, which is inordinate by Coleridge's standards, because Barrett Browning also intended it as reportage, by means of which her English readers might come to understand the Risorgimento. Thematically, too, Barrett Browning has at least a double agenda: as she investigates the connection between Italy's cultural heritage and its present political misfortunes, she finds that she must justify her own contribution to the public conversation, which has been traditionally male in England and even more so in Italy.

The fissures in the poem are revealed more clearly in the details of Barrett Browning's language than in the summary of her argument. In particular, she identifies and critiques a central trope in recent hortatory literature about Italy - the wounded or fallen woman. Ironically, in her discussion of the need for a leader and her worries about the future of the Risorgimento, Barrett Browning's own words echo the stereotypical language which she finds so damaging in other representations of Italy. The first four hundred lines of Part I and the last hundred lines of Part II interrogate the image of Italy as a beautiful, ruined woman - the image which has dominated the nation's patriotic poetry and political rhetoric. The fire in these lines seems to feed off the satirical anger of Browning's speaker in Book IV of *Sordello*, when he describes the siege of Ferrara, the

> lady-city, for whose sole embrace
> Her pair of suitors struggled, felt their arms
> A brawny mischief to the fragile charms
> They tugged for -- one discovering that to twist
> Her tresses twice or thrice about his wrist
> Secured a point of vantage -- one, how best
> He'd parry that by planting in her breast
> His elbow spike -- each party too intent
> For noticing, howe'er the battle went,
> The conqueror would but have a corpse to kiss. (IV. 2-11)

Like *Sordello*, *Casa Guidi Windows* is a study of inherited culture, specifically poetry, in its relationship with the present and the future. There is nothing sentimental in Browning's violent lines. But from Auguste Barbier, who called his country "Juliet of nations," to Filicaja - whose sonnet "Italia, Italia, o tu, cui feo la sorte" Lord Byron freely translated in *Childe Harold's Pilgrimage*[9] - Barrett Browning finds Italy's patriotic poets, sadly sentimental and ineffectual. In a critique of the conventional gendered images of Italy, she regrets these

> Bewailers for their Italy enchained,
> And how they called her childless among mothers,
>> Widow of empires, ay, and scarce refrained
> Cursing her beauty to her face, as brothers
>> Might a shamed sister's, -- 'Had she been less fair
> She were less wretched' (I. 21-26)[10]

Ironically, Barrett Browning suggests, Italy's patriotic literature has had a negative effect: the most dedicated poets and literati are tongue-tied by dying metaphors, and have worked against liberation again and again by casting their motherland in the role of victim instead of emphasizing her strengths. They are

> sonneteering in their sleep,
> And archaists mumbling dry bones up the land,
> And sketchers lauding ruined towns a-heap. (I.148-150)

After critiquing the work of these poets, she concludes, "I kiss their footsteps, yet their words gainsay" (51). An inhabitant of the private sphere, she brings into the public discourse a different kind of music, singing "With birds, with babes, with men who will not fear/ The baptism of the holy morning dew" (I. 156-58).

---

[9] Byron's lines about Italy are, in part, as follows:
> Italia! oh, Italia! thou who has
> The fatal gift of Beauty, which became
> A funeral dower of present woes and past --
> On thy sweet brow is sorrow ploughed by shame,
> And annals graved in characters of flame.
> Oh, God! that thou wert in thy nakedness
> Less lovely or more powerful, and couldst claim
> Thy right, and awe the robbers back, who press
> To shed thy blood, and drink the tears of thy distress (IV. 370-78)

[10] The "others" who were "led on" by Filicaja also included Vittorio Alfieri, Alessandro Manzoni, Vincenzo Monti, Giuseppi Parini, Ugo Foscolo, Giuseppe Giusti, Alphonse de Lamartine, and Percy Shelley (Markus *CGW*, 73).

The poet derives a different kind of inspiration from Renaissance art, created before the Siege of 1530 reduced Florence to political rubble. Dante and Michelangelo, who worked in genres unrelated to patriotic poetry, provide more useful models for her than the artists who came after them, partly because they themselves were not imitators: they did not simply recycle the old, but instead "made it new." (Indeed, Dante's culturally revolutionary work in the vernacular established Tuscan as the literary language of Italy.) Barrett Browning argues that since Michelangelo designed and built military fortifications in response to civic need, and since Dante's political outspokenness earned him years of pain and exile, their art was integrated into, and the product of, political action. Their work was therefore a less literal and more honest response to political realities. Unlike later patriotic poets, these two looked to the future. As Italy's illustrious dead, the poet tells us, they implore "Her future to be strong and not afraid" (215). During its height, she notes, Florence did look forward: "Her very statues send their looks before (216).[11] Barrett Browning's reading of the past recalls the proclamation the city fathers issued in 1296, when ordering plans for the Duomo:

> The Florentine Republic, soaring ever above the conception of the most competent judges, desires that an edifice shall be constructed so magnificent in its height and beauty that it shall surpass anything of its kind produced in the times of their greatest power by the Greeks and the Romans. (qtd. McCarthy 128)

Barrett Browning observes a paradox at work: Italy's cultural legacy is best served, not by repetition or even preservation, but by an art which is ever new, inspired by and respectful of the art of the past, but always looking beyond it.

The loveliest and most powerful passage in the poem is Barrett Browning's description of Giotto's campanile, another legacy from the past which remains as important to the present city of Florence as the statues of Michelangelo or the poetry of Dante. In raising questions which it cannot answer, Barrett Browning's poem indeed mimics the tower:

---

[11] This passage not surprisingly prefigures the mind frame of new historicism as described by McGann: "The critic's focus upon history as constituted in what we call 'the past' only achieves its critical fulfillment when that study of the past reveals its significance in and for the present and the future" (*Historical Studies and Literary Criticism* 18).

How beautiful! the mountains from without
    In silence listen for the word said next.
What word will men say, -- here where Giotto planted
    His campanile, like an unperplexed
Fine question Heaven-ward, touching the things granted
    A noble people who, being greatly vexed
In act, in aspiration keep undaunted? (I. 66-72)

The fourteenth-century landmark is an ambiguous architectural statement. When Giotto died before the completion of the tower, other architects decided that it would be better to leave off the "finishing touch [. . .] a four-sided pyramid fifty armslengths high" (Vasari 32). Thus, the tower was finished by leaving it unfinished, and for Barrett Browning, it is perfect in its imperfection. The beautiful phallic image of Giotto's tower, which resonates with the imagery of Barrett Browning's Sonnet XXXVII (the "sculptured porpoise, gills a-snort/ And vibrant tail, [set] within the temple-gate"), promises a revolutionary reinterpretation of the stereotypically gendered imagery which the poet finds so disturbing - so that male beauty enters the language in which Italy is described (or re-enters, that is, after an absence of three hundred years[12]), and so that masculine imagery may come to include the "space generating and forming the human species" typically associated with the female (Kristeva, "Women's Time" 190). The tower connects the earth and the heavens, the people and the divine will, the past and the present. Although the artifact which Barrett Browning celebrates in this passage is profoundly masculine, these lines may indeed be read as a Victorian anticipation of what Alice Jardine has called "gynesis," a feminine scene of writing characterized by uncertainty, fluidity, consciousness of writing from the body, and acceptance or even celebration of aporia.

After the first four hundred lines, about Italy's past art and present rhetoric, the two principal sections are the crowd scene which echoes Barrett Browning's letter to Henrietta and the meditation on an ideal leader who can channel and educate the passions of *il popolo*. Barrett Browning's description of the crowd seems to be fed, not only by her own immediate positive impressions, but also by a parallel description of all the "Warped souls and bodies" seen by the narrator of *Sordello* from his seat on the palace step in Venice (III.781). However joyous they may be, the Florentines are in a sense "warped," incomplete without a leader to direct and control their impulses. In the first part of *Casa Guidi Windows*, Barrett

---

[12] As I have already observed in Chapter 4, Florentine art of the Renaissance was replete with images of male beauty.

Browning suggests that the Italian people are politically childish and their leaders corrupt - a theme which will become more insistent in Part II. And, despite her claims in the Advertisement that she is responding enthusiastically to the mood of 1847-48, throughout both parts of the poem, she reacts to the spectacle with measured enthusiasm, to the rhetoric of the moment with a modicum of doubt, and to public joy with caution. If Barrett Browning's analysis of recent Italian literature is penetrating and original, her language describing the Italian people reveals a disconcerting dependence on stereotypes: the common people, with their love of color and their naive belief in the hero of the moment - "oil-eaters, with large, live, mobile mouths,/ Agape for maccaroni" - must have a strong leader because they are incapable of forethought and productive action (I. 200-01). (If the leader of Italy's future is to be Mazzinni, she adds in Part II, it is well that he has already, in a speech of 1846, "Set down [the] people's faults," "the want/ Of soul-conviction [. . .] and valour scant/ Because of scanty faith" [II. 527, 528-30].) A true leader is the missing character in the parade under her window - and across the whole Italian political landscape: "But the teacher, where?" (I. 795) cries the poet. She suggests models from the past - Luther, Tell, Masaniello, Brutus, Rienzi - but present leaders seem remarkably unheroic.[13] Other political leaders - Mazzini and Cavour - have not yet consolidated enough power to effect significant chance, and the true heroes of recent years have not survived. The popular Count Calfonieri has been silenced by a fifteen-year imprisonment by the Austrians for his part in the uprising of 1820, and his heroic wife, who interceded for him, died before his release in 1835. The brothers Bandieri, who deserted from the Austrian navy to lead a revolt in Cosenza, were captured and executed by the Austrians in 1844. And even during the relative optimism of 1847, Barrett Browning retained a healthy skepticism of the new Pope and the Austrian Archduke.

The persistent meditation on leadership continues in Part II. In contrast to the energy of Part I, Part II describes stasis and dwells on the failure of Italy's cultural workers to embrace a new, more vital image of Italy.

At first, Barrett Browning harks back to the point made in the framing title - the limitations of the poet and her perspective, and by extension the

---

[13] William Tell was a leader in the revolt of the Swiss against the Hapsburgs in 1291, the protagonist of a play by Schiller and an opera by Rossinni. Masaniello (Tommaso Aniello) led a heroic but unsuccessful revolt against the Spaniards in Naples in 1647. Because he attempted in the fourteenth century to reunify the Italian penisula, Rienzi (Cola di Rienzo) is sometimes regarded as a forerunner of the Risorgimento.

limitations of any single voice that comments on Italy's political struggles. The perspective of the people is incomplete, as are those of the Church, the political leaders, and the rest of Europe, for which Italy's sorrows seem momentarily irrelevant. The roll call of dead heroes and the list of wrongs begun in Part I continues: Anita Garibaldi and Charles Albert of Novara are dead, the rest of Europe has failed to come to Italy's aid, the Grand Duke of Tuscany has, with seemingly unparalleled cowardice, aided Austria once again to consolidate its power in Italy, and the popular Tuscan leader (and writer) Francesco Guerrazzi has aligned his interests with the *status quo*. Worse, the hopes of the Neo-Guelfs for the Pope's leadership in the cause are dashed: his liberal gestures have proven to be empty. Pio Nono's ultimate loyalty is apparently to his own temporal power, which he has shored up, in the long tradition of Italian tyrants, by calling on foreign powers.

Barrett Browning anticipated opprobrium because of the differences in tone between the two parts, and, indeed, this has been one basis for negative criticism. But a more serious problem is a tension between argument and controlling metaphor which persists throughout the poem, becoming more pronounced in Part II. Barrett Browning's position as a *woman* political poet prompted her to critique the current political rhetoric in which Italy is persistently described as a woman, therefore weak, therefore a victim. Barrett Browning's solution to this rhetorical failure was to re-engender the body politic as male, strong, and self-determining and to retain the female imagery in an altered form, as the nurturing mother which she felt Italy to be. Still, by the end of *Casa Guidi Windows*, the image of Italy itself as a damaged woman is persistent, and the radical potential of Giotto's tower has collapsed into more conventional male stereotyping

Part I ends with an argument for a new, powerful image of Italy as a mother who has passed on to her children a rich cultural heritage; this heritage is a potential source of power, but it can only be preserved and continued if proper attention is paid to it and, simultaneously, to the political realities of the Risorgimento. A passage near the end of Part II powerfully suggests psychological and political stasis; the nurturing mother at the end of Part I becomes in Part II Niobe, weeping for her dead children, for the dead future of Italy:

> Still, graves, when Italy is talked upon.
> Still, still, the patriot's tomb, the stranger's hate.
> Still, Niobe! Still fainting in the sun,
> By whose most dazzling arrows violate
> Her beauteous offspring perished! Has she won

Nothing but garlands for the graves, from Fate?
   Nothing but death-songs? (II. 724-30)

Italy must have seemed a Niobe: her most admirable sons and daughters were giving their lives for the cause, while false leaders were thriving. Poetically moving though this description is, however, with the allusion to Niobe, Barrett Browning has come full circle and without irony back to the image of Italy as victimized woman, which she decries in Part I. Niobe, after all, was a figure of hubris: she challenged the gods because her children were so many and so beautiful. Although Barrett Browning is clearly critiquing the image of Italy as Niobe, the figure is so compelling - and apparently, even to her, so apt - that her language makes the Niobe figure even more compelling, rather than deconstructing it.

   Despite her commitment to the present and the future, to the rights of the oppressed and the dignity of women, Barrett Browning conceptualizes nations - both peoples and geographical entities - as feminine and leaders as masculine. In nineteenth-century Western culture, as Linda Shires points out in her study of the Victorian "Woman Question," "Women are [. . .] either rendered invisible or seen only as the immanent matrix of historical progress and fulfillment" (1995: 140); despite her desire to do so, at this stage of her life and her career, Elizabeth Barrett Browning found it difficult to see beyond that conceptual matrix. The submerged logic of her rhetoric is that, if Italy is a woman - damaged or not - her leader must be a man, a whole man, a tower of strength. She deploys such gendered language to depict her idea of a strong *matria* and to support an argument against empowering the papacy: if the people are too emotional (and, by implication, too feminine), then the pope is not emotional enough to be an effective shaper of political action. Barrett Browning's apostrophe to the absent phallus recalls the description of Giotto's tower, but this time the imagery of the incomplete phallus represents not possibility for future growth, but a deficiency in the pope's humanity:

          At best and hopefullest,
He's pope -- we want a man! his heart beats warm,
    But, like the prince enchanted to the waist,
He sits in stone, and hardens by a charm
    Into the marble of his throne high-placed.
Mild benediction, waves his saintly arm --
    So, good! but what we want's a perfect man,
Complete and all alive: half travertine
    Half suits our need, and ill subserves our plan.

Feet, knees, nerves, sinews, energies divine
  Were never yet too much for men who ran
In such hard ways as must be this of thine [. . .] . (I.1034-1045)

In Barrett Browning's scheme, too much or too little revolutionary potency will result in the reassertion of political chaos, leaving Italy more vulnerable than before.

Since Barrett Browning did not reach the theoretical goals of late twentieth-century feminism, such critics as Deirdre David argue that in Barrett Browning's *oeuvre* we find "a contradiction between liberal feminism and patriarchal attitudes" (*Intellectual Women and Victorian Patriarchy* 144). In her own terms, however, Barrett Browning is at least consistent in her inconsistency: she modifies traditional rhetorical strategies just enough to decenter herself as a political speaker, becoming entangled in the web of rhetorical inconsistencies that results from any gendered rhetoric. And, thus her own role as the teacher who leads becomes mired in the gendered rhetoric of the Risorgimento which she is able to critique, but not to escape. She exhorts the rest of the Western world to share the burden of repairing its cultural heritage and protecting the weak, and if doing so means war,

  by this faint heart of my womanhood,
Such things are better than a Peace that sits
  Beside a hearth in self commended mood,
And takes no thought how wind and rain by fits
  Are howling out of doors against the good
Of the poor wanderer. (II. 406-11)

If *il popolo* and the skirted pope are effeminized, so is the woman poet, who thereby undercuts the position of authority which, in the very act of writing, she seems to claim.

In spite of Barrett Browning's pessimism about the Italian people, their leaders, their topical literature, and their political future, *Casa Guidi Windows* does not end without hope. And, in the end, Barrett Browning manages to restore some of the consistency in her gendered imagery as well, by foregrounding her personal involvement as a woman with Italy's fortunes. The final lines re-figure the motif sounded at the beginning, the little child who sings of liberty as he passes in the street.

I heard last night a little child go singing
  'Neath Casa Guidi windows, by the church,

O bella libertà, O bella! stringing
    The same words still on notes he went in search
So high for, you concluded the upspringing
    Of such a nimble bird to sky from perch
Must leave the whole bush in a tremble green,
    And that the heart of Italy must beat,
While such a voice had leave to rise serene
    'Twixt church and palace of a Florence street!
A little child, too, who not long had been
    By mother's finger steadied on his feet,
And still, *O bella libertà* he sang. (I. 1-13)

So begins *Casa Guidi Windows*. When Barrett Browning takes up her
theme again four years after completing "Meditation in Tuscany," she
watches her own child and recalls the child who sang beneath her window:

I wrote a meditation and a dream,
    Hearing a little child sing in the street.
I leant upon his music as a theme,
    Till it gave way beneath my heart's full beat,
Which tried at an exultant prophecy
    But dropped before the measure was complete -- (II. 1-6)

So the poem ends, not with Coleridge's grand rhetorical gesture, but with a
simple domestic scene:

    The sun strikes, through the windows, up the floor;
Stand out in it, my own young Florentine,
    Not two years old, and let me see thee more!
It grows along thy amber curls, to shine
    Brighter than elsewhere. Now, look straight before,
And fix thy brave blue English eyes on mine,
    And from thy soul, which fronts the future so,
With unabashed and unabated gaze,
    Teach me to hope for, what the angels know
When they smile clear as thou dost [. . .].
    And be God's witness that the elemental
New springs of life are gushing everywhere
    To cleanse the water-courses, and prevent all
Concrete obstructions which infest the air!
    That earth's alive, and gentle or ungentle
Motions within her, signify but growth! [. . .]

Such cheer I gather from thy smiling, Sweet!
    The self-same cherub-faces which emboss
    The Vail, lean inward to the Mercy seat. (II.742-51, 761-67, 781-83)

The entire poem is thus framed by a refrain celebrating the poet's own muse, not the draped female figure from outworn tradition, but a little child who sings and smiles. If the Risorgimento is incomplete, "the measure" in a sense is not: the poet has failed to integrate all her themes, but she has managed to restore her own hopes and, through the figure of the child muse, to restore some structural integrity to a fragmented meditation on Italy. As the mother of this "muse," Barrett Browning also suggests the double place of the woman poet in contemporary politics and the idea of political life as a process continuing into the future. Because of her own experience, she can articulate a new image of Italy as a powerful, creative mother, an image which better serves the Risorgimento, the rebirth of a nation. The Niobe image is thus reversed in the final lines of the poem.

Casa Guidi Windows contains beautiful and provocative passages. It literally offers a window on the Risorgimento; the immediacy of Barrett Browning's historical view makes the poem an important historical resource.

More important for my purposes here, Barrett Browning's political meditation on Italy was a watershed in her development. In this poem, she cast a retrospective look at her youthful desire to make of poetry a medium of philosophy and education, and she began to reintegrate these intentions more powerfully into her work. At the same time, the poem anticipates her magnum opus, *Aurora Leigh*, as well as some of the controlled and powerful lyrics published in *Poems before Congress* (1860) and *Last Poems* (1862). *Casa Guidi Windows* served as a rehearsal for Barrett Browning's private conflicts, such as those surrounding artistic nurturance and identity, which she would consider more overtly and perhaps even more consciously in *Aurora Leigh*: in other words, though the two poems are generically quite different, their "plots" are parallel. *Casa Guidi Windows* was also a testing ground for specific themes and ideas: for Barrett Browning's changing understanding of her own potential as a woman poet, and for her developing ideas about the plight of other woman, particularly the fallen woman. Finally, in *Casa Guidi Windows*, Barrett Browning explored a theory about the nature and function of artistic tradition which is clearly articulated in *Aurora Leigh* and which serves as a motivating force for the heroine. Like Browning, Barrett Browning suggests in both poems that, although the artist must know and love the work of the past, she must write for the present and the future, "translating" tradition, rather than attempting to repeat it.[14]

If the mutual influence between the Brownings has been wrongly estimated, it has not been underestimated. Their mutual ideas about politics and poetry developed in a daily dialogue - such as the exuberant celebration of their anniversary at a time of patriotic celebration. *Casa Guidi Windows* reveals as much about the Brownings' relationship as any other work by either of them - perhaps more. The direct address seems to assume complete sympathy of opinions. The poem may indeed be as important a reflection of Robert Browning's thinking as of Elizabeth's - not simply about politics, but also about art and its connection to politics.[15] And the joyous fragment drifting through the window in the opening lines of *Casa Guidi Windows* recalls similar moments in the generically fluid *Pippa Passes*, the poem by Browning that Barrett Browning most "coveted" (*Correspondence* 10.79). The scraps of Pippa's songs, heard through the windows, re-echo in *Casa Guidi Windows*, drifting up to the poet from beneath her window, inspiring her to turn the sights and sounds of Italy into poetry which will once again inspire and invigorate. Indeed, Barrett Browning's child muse is more effectual than Pippa, whose song has no positive effect on events, private or public.

In his study of *Revolution as Tragedy*, John P. Farrell argues that many, if not most, Victorian writers and intellectuals were beset by the desire for revolution on the one hand, for rationality and stability on the other. As a result, they "are trapped because they try to follow revolution in some of its developments but not its totality. Their measured sympathy is always at

---

[14] Gilbert's article on *Casa Guidi Windows* is the definitive statement, I think, about Barrett Browning's projection of her own affiliation hopes and anxieties onto the Risorgimento. Susan Stanford Friedman suggests that *Casa Guidi Windows* had for Barrett Browning a heuristic function in her article on "Gender and Genre Anxiety: Elizabeth Barrett Browning and H. D. as Epic Poets" (208). In "'Because men made the laws': The Fallen Woman and the Woman Poet," Angela Leighton explores the theme of the fallen woman in *Aurora Leigh*, observing a parallel between the treatment of the theme in this poem and *Casa Guidi Windows*. Dolores Rosenblum's comparative study of *Aurora Leigh* and *Casa Guidi Windows* explores theoretical statements in both poems.

[15] Both Alaya and Markus, in an article published shortly after her edition of *Casa Guidi Windows*, argue convincingly that putative disagreements between the Brownings about politics have been exaggerated, if not invented. These critics do not deny eventual disagreement in detail (nor would it be logical to deny that any couple disagreed in detail on a whole range of issues!), but they do suggest that *Casa Guidi Windows* is an accurate index of both Brownings' political feelings and views during their early years in Italy.

odds with revolution's fury against fine distinctions" (19). In *Casa Guidi Windows*, we *hear* Barrett Browning as she comes to this recognition over and over again. In the poems Robert Browning began writing during the last few months his wife worked on *Casa Guidi Windows*, we rarely witness this recognition, but we are aware, nevertheless, of his struggle to make the fine distinctions which were so difficult.

Chapter 6

A Gallery of Voices
1851-1855

The poems Browning wrote between 1850 and 1855 are often considered his finest work. Certainly, they suggest a new level of personal and poetic maturity, and they were no doubt fueled by the very experiences which delayed their composition, while Browning adjusted to life as a husband, parent, and expatriate.

During the earliest years in Italy, Browning spent most of his energy building a life and making a home. Pen's arrival in 1849 of course redefined the Brownings' relationship, and, for Robert Browning, relief at the child's safe delivery was balanced by the new complexities of caring for him. When Pen was two years old, the family embarked on a circuitous journey through Italy, France, and England which would keep them away from Florence for almost a year. In Paris, they visited with other literati and observed the political convulsions associated with Napoleon III's new dictatorship. In London, they visited with family and attended to business with their publisher. Browning's grief at his mother's death was still raw when, during this visit, he learned of his father's involvement with a middle-aged widow, who sued for breach of promise when Browning senior had second thoughts about the relationship.

With external and internal circumstances in disarray, Browning had to work harder at writing poetry. At least by the time the couple returned to Florence in 1853, the hectic activity seems to have fanned Browning's imagination into a brighter fire, and the desultory writing habits he had fallen into after the elopement to Italy changed again. Browning returned to the kinds of materials he had explored in *Dramatic Romances and Lyrics*, reworking them into richer, more complex patterns. He made a new year's resolution to write a poem a day, and though he was of course unable to keep it, he did work at writing shorter poems with enough of the speed and discipline he had exercised before his marriage that, by the summer of 1855, he had completed the fifty-one poems of *Men and Women*.

Apparently, during his early years in Italy, Browning could concentrate only on weighty projects - new editions of his and Barrett Browning's poetry, *Christmas-Eve and Easter-Day*, and the Shelley essay. But he worked on other things as well. A group of poems occasioned by particular experiences with Elizabeth would be the core of *Men and Women*, published in 1855. Browning's emotional growth during the early years of his marriage was perhaps the basis of a central theme of the collection, which Wendell Johnson describes as

> unity, not only the balance of roles but also the ecstatic if momentary sense of oneness in marriage, along with the actual and melancholy experience of alienation, not one-sided coldness and cruelty, in a marriage [. . . . In these poems, there] is not by any means a complete or simple shift in subject matter and emphasis; but Browning's conception of marriage as an idea and as a social and psychological reality appears to have become -- after his own marriage -- a good deal more complex. (216)

A condition of Browning's relationship with Elizabeth Barrett Browning was, of course, life as an expatriate, and the new perspective which resulted from standing outside and away from the institutions of his homeland. Thus Browning also experienced an ideological shift which informs his poetry in subtle ways.[1]

Some of the poems in *Men and Women* which seem to reflect the early years of the Brownings' marriage are among the best known in the volume. "The Guardian Angel," for instance, was written a few days after the Brownings' visit in 1848 to Fano, where they saw Guercino's painting of the angel and the child - famous now mostly because of Browning's poem. "The Patriot" was probably inspired by the events of the Risorgimento which had energized Barrett Browning's "Meditation in Tuscany." In "Up at a Villa -- Down in the City," Browning seems to be describing the house outside Sienna in which the couple took up residence during a holiday in 1850. "Bishop Blougram's Apology" is thematically related to *Christmas-Eve and Easter-Day*. "Memorabilia," a rare lyric in the poet's own voice, has close affinities with Browning's essay on Shelley, written late in 1851. So does "How It Strikes a Contemporary." Both are meditations on poetic fame, always much in the mind and conversation of Browning, whose own infamy as the writer of *Sordello* he seemed unable to live down. Whether or not Browning wrote these poems before 1853, when he is known to have

---

[1] The shift in Browning's poetry which occurred after the Brownings settled in Italy has been noted for a long time by some Browning critics, beginning with Anna Benneson McMahan, whose 1907 study of *Florence in the Poetry of the Brownings* deals with particular poems about Florence in general and the Risorgimento in particular. More recently articles by Alaya and Markus develop and build upon this strain of Browning scholarship.

focused on the project of *Men and Women*, he was at least storing up impressions for later use.

Living in Italy also made the theme of art - always a passion for Browning - more central to his poetry. In the works of visual artists, Browning found a way (obliquely, to be sure) to express a belief about the function and appeal of all art. As his Fra Lippo Lippi says,

> we're made so that we love
> First when we see them painted, things we have passed
> Perhaps a hundred times nor cared to see;
> And so they are better, painted -- better to us,
> Which is the same thing. Art was given for that;
> God uses us to help each other so,
> Lending our minds out. (300-06)[2]

The painter poems in *Men and Women* demonstrate this perennial interest in visual arts and derive from his favorite books, *The Art of Painting* by Gerard de Laraisse and Giorgio Vasari's *Lives of the Artists*. Browning's drawing lessons in Florence perhaps gave an added immediacy to his depictions of working painters which was absent in the earlier painter poems in *Bells and Pomegranates*, "My Last Duchess" and "Pictor Ignotus." The influence of Browning's artistic interests in *Men and Women* shapes not only the content of certain poems, but also the form of other poems and their relationships to each other: the collection is a gallery,[3] and it reflects the Brownings' playful juggling with three concepts: painted portraits, literary portraits, and human models - real "men and women," a title he borrowed from one of the *Sonnets from the Portuguese*:

> I lived with visions for my company
> Instead of men and women, years ago,
> And found them gentle mates, nor thought to know
> A sweeter music than they played to me. (XXVI 104)

---

[2] Jack and Singleton's argument for the dating of *Men and Women* (Oxford Edition) is essential. The often mentioned story of Browning's 1852 New Year's resolution to write a poem a day, they argue, is based on Browning's faulty memory: the period of most intense activity, according to other external evidence, began in early 1853. These editors are reluctant to rely on internal or thematic evidence for the dating of any poem in the collection.

[3] In an article on Browning's narrators David Lawton describes the collection as "a literary scrapbook or collage: extracts from many different contexts reinterpreted, by a potent interpreter, as one' (92). A scrapbook is, of course, by nature chaotic, whereas the walls of a picture gallery appear chaotic only to the eye of the untrained observer.

"Poems are men," asserts Barrett Browning's Aurora Leigh (3.90), in the manuscript Browning was reading while he himself was in the final stages of arranging the poems for his collection. And Browning begins "One Word More," the last poem in *Men and Women*,

> There they are, my fifty men and women
> Naming me the fifty poems finished!
> Take them, Love, the book and me together:
> Where the heart lies, let the brain lie also. (1-4)

And with this introduction to the poem, Browning reveals overtly through his art, for the first time, the nature of his feelings for Elizabeth Barrett Browning, his lover and intellectual companion.

Browning's interest in painting was finally expressed, not only in the poems devoted to art, but in his attention to graphic detail in the delineation of character in the dramatic monologue, his signature genre. Like a good portrait, the dramatic monologue reveals character through the depiction of a single overdetermined moment in a single human life. In "My Last Duchess"(1842), the missing Duchess of Ferrara is a tragic character because she is denied the power to communicate with anyone besides the icy husband who has reduced her to an art object. The Duke's words - "That's my last Duchess painted on the wall" - predict the poet's own proprietary tone in the dedicatory poem at the end of *Men and Women* - and the underlying idea for the volume, a picture gallery. Browning's men and women, however, *do* speak, to anyone who will read the book, just as Browning's relationship with his own wife diametrically opposed the Duke's assumptions about marriage. In "One Word More," Browning in his own voice (he claims) equates the poems in *Men and Women* with portraits, which are simultaneously and paradoxically himself and other characters:

> Love, you saw me gather men and women,
> Live or dead or fashioned by my fancy,
> Enter each and all, and use their service,
> Speak from every mouth, -- the speech a poem. (129-32)

In the 1855 collection, Browning juxtaposes some obviously paired pieces, such as "Love in a Life" and "Life in a Love," just as in the nineteenth-century picture gallery, thematically related pieces would have been placed side by side. But the paired poems in this volume stand in more complex relationships to each other than his earlier paired poems. "Madhouse Cells," first published in his friend Fox's *Monthly Repository* in 1836 and later reprinted in *Dramatic Lyrics* (1842), is a diptych of the homicidal lover in "Porphyria's Lover" and the religious egomaniac who speaks in "Johannes Agricola in Meditation." A second pair in the same volume, "Queen Worship," consists of the monologues of two men, eight centuries apart - one the twelfth-century troubadour Rudel, who falls in love with a portrait, the other an anonymous underling in the contemporary Spanish court, a lover of the notorious Queen Cristina, who was forced to leave Spain in 1840 partly because of her sexual appetites. Both speakers are trapped in a static distance from the object of desire.[4] Similarly, "Fra Lippo Lippi" and "Andrea del Sarto," the portraits of painters in *Men and Women*, are obviously a pair; although they are not juxtaposed in the 1855 *Men and Women*, they were together in two of Browning's later arrangements, 1863 and 1871. Unlike Browning's earlier poems on the same theme, the two speakers in these poems offer radically different interpretations of the nexus between sex and money, sex and art, art and money.[5] The other paired poems in this collection also suggest the complexity of truth by conveying multiple perspectives, which connect within and between individual poems far more deeply than in the linked poems of *Bells and Pomegranates*.

The project represented by these linked poems in *Men and Women* - an exploration of the relativity of truth and the ironies involved in the articulation of truth - is similar to *The Ring and the Book*, which he would write a decade later, and a preview of the insights which fueled it. What Martin calls "the doubleness of the monologue's language and its structures of reciprocity and exchange" are intensified by the relationships between each poem of the collection and its surroundings, just as each monologue in *The Ring and the Book* takes on almost endlessly reverberating ironies as it strikes notes of harmony or dissonance with all the others (167). But the poems in *Men and Women* are not only related thematically: while the characters in the dramatic monologues speak to their silent but responding auditors, they also speak to characters in other poems, to which they are not

---

[4] Thomas P. Walsh remarks that, if "read in isolation," Browning's poems "reveal less than when compared, contrasted, and considered as an emerging commentary" ("Companion Poems in *Men and Women* 71). Walsh is particularly concerned with the "love and hate, sex and aggression, between men and women" in the obviously paired poems.

[5] Economic issues are a frequent theme in critical treatments of "Andrea del Sarto" and "Fra Lippo Lippi." In a fine recent analysis of the latter, "Robert Browning's 'Fra Lippo Lippi' and the Problematic of a Male Poetic," Sussman argues that "the portrait of Lippo shows how the entry or, in Ruskinian terms, the unfortunate 'fall' of the artist into the sphere of commerce generates a debilitating commodification of male energy, both artistic and sexual" (187).

explicitly yoked, from within interconnected landscapes of domestic comfort and urban ruins, and from dialogically resonant mindsets of pleasure, guilt, pain, and love. The pragmatics of *Men and Women* is therefore part of its meaning,[6] and the poems reveal more when they are read intertextually than do the poems of Browning's earlier collections.

This dialogism within and between poems cannot be fully sensed, of course, unless the poems are read in Browning's original order. On the other hand, if the poems are read as one work, the collection becomes so vast and intricate a web of meaning that Browning critics have resorted to a number of strategies to avoid reading it whole, or at least to simplify the task. Studies of *Men and Women* have focused on individual poems, thematic groupings, or generic features.[7] Walsh's study of the framing of the collection, "The Frames of Browning's *Men and Women*," suggests another strategy for understanding the unity of *Men and Women*. Still another approach has been to overgeneralize about Browning's work, as Dwight Culler does when he argues that for Browning, art, love, and religion are different versions of divine love (201), or as William B. Harrold does when he argues that an "overpoem" unifies *Men and Women* by setting up "a dialectic of opposites within the units of poems" (233).

Although a complete analysis of *Men and Women* as a single work would be too vast for this study, I would like to suggest a different strategy for at least thinking of the collection as a whole: that is, a reading based on the arrangement of the poems in 1855. There was nothing accidental about

---

[6] As Woolford has shown in *Browning the Revisionary*, the relationships among poems within the collection are not static, but dynamic: Browning's deep revisions of the collection for the edition of 1863 focus the poems much more strongly on the parallels between divine and human love, and place the work within an emerging Victorian genre, the "structured collection" (101 *et pass.*).

[7] Thematic or generic studies can, of course, contribute significantly to our understanding of Browning's work. In addition to Sussman's provocative and important theme study of "Fra Lippo Lippi" and "Andrea del Sarto," see Penelope Gay's "Desire and the Female Voice in Browning's *Men and Women* and *Dramatis Personae*" which tracks Browning's psychological development and his understanding of marriage as expressed through his poetry before and after marriage. In *The Dialectical Temper*, Shaw suggests another way of reading individual monologues -- as dialectical structures, bracketed as dramatic or performative. Hair also suggests the strategy of reading the individual poems as a "parleying," or a "genuine clash of opposites" in which words are "both instrumental [. . .] and arguable" (*Robert Browning's Language* 294). The two-sided nature of the dialectic is more apparent in individual poems, and multiple meanings emerge in a dialogical approach, such as my own, which emphasizes context.

the sequence. One clear example of Browning's concern with arrangement is his contribution to the 1850 edition of Barrett Browning's poems, published simultaneously with a new edition of his own. Most, perhaps all, of the instructions on the proof sheets for Barrett Browning's poems are in Browning's handwriting,[8] and he changed the order of almost every poem from the 1844 collection, not merely to accommodate the new work, but for added emphasis. For example, his pairing of "L. E. L.'s Last Question" and "Felicia Hemans: To L. E. L." calls attention to the developing tradition of women's poetry, to which Elizabeth Barrett herself had made the most important contributions, and renders both poems more powerful. Browning also insisted that *Sonnets from the Portuguese*, as he called it, be published. The sonnets were placed at the end of the collection, immediately after his favorite of Barrett's early works, "Catarina to Camoens," a dramatic monologue spoken by the dying lover of the Renaissance poet Camoens, in a fever of grief after Camoens is exiled from the Portuguese court. The juxtaposition heightens the effect of both Barrett Browning's dramatic monologue and the sonnets, creating a narrative framework which fictionalizes the sonnets and suggests their importance. This episode in the Brownings' professional relationship demonstrates a high degree of collaboration. Browning's handwriting shows that at the very least he was consulted about every ordering change, and his own habits suggest that his involvement was far greater. Browning's attention to the arrangement of his wife's poems is consistent with the attention he paid to his own.[9]

Browning's lifelong attention to the arrangement and rearrangement of his poems indicates that sequence is always important (if not always for obvious reasons) and that different variables came into play when he made decisions about ordering. An immediate visual influence, of course, was the Pitti Palace, practically across the street from Casa Guidi. Whether or not he consciously referred to it, an even more important spatial model for the 1855 edition of *Men and Women* was the gallery where he spent so many hours as a child. The Dulwich Picture Gallery, which had opened its doors when Browning was a year old, was, he wrote to Elizabeth Barrett, "a green half-hour's walk over the fields" from his parents' home (*Letters* 12.124). Designed by Sir John Soane, the unorthodox structure was one of the

---

[8] The proof sheets for the 1850 edition of Barrett Browning's poems, with Browning's notes, are now in the Wellesley Library.

[9] Browning's interest in arrangement was not new. In "The Arrangement of Browning's *Dramatic Lyrics*," George Bornstein argues that Browning's "earliest collection of mature verse [. . .] displays considerable architectonic skill in its deployment of paired poems punctuated by individual, free-standing ones [. . .] . The independent poems reinforce the implicit [argument] in the pairs [. . .]" (273).

earliest buildings created for the pictures it was to house: it consists of several well-proportioned, high-ceilinged rooms, connected by wide doorways and lit by skylights rather than side windows. Exterior and interior were unadorned, the better to emphasize the paintings. Then, as now, the collection was, with few exceptions, limited to paintings of the seventeenth and eighteenth centuries - historical and mythological narratives, landscapes, and portraits. Although children were banned until the twentieth century, Browning's childhood privileges included frequent excursions to see the pictures. He knew the worth of the honor, years later referring to the Dulwich collection in the letter to Barrett as "that Gallery I so love and am so grateful to - having been allowed to go there when a child, far under the age allowed by the regulations." His favorite pictures included

> those two Guidos, the wonderful Rembrandt of Jacob's vision, such a Watteau, the triumphant three Murillo pictures, a Giorgione music-lesson group, all the Poussins with the "Armida" and "Jupiter's nursing" -- and -- no ends to "ands" -- I have sate before one, some one of those pictures I had predetermined to see, -- a good hour [. . .] .[10] (*Correspondence* 12.124)

---

[10] The general history of the building and the collection are outlined in Giles Waterfield's *Dulwich Picture Gallery* [n. d.]. Waterfield narrates the history of the collection during the nineteenth century in *Rich Summer of Art* (1988). The Dulwich, which started with three private collections and became an art resource open to anyone who could afford the price of a ticket, was representative of a nineteenth-century trend: it came to be considered more appropriate for pictures to be displayed in galleries open to the public than for them to be kept privately as luxuries or investment commodities. (One of Elizabeth Barrett's rare London outings was to see the pictures in the National Gallery [*Correspondence*. 12.119]). As for what Browning actually saw in the gallery, attributions at the Dulwich during its early days tended to be optimistic: both the "Rembrandt" and the "Giorgione" are apparently by other hands. But it is easy to see how the strong images of the Jacob painting and the "costumes and atmosphere of intrigue" (Waterfield 29) of the music lesson would have appealed to Browning. When Browning was writing his tribute to the Dulwich, the gallery guide listed fourteen paintings by Poussin, which illustrated mythological or historical stories, and two by Watteau. There were six by Guido Reni; Browning was probably most drawn to the large, dramatic, and prominently displayed portraits of John the Baptist and Saint Sebastian. Of the ten paintings attributed to Murillo, it seems likely that Browning's favorites included at least one of the two intimate and naturalistic paintings of urchins playing among ruins. One can detect, too, the influence of the Dulwich landscapes attributed to Gerard de Laraisse and the treatise Laraisse wrote when blindness ended his painting; a reference to this work appears in "Parleying with Gerard de Laraisse" (1887).

In the nineteenth century, collections tended to be generically more homogeneous; the salon hanging typical of the nineteenth-century gallery (and which still obtains today in the Dulwich) may be determined on the basis of subtle differences in theme or style, or size and color. In this gallery style, there are only two constants. Frames are more important than in the modern gallery, where works are separated instead by space. And works considered inferior, or less valuable, are relegated to the top row, so that the viewer must risk eye strain or twisted neck muscles to study them. In a curious foreshadowing of Whistler, who in the 1890s initiated the move away from the crowded salon groupings typical of the nineteenth century, Browning reduced the number of poems in the 1863 version of *Men and Women* from fifty to twelve, and these twelve, in fact, included four from earlier collections. The 1863 *Men and Women*, according to Woolford, is more obviously "a thematic structured collection" (101) than a crowded gallery of voices. In this second version of *Men and Women*, Woolford notes that the characters more obviously conflate the love of art with the love of other human beings, and, as they are more obviously obsessive in their loving, the collection resonates strongly with Browning's early interest in psychological perversity. The frames of the poems thin out, and the separate works of the first version merge more closely into a "surrogate long poem," a substitute, perhaps, for the huge sustained poems of his early and late career (Woolford 88-89). In the second version of *Men and Women*, Browning omitted the poems which did not contribute to the theme, and perhaps he also pared down the collection by rejecting the "top row."

But, in fact, Browning's arrangement of the poems in the 1855 *Men and Women* was no less careful than the more obviously tight structure of the 1863 collection. Proximate poems of the 1855 collection almost always overlap in some way - thematically, in terms of genre, psychologically, or symbolically. In *Problems of Dostoevsky's Poetics*, Bakhtin has this to say about discursive proximity:

> Two discourses equally and directly oriented toward a referential object within the limits of a single context cannot exist side by side without intersecting dialogically, regardless of whether they confirm, mutually ·supplement, or (conversely) contradict one another or find themselves in some other dialogic relationship (that of question and answer, for example). Two equally weighted discourses on one and the same theme, once having come in contact with each other, must inevitably orient themselves to one another. Two embodied meanings cannot lie side by side like two objects -- they must come into inner contact [. . .]. (188-89)

Browning's arrangement exploits this principle. One key to discerning the links between proximate poems in *Men and Women* is discovering the area of overlap; another is defining the interactions between proximate poems, which is not always one of opposition.

The rest of this discussion of *Men and Women* will be devoted to the first six poems of Volume II: "Andrea del Sarto," "Before" and "After," "In Three Days" and "In a Year," and "Old Pictures in Florence." Almost any series of poems from *Men and Women* could demonstrate the principle, but I am especially interested in this one because it opens with "Andrea del Sarto," one of Browning's strongest dramatic monologues, and closes with another very different poem about the visual arts, "Old Pictures in Florence." "Andrea del Sarto" is usually considered with the other poems based on Vasari's *Lives*, not with "Before" and "After," the pair of poems about dueling, and "Old Pictures in Florence." At first glance, Browning's jovial first-person account of his passion for old pictures and his lament for the decay of Florence's Renaissance heritage appears to have little in common with the pair of poems preceding it, "In Three Days" and "In a Year." These are studies of the tensions in long-distance erotic relationships. Nevertheless, despite the disparities revealed even by the titles, all six poems explore distance and desire and are organized around erotic tensions.

Schematically, these works form a cluster, a work within a work, which opens out from the concerns of an individual to those of friends and lovers, and, finally to the concerns of the polity. All of these poems explore failure or vexation, or near failure. "Andrea del Sarto" portrays a failed husband and artist; "Before" and "After," a failed friendship. "In Three Days" and "In a Year" show the failure and instability of romantic love. "Old Pictures in Florence" suggests the cultural and political failure of a society, revealed in the betrayal of its artistic heritage. Even the connections between the sets of paired poems are by no means as simple as their titles suggest, and the two poems about art, which seem unrelated to the ones they bracket, nevertheless enter into dialogue with their neighbors.

The dynamics among these poems are an important part of their meaning, but relationships among the poems also reveal another dimension of the Brownings' interaction as artists and lovers.

During their courtship - ten years before the publication of *Men and Women* - Browning and Barrett had two serious disagreements, both of which illustrate the almost stereotypical differences between male and female morality as described in Carol Gilligan's *In a Different Voice*. In Gilligan's analysis, male ethics are typically based on more or less absolute principles, female ethics on relationships, the preservation of which almost always takes precedence over rules. One quarrel between Browning and Barrett was over the moral rectitude of negotiating with dog snatchers. When Flush was stolen (for the third time!) on August 31, 1846, soon before the lovers' scheduled departure for Italy, Browning had the misfortune to speak of him in the past tense and to recommend withholding the ransom, as a matter of principle. Barrett responded tartly that she hoped he would not react the same way if she were kidnapped. The story ended happily. Barrett did pay the ransom (against the advice of her lover, her brothers, and her father), seeking out the dog snatcher with the trusty Wilson in tow and negotiating with his rough-speaking wife for Flush's life. Flush eloped with the couple to Italy a few weeks later, and Browning's principles about paying ransom money were never tested, on behalf of Flush or his wife.

The other disagreement - sparked by an actual event in the French world of letters, witnessed by Dumas, - was about dueling. The arguments the poets carried on at length in their letters of April 1846 are consistent with their respective responses to Flush's misadventures. Browning's position was that, in a situation which ends in a duel, there is "an impersonal conflict of claims" (Gilligan 32), which should be sorted out on a level playing field between two men with weapons, if that is the solution both choose. "Sin is sin every where and the worse, I think, for the grossness -- Being fired at by a Duellist is a little better, I think also, than being struck on the face by a ruffian" who does not rue his action, he wrote (*Correspondence* 12.211). Barrett's response to Browning's support of dueling seems rooted in the belief that "in morality lies a way of solving conflicts so that no one will be hurt" (Gilligan 65). Each wanted the last word. After a "duel" of two letters from each on the subject and some conversation in between, Barrett sends a third message, in which she pretends to lighten the tone:

> Well! Because I do 'not rue' (& am so much the more unfit to die) I am to be stabbed through the body by an act of 'private judgement' of my next neighbor. So I must take care & 'rue' when I do anything wrong -- and I begin now, for being the means of tiring you, . . & for seeming to persist so! You may be right & I wrong, of course -- I only speak as I see. And will not speak any more last words. . taking pardon for these. I rue --" (*Correspondence* 12.228)

Browning made another pass on this issue in "Before" and "After," written perhaps at the time, perhaps years later. Either way, however, he neither gave in nor persisted in his own unmodified view, but approached the subject of dueling from another angle. Browning's thinking in his paired poems is more complex and more ethically detached than his stereotypical "masculine" position in the letters, and it avoids Barrett's stereotypical "feminine" position as well. (The poems about dueling are also among the most obvious testaments to the kind of conversations which fueled the Brownings' poetic energies.)

This pair of poems is typical of Browning's response to any kind of intellectual problem - that is, chromatic refraction which creates, not one or even two, but several perspectives, with the implication that truth takes shape in a space between. In this pair of poems, not two, but three voices, are represented directly or indirectly. The worldly narrator of "Before" is a second to one of the duelists; he defends the practice of dueling with the familiar notion that active defense of honor is superior to passive acceptance of a wrong. The auditor in the poem is, apparently, a passionate onlooker, who has been arguing against dueling from a Christian perspective of forgiveness. The issue is so ideologically charged that the speaker reacts to his auditor's gesture of rebuttal - "But you must not end my friend ere you begin him"(35) - and he seizes the last word when he announces, "Both fighters to their places!/ While I count three, step you back as many paces" (39-40). The energy of the speaker - especially as the poem follows the monologue of the passive Andrea del Sarto - is obvious, and he makes an argument for action often heard in Browning's works:

Better sin the whole sin, sure that God observes;
Then go live his life out! Life will try his nerves,
When the sky, which noticed all, makes no disclosure,
And the earth keeps up her terrible composure. (13-16)

But the speaker of "Before" no more has the last word than Browning had in his argument with Barrett. "After" makes it clear that the last word is not granted to Barrett, either: instead of addressing the ethical question directly in "After," the speaker, the wronged man and therefore the "right" winner in the conflict, sidesteps the question of right and wrong by describing in highly formal language his grief at the death of a man who was once his friend, and who is now beyond the concerns of this world:

absorbed in the new life he leads,
He recks not, he heeds
Nor his wrong nor my vengeance [. . .].

The words of the victor are less an elegy to the dead man than an elegy to innocence, lost long before the duel or the insult:

I would we were boys as of old
   In the field, by the fold:
His outrage, God's patience, man's scorn
   Were so easily borne! (5-7, 13-16)

The language of the speaker in "After," which is both formal and passionate, does not concern itself with possible alternatives to this death, which seems tragic but inevitable. And Browning leaves unanswered, as he must, questions about the feelings of the dead man, the true opposite of the victor's feelings. The unusual stanza form in "Before" - a heptameter couplet followed by a hexameter couplet - gives the impression of the emotional and rhetorical control which would be required of the second in a duel. The alternating tetrameter and dimeter lines of "After" imply the shortness of breath, which would be experienced after a fight, and the victor's self-control, achieved by formality. Each speaker in the dueling poems is conscious of presenting a particular static face to the world; and in this way, they are like the passive Andrea del Sarto, for all their headlong rush to participate in worldly action.

Together, these two poems exemplify not so much influence between the Brownings as cross-fertilization of feelings and ethical ideas, and the existence of a dialogic space in which these feelings and ideas could be exchanged and turned into art. When Browning was questioned about what the poem meant in 1864, by a Mr. Ball at Trinity College, Dublin, he responded with a comment about ethics. The killing is, in Browning's view, a "sin," which may not be punished in any visible way. However,

> let things go smoothly as they may, his conscience will soon become aware that there is a Retribution certainly waiting him [. . .] and that all the toleration and indulgence of [. . .] the present serve, like the luxuries conceded to a condemned felon, to enhance the final punishment [. . .]." ("Two Unpublished Browning Letters" 42)

Reading backwards from this pair of poems also illuminates "Andrea del Sarto," one of Browning's most complex dramatic monologues, usually considered within the context of Browning's other artist poems, or the poems about the exercise or repression of sexual energy. Analyses of this poem usually conclude with a negative judgment about Andrea del Sarto's art, supported by Vasari's *Lives*, or a negative judgment about the painter's passive enslavement to his wife Lucrezia's more vigorous sexual and material desires; such readings are also supported by comparison to other poems such as "The Statue and the Bust," in which two lovers waste their lives waiting for the best moment to run away together.[11] However, juxtaposing "Andrea del Sarto" with "Before" and "After," poems about traditions of masculine honor, brings to the surface of Andrea's monologue a concern about the price of choosing honor over dishonor. Andrea admits that he has let his parents die in want and failed to fulfill his commission as an art buyer for the French king. Instead, he has spent the king's money to please his beautiful and grasping wife. However, since he has made an unwise choice in marrying, his alternatives are limited. He can live with Lucrezia, struggling to make the best of each moment, or he can strike out at the lovers she flaunts in front of him, kill them in duels, an alternative suggested by the dueling poems just before this monologue, or be killed himself - a likely fate for an enervated man whose life choices have deprived him of nerve.

In spite of his shame, Andrea del Sarto is aware that he makes choices.[12] As he looks out through the window at Florence (an ironic parallel to the position of the poets in *Casa Guidi Windows*), the artist tells his wife that, in his daydream, heaven has four walls, which God has reserved for "Leonard, Rafael, Agnolo and me to cover." Even in his own fantasy, he knows that he will be bested, "Because there's still Lucrezia -- as I choose" (263, 66). Like Pio Nono as Barrett Browning portrays him in *Casa Guidi Windows*, Andrea del Sarto is a "half man" who has lost his honor, but the cost of maintaining his honor is one he simply cannot pay.[13] The

---

[11] One of the most interesting readings of this poem is in Martin's *Browning's Dramatic Monologues and the Post-Romantic Subject*. Martin sees "Andrea del Sarto" as a study of the painter's failure of energy, ironically coupled with his drive to possession -- the possession of a woman, of fame, even of a link with divinity. "Andrea del Sarto" has been, of course, one of Browning's most popular poems; the two most important themes in the extensive critical literature about it are the idea of choice, which Andrea insists upon in the next to last line, and the possibility of a biographical connection between the painter and the poet (see notes 12 and 13).

[12] Readers have usually felt that Browning leaves little choice to the characters in both "Andrea del Sarto" and the dueling poems. Thomas Walsh argues that "Andrea del Sarto" as well as the companion poems which follow it depict characters who believe that their choices are circumscribed by predestination (72-74). Similarly, Warwick Slinn argues that the "choice is an illusion" for Andrea del Sarto (*Browning and the Fictions of Identity* 16). Keith Polette argues that the poem is structured as a series of walls within walls, built mostly by the speaker himself; Andrea's "adversity," he writes, is "self-scripted and self-inflicted" (504).

[13] Sarto's ennervated sexuality has inspired a spate of psychobiographical readings, including the one in Miller's biography, which implies a parallel between Browning's presumed dissatisfactions with Barrett Browning and Sarto's

dimensions of the poem which emerge from a comparison to the dueling poems do not make Andrea del Sarto sympathetic, but they problematize the judgments against him which are inevitable when it is read alone or with "Fra Lippo Lippi," the apologia of a lusty monk whose life is full of action, and whose art is full of life.

The dueling poems connect differently with the two poems that follow them, "In Three Days" and "In a Year." The first of these two poems is spoken in the panic-stricken voice of a man who is separated from his love, apparently for the first time. He recites, as a mantra,

> I shall see her in three days
> And one night, now the nights are short,
> Then just two hours, and that is morn. (34-36)

The speaker in the second poem of the pair is equally distraught: here, a woman abandoned by her lover obsessively recalls details of their life together and imagines dying of grief over their separation. "Before" and "After" certainly recall one of the Brownings' early quarrels. Miller suggests that "In Three Days" also may narrate an incident in the Brownings' life together, a short painful separation rather than a disagreement, when Browning went to Paris to settle his father after the lawsuit for libel and breach of promise. Eleanor Cook argues, instead, that the poem is based on the usual interval between the poets' meetings during their courtship (212). In either case, the incident is dramatized and fictionalized, according to Browning's usual practice. "In a Year" is evidently entirely fictional, but the theme of a woman in love is a persistent one in Browning's poetry.

The asymmetrical relationship between the poems within the pair, and the generic and prosodic similarities between the two pairs, are immediately obvious. In "Before" and "After," contrasts between the views of the speakers are reinforced by differences in verse forms. The relationship between the verse form of "In Three Days" and the verse form of "In a Year" is similar. The speaker in the first poem, a man whose passion for his lover can hardly be restrained for the three days which must elapse before he sees her, expresses his emotions in four tetrameter stanzas

---

alienation from Lucrezia. Both Avanzo and Bieman argue that the gold-silver imagery of "Andrea del Sarto" derives from a Renaissance archetype and suggests that Andrea's betrayal of his own homosexual nature has resulted in a failed relationship with his wife and his art.

of seven, seven, nine, and fifteen lines. The increasing length of the stanzas suggests a barely successful effort to hold his passions in check, for

> 'years must teem with change untried,
> With chance not easily defied,
> With an end somewhere undescried'. (29-31)

The stanza form of the other poem in the pair, "In a Year" - an octet of alternating trimeter and tetrameter lines - implies the speaker's lack of emotional control. She realizes that, after a year of passion, she has been abandoned. Pathologically, she wishes for death, imagining that the man who has become bored with her "should smile" and ask himself,

> 'Dying for my sake --
>   White and pink!
> Can't we touch these bubbles then
>   But they break?' (68-72)

"In Three Days" and "In a Year" explore the problem of erotic emotion and distance. The man who speaks in the first poem admits that it will not be long before he sees his lover - three days, two nights - but he struggles palpably with his irrational fear that disaster may strike before his journey ends. If he manages, just barely, to maintain self-control, the speaker in the companion poem "In a Year" has lost it. As she remembers the passions which have cooled since her love affair began a year ago, she becomes suicidal, imagining that her death might please the lover who has gone away.

The speakers in these two poems live intensely in the present, driven by desire to extremes of language. They give the impression of coming to understand their feelings as they speak. Each utterance is addressed to an auditor who is not present, and yet each speaker has a heightened consciousness of how his or her words would reverberate against the language of the other: the poems illustrate Bakhtin's psychological observation that "A person has no internal sovereign territory, he is wholly and always on the boundary; looking inside himself, he looks *into the eyes of another* or *with the eyes of another*" (*Problems of Dostoevsky's Poetics* 287, Bakhtin's emphasis). These poems are double-voiced in a way which is different from the static double-voicedness of "Andrea del Sarto" and the dueling poems, in which the audiences are actually present. Instead of consciously speaking to another who is present, the speakers of "In Three Days" and "In a Year" experience their words splitting in two: the word represents the semantic position of the speaker and is also "someone else's semantic position." As Bakhtin notes in his analysis of Dostoevsky's language, "Thus dialogic relationships can permeate inside the utterance, even inside the individual word, as long as two voices collide within it dialogically [. . .]" (184). Forced into external stasis, the speakers compensate by frantic emotional and linguistic activity.

"Old Pictures in Florence," which follows "In Three Days" and "In a Year," is like one of those omnibus collectors' paintings, so popular with collectors and artists from the time of the Renaissance. In these works, the spectator observes from eye level a large, light room filled almost from floor to ceiling with pictures, all of which are rendered in as much detail as the dimensions of the frame allow. Sometimes, the painter or collector stands in the middle of it all, gazing at his treasures with satisfaction. George Mignaty's painting of the Brownings' salon at Casa Guidi is an example of the genre, though less replete than most. It shows a large, formal, high-ceilinged room, furnished with stiff, curious pieces of furniture and impossibly high book cases, combined with book-laden tables, comfortable couches, and Elizabeth's green velvet lounge chair. Over everything else preside more than a dozen paintings, large and small, as if merely living in Florence were not enough to remind the Brownings that they were surrounded by, and part of, history.

"Old Pictures in Florence" is also a meditation on politics and art, contrasting to, but also related to, the preceding poems by the theme of distance and obsessive desire, and also by the dialogical position of the speaker, whose primary auditor, Giotto, does not literally exist in the poem's present. The secondary audience, Elizabeth Barrett Browning, does exist in the poem's present, of course, and the poem is a continuation of the dialogue that she first suggested in print in *Casa Guidi Windows*, which is directly addressed to her husband. In "Old Pictures in Florence," Browning reflects upon Barrett Browning's suggestion that a country's artistic tradition, if rightly understood, can be a source of social and political strength, and he echoes her argument that a nation's artistic practice dictates the quality of its political life.

Both Barrett Browning's poem and Browning's are personal narratives, but the two poets' construction of themselves as narrators are predictably different. Whereas in her political poem Barrett Browning frames herself as a teacher, who brings to contemporary political discourse the hitherto missing woman's perspective, Browning's self-representation in "Old Pictures in Florence" is, like the persona in *Christmas-Eve and Easter-Day*, sardonic, manic, irreverent. "Old Pictures in Florence" carnivalizes the themes of distance and desire. Instead of Andrea del Sarto's desire *to* desire, or the pain of frustrated erotic desire in "In Three Days" and "In a Year," or the desire to avenge a slight against masculine honor which drives the dueling poems, "Old Pictures in Florence" describes a petulant, frustrated, and comic desire for "old pictures," especially for old pictures painted by Giotto, the versatile artist who also designed the campanile featuring so prominently in *Casa Guidi Windows*. The poem is as autobiographical as anything Browning ever wrote, as self-revelatory, I think, as "One Word More," and based on the collector's greed which overtook Browning during his years in Florence. In a witty letter to Eliza Ogilvy, written in May 1850, Barrett Browning describes Browning's avid collecting. Encouraged by the couple's learned and colorful friend, Baron Seymour Kirkup,[14] she optimistically attributes her husband's bargains to famous painters:

> Robert has been buying pictures and covering himself with glory, at the expense of some scudi [. . .]. Well -- the other day, an accident took Robert into a cornshop, a mile beyond the gates, and there he fell on a deposit of pictures [. . .]. Robert made his way up stairs; & into the bedroom & behind a bed, were other pictures [. . .]. He bought five pictures in all; and when he had placed them in a good light, he went to fetch Mr. Kirkup, & we were encouraged to name names which you will scarcely believe in perhaps -- 1. Giottino, 2. Ghirlandaio, 3. Cimabue, 4, a very curious crucifiction, supposed to be too crude to be a Giotto, but of his time [. . .] 5, a virgin & child of a Byzantine master. All are in beautiful preservation. (Barrett Browning & Ogilvy 7-8)

There is nothing static about Barrett Browning's description of Browning's new passion, and the poem describing his search for pictures, which Browning wrote three years later, is, likewise, all motion (Markus, " Old Pictures," 54). The speaker, who resembles Browning himself enough that he may be safely referred to *as* Browning, simultaneously reveals and conceals himself, as the poet almost always does when representing his own thoughts and emotions - in this case, his feelings about losing Giotto's *Death of the Virgin*. This painting had been misplaced for centuries, found again, and snapped up immediately by another collector (54-55). Browning was known among his friends as an indefatigable and noisy talker, and the

---

[14] In Irvine and Honan's *The Book, the Ring, and the Poet*, Kirkup is described as "a deaf, white-bearded, skinny-handed, glittering-eyed old necromancer of a man who inhabited several dusty, book-and-manuscript-crammed Faust chambers hanging over the Arno" (324) An atheist, Kirkup was nevertheless an expert on the occult. He fed Robert Browning's interest in occult history and encouraged Elizabeth Barrett Browning's interest in spiritualism, as he succumbed to the fad himself.

dramatized Robert Browning in this poem bears a strong resemblance to the public Browning persona. Chattering on, he carnivalizes himself and takes liberties with his subject matter in order to stress the necessity and inevitability of political, personal, and artistic renewal.

The "conversation" begins when the poet situates himself within the Florentine landscape: "I leaned and looked over the aloed arch/ Of the villa-gate this warm March day" down toward the valley where "white and wide/ And washed by the morning water-gold,/ Florence lay out on the mountain side" (3-4, 6-8). For the poet, "the best to see":

> Was the startling bell-tower Giotto raised:
> But why did it more than startle me? (14-16)

And thus begins the dialogue with the versatile Giotto, as the narrator begins to confide in him his own ruminations about the sorry state of Florence's artistic heritage and the stupidity of contemporary observers. Next, Browning skims over to thoughts about one of his most persistent themes, the contrast between supposedly perfect Greek art and the more vital art of the early Renaissance, represented for him by Giotto's work. In a sense, classical Greek representations of the human form are inauthentic:

> So, you saw yourself as you wished you were,
> As you might have been, as you cannot be [. . .] (89-90)

In contrast, artists such as Giotto

> Make new hopes shine through the flesh they fray,
> New fears aggrandize the rags and tatters [. . .] (149-50)

The speaker's reflections on art history remind Browning that he has failed to acquire a certain picture by Giotto on which he had set his heart. Finally, Browning explains his special deserts: better than anyone else (although he does give a nod to his wife in *Casa Guidi Windows*), he claims to see the link between the artistic heritage of Florence, the city's present political woes, and its glorious political future. Like the verse of *Christmas-Eve and Easter-Day*, the eight-line stanzas are riddled with hudibrastic rhymes, and as in the earlier work, these rhymes in "Old Pictures in Florence" have the effect of destabilizing the speaker himself in his role as a satirist of contemporary life.

In "Old Pictures in Florence," Giotto (and a second Renaissance for Italy) is Browning's object of frustrated desire: "how, with that soul of yours," Browning queries Giotto, "Could you play me false who loved you so?" (17-18). (Browning's pre-publication title, OPUS MAGISTRI JOCTI, focused the poem even more clearly on Giotto.) If other Renaissance artists have not granted Browning ownership of lost and coveted paintings, that is to be expected, but Giotto, a kindred creative spirit, should have reached out over the centuries to channel his works into the poet's hands: "the thing grows hard to bear/ When I find a Giotto join the rest" in the hands of greedy art dealers and ignorant collectors. The stanzas addressed to Giotto are technically apostrophes, but the great distance normally between speaker and audience in apostrophe shrinks to intimate space: instead of distance and adoration, Browning conveys a feeling of kinship which is perfectly in keeping with what he knew about Giotto's personality. Vasari calls the painter "a very clever and charming man," remembered for his "witty retorts" and pranks, such as embellishing the nose of a portrait by Cimabue (his teacher) with a fly so lifelike that his fellow students tried to shoo it away (33, 35).

One of most the striking features of the poem is the erotic subtext which rises to the surface in the striking and ambiguous system of visual imagery, the O and the tower, vaginal and phallic images. Both images refer to Giotto - and they are graphically juxtaposed at the end of line 135:

> Things learned on earth, we shall practise in heaven:
>> Works done least rapidly, Art most cherishes.
> Thyself shalt afford the example, Giotto!
>> Thy one work, not to decrease or diminish,
> Done at a stroke, was just (was it not?) 'O!'
>> Thy great Campanile is still to finish.

Browning's parenthetic advice in stanza IX for the reader to "(See Vasari.)" (72) is worth taking again at this point. According to Vasari, Giotto (1266/7-1337) was discovered by the master Cimabue during a country walk. Giotto, who had taught himself to draw on the ground with a stick, was further trained by Cimabue until his narrative originality and lifelike portraits amounted to a paradigm shift in Italian art. Hearing of Giotto's fame, the Pope sent an emissary for a sample of his art, and, in response, Giotto drew, in one stroke, a perfect circle. The saying "rounder than Giotto's O," Vasari points out, is a pun; in the Tuscan dialect, *tondo* means both perfectly round and dull-witted.

2   *Campanile, with Cathedral and Baptistry*, photographer unknown. *Florence in the Poetry of the Brownings* (1907), Ed. Anna Benneson McMahan

Vasari goes on to describe the design and construction of Giotto's bell tower for Santa Maria del Fiori, left unfinished at his death. In Giotto's design, Vasari writes,

> this bell tower was supposed to have as its finishing touch above what is now visible a point or, rather, a four-sided pyramid fifty armslengths high, but since it was a German construction in the old style, modern architects have always advised against adding this, believing it to be better as it now stands. (32)

In *Casa Guidi Windows*, Barrett Browning follows Vasari in praising Giotto's "unperplex'd Fine question Heaven-ward" (69-70): for her, the tower is best as it stands, representing the beauty and openness of the future. But Browning, like Barrett Browning in *Casa Guidi Windows*, lacks complete control of the gendered imagery he employs. Curiously, despite Vasari's analysis of the architectural problem and the doctrine of the imperfect which informs so much of Browning's own poetry, Browning claims to wish to see the tower finished. When Florence has a "kind of stern Witanagemot/ (Ex: 'Casa Guidi,' *quod videas ante*)" leading to freedom, its citizens "shall ponder [. . .] How Art may return that departed with her [freedom]" (259-62). As a sign of the Risorgimento, the city will turn

> the bell tower's *alt* to *altissimo*:
> And fine as the beak of a young beccaccia
>   The Campanile, the Duomo's fit ally,
> Shall soar up in gold full fifty braccia,
>   Completing Florence, as Florence Italy.

In Browning's political fantasy, he himself - the comic dilettante poet in place of Barrett Browning's teacher poet - will be the hero. The stanza is dominated by a burning question:

> Shall I be alive that morning the scaffold
>   Is broken away, and the long-pent fire,
> Like the golden hope of the world, unbaffled
>   Springs from its sleep, and up goes the spire
> While 'God and the People' plain for its motto,
>   Thence the new tricolour flaps at the sky?
> At least to foresee that glory of Giotto
>   And Florence together, the first am I! (276-88)

Within this system of imagery, Giotto is doubly represented by the feminine image of the O and the masculine image of the tower. He is masculine in his daring and vision, feminine as an object of desire and in the perfection of the simple O, and symbolically castrated until his famous tower is completed, or at least until, as Lawrence Starzyk suggests, it becomes "something other than it presently is" (31). Self-consciously torn between the "passion for telos" and the resistance to closure, Browning's vision restores the half-completed masculine power of Giotto's tower. Browning imagines in this comic vision that he, too, will recapture some of the glory of his earlier days (Starzyk 30).

Like most of the poems in *Men and Women*, "Old Pictures in Florence" resonates with other poems in the collection. These final stanzas on Giotto's Florentine bell tower stand in comic contrast to the dark, broken tower in the middle of nowhere, the object of Childe Roland's morbid quest. In a move of pure bravado, the speaker of "Old Pictures in Florence" expresses the wish and even asserts the possibility of reversing history. "What if I take up my hope and prophecy?" he cries in stanza 31 (248), to foresee the new Italy and the preservation of the old Italy's treasures. Browning imagines himself the "rescuer," a Saint George fighting against greedy art dealers and the dragon of Austrian military might - the imperfect poet of the imperfect, wishing that the force of his own will could save the riches of a disappearing past and thus insure Italy's future. The reverberations of the bottomless irony in this assertion can be heard more clearly within the context of the other poems of *Men and Women* than in isolation from them. As Valentine Cunningham has observed, "the ruinous pastness of the past is given still more extraordinary life in Browning" than in the work of Romantic poets; it is a "key element in his [poetic] composition" (172).

Browning's irony is also more complex than that of Barrett Browning in *Casa Guidi Windows*. Barrett Browning critiques the patriotic poetry of the past, which has over and over again reinscribed the image of Italy as a damaged woman, and she asserts the possibility of a more powerful and positive political poetry for the future. In contrast, Browning's comic persona both asserts and denies that poets can affect history at all. His stance is more complex than hers, his optimism more guarded. His poem is an answer to hers, evidently written after Barrett Browning had finished *Casa Guidi Windows*, after the historical tide in Italy had changed for the worse, and within the dialogue both poets must have carried on continually about the fate of their adopted country.[15]

---

[15] Markus traces the history of the composition of both poems in "'Old Pictures in Florence': Through *Casa Guidi Windows*" (1978), and argues that the two poets' views of Italian politics did not diverge significantly, but that their two poems about Florence actually convey shared opinions, at two different points in time.

"Had you [. . .] but brought a mind!/ Some women do so. Had the mouth there urged/ 'God and Glory! Never care for gain' [. . .] I might have done it for you," Andrea del Sarto complains to his wife (126-28, 133). Joyfully aware of the contrast between his wife and Andrea's, the differences between Andrea's role as the faultless painter living at the decline of the Renaissance and his own role as a faulty poet during a time of great political ferment, in "Old Pictures in Florence," Browning playfully manipulates the confessional form of the greater romantic lyric to make a statement which is aesthetic, personal, and political. As a poet of Italian freedom, he is a comic rival to EBB, "covering himself with glory," comically deconstructing his own persona, and always celebrating the power of renewal and desire.

Although his decisions about the content of *Men and Women* were determined in part by the demands of the Victorian reading public, it seems clear that the visual and plastic arts at this point in his poetic development functioned as a language through which Browning could consider his own art from the outside. Stories of Raphael's lost sonnets and Dante's foiled attempt to paint an angel gave Browning access to new dimensions in his own poetry. In the last poem of the collection, "One Word More," Browning dedicates his work to Elizabeth with a rare gesture, speaking in "this once in my true person" (137) rather than as a carnivalized version of himself or a historical or fictional character. Because he understands the impulse toward parallel vocabularies, he would rather read the sonnets than any other book, and he lives with the image, he says, of Dante's angel:

Ay, of all the artists living, loving,
None but would forego his proper dowry, --
Does he paint? he fain would write a poem, --
Does he write? he fain would paint a picture,
Put to proof art alien to the artist's (65-69)

Inspired by the other poet in his life, Browning wrote in his conclusion what he considered her kind of poetry. His reason for the experiment is familiar: Browning was constantly trying to see things from new angles and to speak about them with different vocabularies. His self-portraits in *Men and Women* are only two portraits in a gallery of many. The placement of the second self-portrait as the dedicatory conclusion to the book reconfirms

---

Although they hesitate to date poems without overwhelming external evidence, Jack and Inglesfield do indulge in a speculation that "Old Pictures" is one of the earlier written poems in *Men and Women* and even that it might have been written over a period of time (V. 293).

the autonomy of the other voices and the poet's conviction of the shiftiness in his own lyric authority.

Chapter 7

"What Form Is Best?"
1852-1856

The Brownings never stayed in one place very long. After returning from Paris and London in 1852, Elizabeth suffered a bout of illness, but in a few months, she was strong enough that they could abandon Casa Guidi temporarily for Rome in the winter of 1852-53. There, the Brownings cultivated a vivid and varied circle of English and American friends which included Alfred Tennyson's tongue-tied brother Frederick, the novelist Bulwer Lytton's son Robert Lytton, and the American sculptor Hiram Powers. Tennyson and the Americans were much taken with spiritualism, to Browning's dismay, and he was given to occasional outbursts of temper when Elizabeth strayed with them past the boundaries of good sense, a subject he later took up for "Mr. Sludge, 'The Medium,'" in his 1864 collection, *Dramatis Personae*. Life was busier than ever partly because more of the Brownings' time was now devoted to parenting and teaching Pen, an affectionate and lively child who entertained his parents with nightly tambourine concerts, but evidenced a short attention span for lessons. Although they renegotiated teaching duties from time to time, his father was usually responsible for teaching him music and art, his mother for reading and languages.

Despite their travels and their worries about the political troubles in Europe, the cheerful furor that surrounded their child, and the attention to fads, the Brownings' lives were still anchored securely in Casa Guidi, and their relative ease of existence enabled them to settle down for the sustained work which is considered by many readers to be the best they ever wrote.

During the summer months, when they customarily rented houses in the villages outside Florence to escape the heat, they explored the Tuscan countryside with the same enthusiasm they had for traveling around the country during their first three years away from England. Love for this landscape informs Barrett Browning's *Aurora Leigh* no less than the poems in *Men and Women*. In *Aurora Leigh*, the life narrative of the woman poet is framed at the beginning and end, with topographical precision, by descriptions of Florence and its surrounding hills. The last three books of the poem, especially, are fully situated in the places and customs of contemporary Italy. Italy has been both fatherland and motherland for Aurora: her Italian mother dies when she is an infant, and her English father, who dies after a few years of widowhood, is buried with his wife in Italy. Then, at thirteen, the child is pulled up from her roots and sent to England, where she lives in cold companionship with a maiden aunt. Although Florence becomes her home once more at the end of the story, Aurora discovers that living in her father's house would be too painful. From the villa she chooses for her home instead, she is able to take in the city and the surrounding landscape:

> I found a house at Florence on the hill
> Of Bellosguardo. 'Tis a tower which keeps
> A post of double-observation o'er
> That valley of Arno (holding as a hand
> The outspread city,) straight toward Fiesole
> And Mount Morello and the setting sun,
> The Vallombrosan mountains opposite,
> Which sunrise fills as full as crystal cups
> Turned red to the brim because their wine is red [. . .] .
>   From the outer wall
> Of the garden, drops the mystic floating grey
> Of olive trees (with interruptions green
> From maize and vine) until 'tis caught and torn
> Upon the abrupt black line of cypresses
> Which signs the way to Florence. Beautiful
> The city lies along the ample vale,
> Cathedral, tower and palace, piazza and street,
> The river trailing like a silver cord
> Through all [. . .] . (VII. 515-23, 529-38)X

Not based on a single location, Aurora's villa is evidently a synthesis of many places the Brownings visited during their years in Florence - the novelist Bulwer-Lytton's house in Bellosguardo, the view of Florence from Fiesole, the landscape around Siena, and probably Bagni di Lucca, the Brownings' favorite summer resort.

The reunification of their adopted country might have been the most immediate of the Brownings' political concerns in the 1850s, but it was not the only one. Like *Men and Women*, Barrett Browning's next big poem, after her burst of creativity in 1848-1850, was big enough to express and accommodate a range of themes, interests, and ideas. *Aurora Leigh* is not an autobiographical poem in the strictest sense, but it does reveal the pleasures and conflicts of Barrett Browning's life at this time. There is room in this poem - about ten thousand lines - for the discursive as well as the narrative, the political as well as the personal. Five years before the publication of *Aurora Leigh*, *Casa Guidi Windows* had been a deliberate experiment with the nature of authorial voice. Barrett Browning had been dismayed to learn that, in terms of reception, at least, the experiment failed: the public wanted neither that kind of honesty nor the political views of a woman poet. The feminist theme in *Casa Guidi Windows* - the problematic place of the woman poet - was thus reinforced by negative reactions to it, and, once more, the poet considered the difficulties imposed upon women of all classes by the separate sphere ideology. Although she had already explored this theme in shorter poems such as "The Runaway Slave at Pilgrim's Point" and her numerous ballads for the popular press, the length and form of *Aurora Leigh* would allow for the development of theory, practice, and illustration of what she had learned about the woman question. She was ready to try again to understand and explain the special insights of the woman poet and her necessary participation in the public sphere.

So, in the fall of 1852, after years of mulling it over, Elizabeth began her novel poem *Aurora Leigh* in earnest, devoting every morning to it while Robert worked on his own poems in another room. This would be her *magnum opus*, as she informed her brother George a year later:

> my poem is growing heavy on my hands -- & will be considerably longer than the 'Princess' after finished I mean it to be beyond all question my best work [. . .] .
> (*Letters of the Brownings to George Barrett* 200)

If *Sonnets from the Portuguese* was inspired by Browning and *Casa Guidi Windows* addressed to him, Barrett Browning was equally indebted to her husband for *Aurora Leigh*, not simply because her life with him is in some ways mirrored in the plot of her great work, but because his poetry and his presence in her life validated her urge for large-scale experimentation and her poetic of involvement with contemporary life. As Mermin points out in *Godiva's Ride*, Barrett Browning also published works that openly challenged social and political anthropocentricism

> when she was respectably married, living abroad, and could afford not to worry about annoying her male relatives or affronting English decorum. As a wife and mother she would not be accused of publishing erotic daydreams or advertising for a lover. Marriage and maternity gave her both the freedom and the confidence to use the skill she had acquired through long years of literary

apprenticeship. And her life, with its princess-like seclusion, long close brush with death, and romantic elopement from paternal tyranny, was a revision of romance that could be generalized to good purpose [. . .] ." (67)

In short, writes Mermin, "No other poet of the century had such experience, such freedom, or such vision" (67).

Quite simply, *Aurora Leigh* could not have been written without Robert Browning. The generative power of Browning's presence in Elizabeth Barrett's life can be felt throughout the courtship correspondence, in which *Aurora Leigh* began to take shape fully a decade before it was completed. That early correspondence suggests that Browning's presence in her literary life was more than simply supportive or enabling - for both of them, their life together was a process of mutual teaching, the results of which become most pronounced in *Men and Women, Aurora Leigh* and, as we shall see, the poetry Browning wrote during the 1860s and early 1870s. In Vygotsky's terms, each pulled the other forward into greater scholarly and creative complexity. As I have suggested before, this action and reaction indicates both rivalry and sharing. Throughout the letters, as the two poets discussed the details of Browning's work and its ability to communicate to contemporary readers, a less overt dialogue about Elizabeth Barrett's work was taking place, a quiet conversation about Barrett's vexed relationship with male literary tradition and about her need to challenge and change received literary forms. (Her interest in translation is a psychologically complicated example of Barrett Browning's deep interest in learning about, transmitting, and transforming tradition.)

Barrett's often quoted letter of 27 February 1845, written to Browning even before they met, combines commentary on his plays with an apology for her own, supposedly botched translation of the *Prometheus*, a short narrative of her own literary life, and irreverently expressed plans for future work.[1] The letter suggestively juxtaposes Barrett's interest in tradition with her lifelong interest in building out of tradition, as she jumps from Greek drama to the contemporary novel:

And then, I have in my head to associate with the version, . . . a monodram of my own -- not a long poem,. but a monologue of Aeschylus as he sate a blind

---

[1] Alice Meynell, one of Barrett Browning's most sympathetic early editors, disagreed about the value of the 1833 translation and chose it over the 1845 translations as the copy text for her edition of *Prometheus Bound and Other Poems* (1896).

exile on the flats of Sicily and recounted the past to his own soul, just before the eagle cracked his great massy skull with a stone.[2]

But my chief <u>intention</u> just now is the writing of a sort of novel-poem -- a poem as completely modern as "Geraldine's Courtship," running into the midst of our conventions, & rushing into drawingrooms & the like "where angels fear to tread"; -- & so, meeting face to face & without mask, the Humanity of the age, & speaking the truth as I conceive of it, out plainly. That is my intention. It is not mature enough yet to be called a plan. I am waiting for a story -- & I wont take one, because I want to make one -- & I like to make my own stories, because then I can take liberties with them in the treatment. (10.102-03)

Browning's next two letters comment richly on the *Prometheus* and Barrett's translation of it, with which he was already familiar. On March 11, he enthusiastically endorses her "intention" for the novel poem and appears to understand it as part of a poetic project which resembled his own:

The Poem you propose to make, for the times, -- the fearless fresh living work, you describe, -- is the <u>only</u> Poem to be undertaken now by you or anyone that <u>is</u> a Poet at all, -- the only reality, only effective piece of service to be rendered God and man -- it is what I have all my life been intending to do, and now shall be much, much nearer doing, since you will be along with me. And you <u>can</u> do it, I know -- and am sure -- so sure, that I could find in my heart to be jealous of your stopping in the way even to translate the Prometheus [. . .] . (10.118-19)

A few months later, in August, Barrett writes to Browning that she is hard at work on the *Prometheus* and the sonnets, about which she is vague, but she notes that her current project is "not a part of the romance-poem which is to be written someday if I live for it" and which has evidently been the subject of conversations in between letters (11.19). Six months later, in January, 1846, Barrett notes with interest Tennyson's new project in progress, *The Princess*, about which her lawyer brother has reported to her, a

new poem -- he has finished the second book of it -- and it is in blank verse & a fairy tale, & called the University, the university-members being all females. If George has not diluted the scheme of it with some law from the Inner Temple, I

---

[2] The poem about Aeschylus is "Aeschylus' Soliloquy," which has been wrongly attributed to Browning because it is a monologue and because the fair copy made in his hand is the only surviving manuscript in the Browning papers. (See Reynolds & Rosenbaum.)

don't know what to think -- it makes me open my eyes. Now is'nt the world too old & fond of steam, for blankverse poems, in ever so many books, to be written on the fairies? (12.29) .

Browning agreed in his next letter. Tennyson was ill at the time, and Browning snidely conflates Tennyson's physical condition with the condition of the new work:

> I am sorry to hear of poor Tennyson's condition -- the projected book, title, scheme, all of it, -- that is astounding: -- and fairies! -- if Thropès [Thorpès] and barnes, sheep-pens and dairies -- this maketh that there ben no fairies" -- locomotives, and the broad or narrow gauge must keep the very ghosts of them away [. . .] . (12.36)

Clearly, he felt Elizabeth's conception was superior. Indeed, when it was finished, *Aurora Leigh* became a logical culmination of trends in his own poetry as well has hers. In 1855 and 1856, the themes of the two poets' works resonated more strongly than ever with each other, and, for the first time, Barrett Browning confidently engaged in the "genre violations" which Browning had continually risked since the publication of *Sordello* in 1835.[3] Even as early as *Essay on Mind*, she had hinted at the need for this kind of experimentation, but never before had she so thoroughly put into practice her belief that generic boundaries had to be challenged and broken.

The Princess was first published in 1847, and by 1853, the poem had gone into its third edition, an expanded version which now included the lovely lyrics for which the poem has been chiefly remembered. But Barrett Browning eschewed the fantastic elements of Tennyson's work in favor of domestic realism, the dominant trend of most fiction written by women in her day.[4] Thus, the plot of Barrett Browning's poem also demands comparison with plots of novels by Charlotte Brontë, George Sand, Mme. de Staël, and the new French realists both Brownings were reading in the 1850s - Balzac, Sue, and Flaubert.[5] Perhaps because *Aurora Leigh* emerges

---

[3] Maryellen Bieder uses the term "genre violations" in her discussion of the late nineteenth-century Spanish novelist Concepción Gimeno de Flaquer, whose work was an attempt (unsuccessful in Bieder's opinion) to blend women's concerns with literary realism.

[4] Vineta Colby narrates the development of domestic realism by women writers in *Yesterday's Women: Domestic Realism in the English Novel*.

[5] In *The Brownings and France*, Roy E. Gridley gives a full account of the Brownings' interest in and extensive knowledge of French literature.

from the matrix of domestic fiction, which she had read avidly since girlhood, Barrett Browning's innovative alterations of the conventional long narrative poem, as Stone argues, are more "radical" and "consistent" than Tennyson's ("Genre Subversion and Gender Inversion" 104). In contrast to that of Tennyson, Barrett Browning's story takes place across a variety of settings (not a university) and includes episodes of rape, prostitution, seamstress sweatshops, unwed mothers, and Grub Street, within an "ironically self-mocking" form (Stone 120).

Within the parameters of the poem, not to mention her statements outside it, the poet who began her career as a published poet with a miniature epic about the Greeks now claims to be writing both a novel and an epic. And she argues in the theoretical sections of her book that, as the stuff of epic changes with history, so must the forms in which epics are written. *Aurora Leigh* resonates with the novel as it is described by Bakhtin - a polyphonic work of many layers, voices, and genres. Barrett Browning's text contains a weave of (fictional) autobiographical narrative, reconstructed from a diary; interpolated letters; the stories (both *verbatim* and summarized) of secondary characters' lives; lyrical passages such as Aurora's description of her home in the hills; and discursive passages in which the hero comments on society or develops a literary theory reflecting her own life and art.

Aurora Leigh catches the spirit of the novel as well as the form, more surely than anything Barrett Browning had ever written before. The mix of genres Bakhtin describes as an essential feature of the novel results in "an indeterminacy, a certain semantic openendedness, a living contact with still-evolving contemporary reality" ("Epic and Novel" 7). The description applies as well to *Aurora Leigh* as to *David Copperfield* or *Crime and Punishment*. If the traditional epic hero is, in Bakhtin's words, "fully finished" (34), Barrett Browning's hero is characterized by "unrealized potential," and responsive to "unrealized demands" (37) - as Bakhtin said of the hero of the modern novel. If the plot of the epic is part of a completely known series of past events, the plot of the novel "speculates on the unknown" and projects into the future (32); so does *Aurora Leigh*. Both the author and the reader of the epic are "absolutely fixed into unfreedom" (17), according to Bakhtin, because the epic concerns "the absolute past" (15). The novel, however, is participatory: both reader and writer enter into the world of the novel, and the novelist herself can claim only the ambivalent authority of Socrates: "I am wiser than everyone, because I know that I know nothing" (24). In *Aurora Leigh*, Aurora lays open her own creative and emotional processes and, like many of Browning's monologists, continually invites the reader to deconstruct her literal statements, as she herself is conscious of doing throughout the narrative. By this strategy, in fact, she trajects her own story beyond the boundaries of epic, even while epic provides her frame of reference.[6] Novels are not necessarily prose: and Barrett Browning's rough versification recalls, not the stylized language of epic or even the authoritarian sonorities of neoclassical blank verse, but the conversational blank verse of Shakespearean drama (one of many allusive webs running through the poem). It is through the jagged scansion, the lacunae, the self-contradictions that we are enabled to understand the hero better than she understands herself.

Work on the poem picked up speed in 1854. From spring until fall of 1855, however, progress was slow. The Brownings were preparing for another journey to Paris, and thence to London. Once *Men and Women* had been delivered to the publisher, the proofs of Browning's collection had to be read and returned. Barrett Browning's letters from Paris to friends reveal frustration at the pace of her own project. In March, before leaving Casa Guidi, she reported to Eliza Ogilvy that she had "between five & six thousand lines *in blots* . . not one copied out. . & I am not nearly at an end of the composition even" (qtd. Reynolds, *Aurora Leigh* [1992] 86). In May, she wrote to Anne Braun that:

> We go to England in a week or two or three and we take between us some sixteen thousand lines, eight on one side, eight on the other, which ought to be ready for publication. I have not finished my seventh thousand yet; Robert is at his mark. (qtd. Reynolds, *Aurora Leigh* [1992] 86)

Back in Paris in the fall, they found themselves booked into unsatisfactory rooms, and the manuscript of *Aurora Leigh*, when finally dug out for renewed work, was disorganized.

Barrett Browning was pleased at the prospect that Browning might finally receive the praise he deserved, but vexed that publication of his work slowed her progress on *Aurora Leigh*. Letters to friends at this point reveal even greater frustration. In a letter to Jameson written in January, 1856, Barrett Browning still complained of a manuscript so "dishevelled

---

[6] Graham writes that, during the Victorian period, "Epic remains as the substantial shadow of a genre, argued with but rarely used" (3); for Graham, *Aurora Leigh* and *The Ring and the Book* are exemplary.

[. . .] it seemed scarcely possible to draw a poem out of it all. I was desperate. ." (*Aurora Leigh* 1996, 331).[7]

Indeed, the first draft - all but the last four hundred lines of the last book - is written in a thick blank book, four and a half by seven inches, with marbled covers, a gift from her sister.[8] The manuscript fills the whole book, even the space around the inscription: "E. B. B. with Arabel's love." Typically, Barrett's tiny handwriting begins, with the first line on every page, to slope downward, so that, by the time she reaches the bottom of the page, the right-hand margins become increasingly crowded; to compensate for the crowding, lines near the bottom sometimes wander back up the right-hand margin. Interlined revisions are almost microscopic, and it is sometimes difficult to place them in the poem. Revisions of revisions are almost impossible to read because they are even tinier. Nearly every page is obscured by writeovers and ink blots. Browning had read the first six books by March 1856 and read the rest soon thereafter. (His involvement at this point no doubt compensated for the time Barrett Browning had invested in seeing *Men and Women* through the press!) Inside the marbled covers is such a desperate tangle that Robert must have needed several prompts per page. Even getting through this manuscript would have required a fully collaborative effort. If we had no more information about the Brownings' working relationship than the clues left in the first draft of *Aurora Leigh*, we would have to conclude that it involved deep and constant dialogue. Barrett Browning in fact reports in her letters that Robert read the poem in installments. "He keeps saying -- 'Out and out superior to anything you have done!'" (*Aurora Leigh* 1996, 330).

But there is also evidence throughout the finished poem that it results from a marriage of true minds. Barrett Browning's attention to her husband's work may have interfered for a time with her own poem, but *Men and Women* also validated and reinforced its central premise, that the best work comes from sharing, dialogue, and resistance to closure. Conceived even before she began to correspond with Browning, and begun in earnest two years after the publication of *Casa Guidi Windows*, *Aurora Leigh* pushes the experiment of *Casa Guidi Windows* one step further: whereas the earlier poem problematizes and contextualizes the poetic subject in order to claim artistic authority for the woman poet, *Aurora Leigh* novelizes the poetic subject while it analyzes contemporary poetic discourse. In this novel poem, she works out another hybrid form which

---

[7] The letters to Jameson, Ogilvy, and Braun appear in a selection of letters which Reynolds includes in her Norton Critical Edition of *Aurora Leigh* (1996). This selection is essential reading.

[8] The first draft of *Aurora Leigh* is in the Wellesley collection.

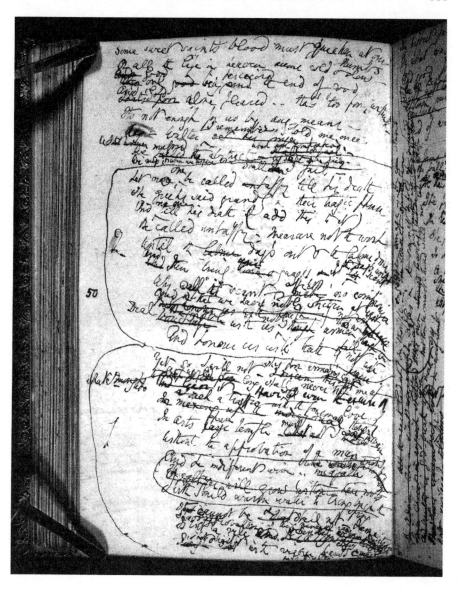

3 *Aurora Leigh*, Book V, ll. 51-67, first draft.
Courtesy of Wellesley College Library

expresses a dramatic indeterminacy similar to Browning's at his most subtle and complex. *Aurora Leigh* is a kind of dramatic monologue, consisting of nine books and over ten thousand lines, and including several outside voices in ironic suspension. Like so many of Browning's characters, Aurora and Romney Leigh are works in progress.

In March, about the time Browning was finishing his collection, Barrett Browning reported to her cousin John Kenyon (to whom she later dedicated *Aurora Leigh*) that she had "Between five & six thousand lines written, & still more to write -- Blank verse --. Why not? -- An autobiography of a poetess -- (not me) [. . .]." (*Aurora Leigh* 1996, 330).[9] Browning's collection portrays individuals, "my fifty men and women," in all their complexity at critical moments in their lives. If *Men and Women* is a picture gallery, *Aurora Leigh* is a portrait, not a self-portrait of the author, but the self-portrait of a fictional "poetess" whose life in some ways parallels Barrett Browning's. At the beginning of her narrative, Aurora proposes to write about herself, for her "better self,"

> As when you paint your portrait for a friend,
> Who keeps your portrait in a drawer and looks at it
> Long after he has ceased to love you, just
> To hold together what he was and is. (1.4-88)

Yet Aurora Leigh also admits the difficulty of her project:

> Let who says
> "The soul's a clean white paper," rather say
> A palimpsest [. . .]". (I.824-26)

The points of contact between poetry and portraiture are reinforced in several ways, beginning with the portrait of Aurora's Italian mother, painted after her death, an image of loss which dominates Aurora's earliest memories.

---

[9] The feminist scholarship which has returned *Aurora Leigh* to its place within the canon has, on the whole, stressed the poem's feminist content and its continuity with a female literary tradition. That is to be expected: *Aurora Leigh* has attracted feminist scholars because it speaks directly to us: like Barrett Browning and her poet hero, professional women still suffer from emotional binds and double standards in their public and private lives. Understandably, readings of the poem which foreground gender issues have also stressed similarities between the poet's hero and herself, though the relationship between Barrett Browning's life and that of her character is not simple or straightforward.

The most sustained references to painting are in Aurora's exchanges with the painter Vincent Carrington. This friendship consists of conversations and letters about the slippery relationship between the meanings of images and the material from which they are created. Carrington the painter is a foil for Aurora Leigh the poet: her narrative self-portrait is foregrounded against his portraits of mythical subjects (for example, Danae, about to be raped by Jupiter) and against Carrington's spirited discussions with his fiancée Kate Ward about how she is to be painted (Kate wins the contest, so he paints her holding Aurora Leigh's latest book rather than his palate and brushes). Each of Carrington's paintings demands interpretive choices, and sometimes he can make these choices only by producing two different images of the same subject.

Similarly, as Aurora attempts to portray herself on paper, images of the self continually coincide, diverge, and enter into new relationships in a way reminiscent of Browning's practice. The "struggle to achieve a determinate and stable image of the hero," according to Bakhtin in his meditation about the relationship between author and character, "is to a considerable extent [the author's] struggle with himself" (*Author and Hero* 6). To create the image of the woman poet in a novel poem, Barrett Browning had to break out of the boundaries within which she had previously worked. In the Brownings' own critical language, *Aurora Leigh* had to be more objective and less subjective than her previous poetry. This idea would have been especially fresh in her mind then - when her work on *Aurora Leigh* began in earnest, Browning had just finished revisiting the same theme in the Shelley essay. As a novelist, she had to "exert a double vision" (V. 184), to develop the novelistic potential which had always informed but never dominated her work. Bakhtin's theory of the dialogic relationship between author and character speaks to Barrett Browning's practice in *Aurora Leigh*. The author, Bakhtin writes, struggles to allow the hero a separate and distinct identity:

> The hero [. . .] may coincide <u>as a human being</u> with the author <u>as a human being</u>, and that, in fact, is what occurs most of the time. But the hero of a work can never coincide with the author -- the <u>creator</u> of that work, for otherwise we would not get a work of art at all. If the author's reaction merges with the reaction of the hero [. . .] the author begins to act and cognize together with the hero, but loses the artistic, consummating vision of the hero. (*Author and Hero* 222)

However much Aurora Leigh may coincide with Elizabeth Barrett Browning "as a human being," Barrett Browning tells Kenyon, she is "not me." However much Aurora is not Barrett Browning however, her emotional and artistic evolution could only have been imagined by someone who had evolved in a similar way.

The first person narrative of *Aurora Leigh* is crisscrossed by inner turmoil and conflict, broken chronological threads, patches of extra-literary genres, embedded narratives from other lives - all of which effect aesthetic distance between author and hero, and between the writer hero and her hero. Furthermore, Aurora's continual questioning of her own narrative authority scatters the unitary focus to which Bakhtin claims poetry aspires (*Discourse in the Novel*, 286 *et pass.*). The generic variegation of *Aurora Leigh* prompts Cora Kaplan to call it a collage or quilt (5) and Stone to label it a "novelized epic" ("Genre Subversion and Gender Inversion" 104).[10] Whether Aurora is questioning her responses to the "fallen woman" Marion Erle, her misreading of her earnest cousin Romney Leigh, or her compromises with the literary marketplace, she continually sacrifices narrative authority for authenticity. Despite the epic scope and unifying blank verse, at every level - narrative structure, plot, language - the idea of a unitary consciousness and the authority of the author is undermined. Browning had experimented from the beginning with decentering narrative - now Barrett Browning followed his lead.

One way Barrett Browning undermines the notion of authorial authority is by demystifying the process of writing itself. "I who have written much in prose and verse/ For other's uses, will write now for mine" (I.2-3), Aurora Leigh begins. Closure and elegance are irrelevant. Later she calls her story a "broken tale" (III.156). Its twisted time frame bears witness to

---

[10] Beverly Taylor contrasts Tennyson's "tact" in speaking about female sexuality ("'School-Miss Alfred' and 'Materfamilias'" 7) with Barrett Browning's daring; in fact, readers disapproved of both approaches to the subject. Stone compares *Aurora Leigh* to Tennyson's *The Princess*, and her analysis of generic features of both works includes a detailed analysis of Barrett Browning sources-- including Wordsworth's *The Prelude* and a number of eighteenth- and nineteenth-century novels by women, particularly *Bildungsromane* ("Genre Subversion and Gender Inversion"). Forster's biography also suggests Barrett Browning's indebtedness to other Romantic and Victorian literary models by including an account of her reading. Mark Weinstein points to the similarities in critical treatment of Barrett Browning's *Aurora Leigh*, Browning's *Men and Women*, and Tennyson's *Maud*, also published in 1855: all were branded as "Spasmodics" by the influential critic W. E. Aytoun, despite the fact that the spasmodic fad was passé by the mid 1850s. The Spasmodics (Joanna Baillie, Sidney Dobell, Alexander Smith) did challenge "classical conceptions of unity and coherence" and value overt expressions of passion, but, unlike the Spasmodics, Tennyson and the Brownings labored more consciously to revise traditional literary forms (*The Spasmodic Controversy* 172).

her claims of authenticity. In fact, the disorder is an illusion: as Reynolds points out, the shape of the plot is a palindrome (*Aurora Leigh* 50). Furthermore, the timing of the composition is an essential part of the scene of writing.[11] If the book is epic in length, it also takes over from epic the convention of the broken narrative; the tectonic plates of the story collide and pile up, and the important episodes are distributed against the structure of the poem's division into books. It is typical of the poem's structure that the story of Marion's childhood crosses Books III and IV; Book V contains both the most theoretical section of the poem and the most banal episode; and Romney's tale of failure and betrayal stretches across Books VIII and IX. Although Aurora's own narrative is presented in a rough chronological order which partially conceals the temporal discrepancies, its composition, we discover in the process of reading, stretches out over at least three years of her life.

Although a plot summary certainly cannot convey the novelistic spirit of the book, it can suggest the parallels between life and writing, books and the world, which Aurora discovers in maturity.

The first two books narrate Aurora's childhood in Italy, the loss of her parents, the rigid English education she received from her puritanical aunt, the difficult relationship with her cousin Romney Leigh, and her early career. When she writes these two books, she is twenty-seven. In later years, when Aurora takes her story from its drawer, Books I and II will remind her of who she was as a child and how she came to be a poet, in spite of all the forces around her which were hostile to this vocation. She will remember her painful separation from Romney before seizing her independence at the age of twenty and earning her way in London as a popular poet.

Book III records the first seven years in London, during which she makes a lonely passage into adulthood and the literary-artistic London establishment. Aurora's moral and artistic isolation are conveyed through numerous scraps of reviews which, whether hostile or friendly, always misrepresent her work and bracket it as the work of a woman, not a poet. The events Aurora records in Books III and IV lie within her past: she believes she has come to terms with them, and she thinks she understands their influence on her subsequent life. Written later than Books I and II (exactly how much later is unclear), they chronicle Aurora's introduction to Romney's working-class fiancée Marian Earle. They tell of Marian's

---

[11] In her Critical Introduction to the 1992 edition (28-30), Reynolds defends Barrett Browning's narrative experimentation against a critical tradition which has attributed the narrative and temporal inconsistences of *Aurora Leigh* to carelessness (68n). Forster's analysis here is essential reading.

terrible childhood and the disastrous engagement between Marian and Romney. The cruelty and privation Marian has suffered contrast with the privileged existence of the Leighs, but Marion's loneliness and her orphaned state are perfectly parallel to theirs.

Like Tennyson's Ulysses, Aurora is part of all the people she meets, especially the people she loves, so Marian's narrative is appropriately embedded in Aurora's story. Like the first two books, Books III and IV are narrated from a perspective somewhat removed from the action by the passage of time, but Aurora's language begins to betray how difficult it is to maintain psychic distance; as she writes, memories of these events are hotter and less emotionally integrated than her earlier memories, her language less controlled. If she is temporarily close to the events she narrates, she is much closer to a self awareness.

> Why, what a pettish thing I grow [. . .]
>   a mere flaccid nerve,
> A kerchief left out all night in the rain,

she remarks after complaining about her maid's "buzzing in the room" while she tries to write (III. 36-38, 28). More significantly, if she refuses to admit her love for Romney, she does admit to loneliness and a sense of incompleteness.

After Marian abandons Romney at the altar and Romney immerses himself without restraint into Fourierism, Aurora waits eighteen months before summoning the resources to continue her story in Book V. In the interval, she has fully realized that her place in the world of letters will always be undermined by the conventionalities expected by her reading public. expects. At this point, Aurora turns to a lengthy discourse on literary theory. Literary theory is always part of her equipment for living; according to Susan Walsh, "From her mid-twenties onward, Aurora's poetic aims do not essentially change. We are to believe her about her art" (181). But focusing her attention on poetics at this moment, when she can no longer accept her social or professional surroundings, also seems to provide an interval of objectivity as Aurora tries to make sense of her conflicting emotions. The theory in Book V centers the palindrome shape of the whole. Book V also ends with the most conventionally novelistic scene in *Aurora Leigh* - a party scene which demonstrates Aurora's theory that the heat of real life in the nineteenth century is generated in the drawing room. The trivial and spiteful conversations among the guests remind Aurora that she and her poetry are commodities exchanged among the useless classes. In reaction, she sells the books her father left her and spends the money on passage to Italy, perhaps to recapture a golden age of artistic purity and spiritual independence.

Aurora begins writing Book VI some weeks (or months) later in Paris, where she has paused on her way to Tuscany. In Paris, she discovers Marian Earle; she hears about Lady Waldemar's interference with Marian's engagement and Marian's subsequent abduction and rape, a story continued in Book VII. Book VI also contains Carrington's newsy letter about Romney's purported marriage to Lady Waldemar, who has long wanted Romney for herself. After reading the letter from Carrington, Aurora sends an accusing letter to Lady Waldemar, whom she holds responsible for all the recent tragic events in Marian's life. Book VII ends with Aurora, Marian, and her child peacefully settled in a Tuscan villa. By this time, Aurora Leigh is thirty. She is less lonely than during her London years, but:

> Ten layers of birthdays on a woman's head
> Are apt to fossilize her girlish mirth
> Though ne'er so merry". (VIII 532-34)

The last two books, the final installment of her autobiography, narrate only the conversation of one evening, but this conversation calls up intensely mixed emotions and, finally, resolves the conflicts which have followed Aurora and Romney Leigh throughout their adult lives. One starlit evening, Romney Leigh appears on Aurora's terrace, tells the story of his failed experiments in social engineering and his rejection of Lady Waldemar, and offers to honor his commitment to Marian Earle. When Marian releases him from his sense of obligation, he declares his love for Aurora Leigh, his admiration for her poetry, and his desire to support her in that work. The account of this evening is written some time later, when Aurora is willing to assess its significance, but the weight and momentum of the entire narrative carry the story beyond the ending. Since Aurora is assembling the narrative after the events, we know that she does continue to write. She and Romney have admitted mutual dependence and learned mutual support.

As Aurora nears the end of her narrative, the distance between the events and their telling diminishes. The result is a double pattern of increasing objectivity about the past and increasing consciousness of subjective complexity. Aurora is more mature and assured as a writer when she composes the last installment, but she has also learned to distrust monologic discourse, even her own, and to be flexible, especially as she tries to match theory and practice. In Book VII, Aurora returns to theoretical considerations. In reaction to the ossified conventions of early Renaissance painting:

Make them forget there's such a thing as flesh.
Your business is to paint the souls of men --

Browning's Fra Lippo Lippi says that:

If you get simple beauty and nought else,
You get about the best thing God invents [. . .] .
        This world's no blot for us,
Nor blank; it means intensely, and means good:
To find its meaning is my meat and drink. (182-83, 217-18, 313-15)

Like Brother Lippo, Aurora now considers the religious significance of the poetic theory she has worked out in Book V:[12]

            Without the spiritual, observe,
The natural's impossible, -- no form,
No motion: without sensuous, spiritual
Is inappreciable, -- no beauty or power [. . .] .
But man, the two-fold creature, apprehends
The two-fold manner, in and outwardly,
And nothing in the world comes single to him,
A mere itself -- cup, column, or candlestick,
All patterns of what shall be in the Mount [. . .] .
            "There's nothing great
Nor small," has said a poet of our day,[13]
Whose voice will ring beyond the curfew of eve [. . .] .
            Art's the witness of what Is
Behind this show". (VII 773-76, 802-05, 834-35)

The erratic textual history of Aurora's own narrative - revealed in fits and starts, in asides and subordinate clauses - reinforces the difficult nature of her task.

Even more obviously dialogic than Aurora's theory is the shifting narrative center. A novel of education such as *Aurora Leigh* necessarily shows the main character in conflict with other people who teach lessons. *Jane Eyre*, to which Barrett Browning's poem is often compared, offers an interesting parallel - and an interesting contrast. If both are

---

[12] George M. Ridenour traces similarities between Fra Lippo Lippi's aesthetic theory and Aurora Leigh's -- and notes as well a continuation of the mutual influence between the Brownings in the similarities between Marion Erle and Pompilia in *The Ring and the Book* ("Robert Browning and *Aurora Leigh*").

[13] The "poet of our day" is Robert Browning, the allusion to the Introduction of *Pippa Passes*.

Bildungsromane, narrating the processes through which a woman comes to understand both autonomy and relationship, the attitudes of the heroines are radically different. Jane does not admit doubt or error: Aurora, on the other hand, is constantly beside herself, continually interrogating herself about how she might have felt, thought, acted differently - and, by the end of the book, she is indeed able to take in her younger, immature selves and to evolve as an artist and a human being. Unlike Jane Eyre, she abdicates control of the narrative in other ways as well - through inserted letters and monologues by other speakers - Marion Erle; Marion's rival for Romney's love, Lady Waldemar; and finally Romney, whose narrative fills most of Book IX. Distributing the narrator's control over her life story into a number of different "semantic centers" is Barrett Browning's method for showing how much Aurora needs to change, and how much she does change (Bakhtin, *Problems of Dostoevsky's Poetics* 204). Aurora's most important lesson is the human propensity to misconstrue the actions and motives of others, and the ease with which we violate others' words.

Despite her efforts to understand, Aurora continually misunderstands, but by interpolating other voices, she partly compensates and atones for her errors.

In Marian's two stories, the first in Books III and IV and the second in Books VI and VII, Aurora gives up narrative control for the longest periods of time. She may ridicule Romney's life "by diagrams" and the "formal universals" (III. 744, 747) with which he codifies compassion, but Aurora is also limited. From her childhood, Aurora has been headstrong in her passions and headlong in her judgments, but curiosity and compassion sometimes compensate.

If she first seeks out Marian Earle in a London slum to show that she is above quarreling with her cousin about an inappropriate marriage, Aurora stays to listen because she is interested in the story, sympathetic with Marian, and proud of her own ability to rise (sometimes) above the prejudices of class. Unable to imitate Marian's language, Aurora tries to replicate the story of Marian's harsh childhood in a style which does not betray it,

> with fuller utterance,
> As coloured and confirmed in aftertimes
> By others and herself. (III. 828-39)

As Aurora writes down Marian's terrible account of privation, parental cruelty and alcoholism, illness, and rescue, she says:

> I tell her story and grow passionate.
> She, Marian, did not tell it so, but used

Meek words that made no wonder of herself
For being so sad a creature. (III. 847-59)

When Aurora hears the story, she is curious and benign rather than
otherwise, but she is not morally or emotionally engaged. In fact, although
she is sympathetic to Marian's story, she is not really touched by it until
later, when she writes it down. From the perspective of greater sadness and
wisdom, she realizes,

> I have been wrong, I have been wrong [. . .] .
> I had not been ungenerous on the whole,
> Nor yet untender; so enough. I felt
> Tired, overworked; this marriage somewhat jarred;
> Or, if it did not, all the bridal noise. . .
> Was scarce my business: let them order it [. . .] . (IV. 439, 456-59, 463)[14]

When she is finally ready to narrate Marian's experience, Aurora
is prepared to engage dialogically with Marian as a human being and as
a character. Bakhtin's description of the way Dostoevsky handles point
of view applies to the way Aurora Leigh handles Marian's: Aurora
is "guided by the principle: never use for objectifying or finalizing
another's consciousness anything that might be inaccessible to that
consciousness, that might lie outside its field of vision" (278). Aurora's
ability to observe this principle indicates her growing maturity as an artist
and as a woman.

But she still has much to learn. In Book VI, Aurora glimpses Marian
with her child in a Paris street, seeks until she finds Marian again in the
flower market, follows her home, and demands an explanation for this
appearance of sin. This time, Aurora is limited not by her imperfect control
of language or even her ability to extend herself emotionally, but by
conscious and unconscious moral prejudices. A change in narrative method
- more immediate and less retrospective - reveals that curiosity and

---

[14] Many critics have felt the need to blame or justify Barrett Browning's class
prejudices, especially as they surface in her Book III description of the slum
dwellers and her description of the crowd in Book IV. See, for instance, Caplan's
introduction to the 1978 edition of *Aurora Leigh* and David's *Intellectual Women
and Victorian Patriarchy*. Barrett Browning certainly had these prejudices, but to
argue that they are unconscious and unmitigated is to overlook the implications of
the book's narrative construction and its shifting narrative center. (It is also
interesting to note that Barrett Browning's crude descriptions in these scenes
resemble Browning's similar descriptions in "Christmas-Eve" so closely that lines
from the two poems could be switched without tearing the fabric of either text.)

compassion do not compensate until Aurora has exposed her rigid moral code to Marian and to herself: instead of writing retrospectively about the interval in Paris, she writes in the present as she experiences, revealing a series of wrong judgements. The story has the immediacy of a series of journal entries, revealing raw emotions rather than passions controlled and understood. First, Aurora assumes that the child with Marian is Marian's and that it is illegitimate. Although both assumptions turn out to be true, she has no basis for them. Her inadequate and judgmental logical process is revealed when she catches sight of Marion in a crowded Paris street, carrying her baby:

> Who finds an emerald ring
> On a beggar's middle finger and requires
> More testimony to convict a thief? (VI. 350-52)

After agonizing about telling Romney of her discovery, she realizes,

> I go too fast [. . .] in haste to take
> The first stir in the arras for a rat [. . .]. (VI. 366-68)

But at first she questions only the assumption that the child is Marian's, not her assumption that, if Marian's, the child would be a sign of sin. Eventually, Aurora finds Marian again, and when she sees the sleeping child in Marian's attic, she is speechless, "For, oh, that it should take such innocence/ To prove just guilt" (VI. 582-83). Aurora demands an explanation, challenging each detail silently or aloud, for she now assumes that Marian has been seduced - that she is guilty of weakmindedness, at best. Several times during Marian's account (seven hundred lines), Aurora accuses her aloud of "stealing" her child - emphasizing the baby's illegitimacy - and only when she hears the story of Marian's betrayal, rape, destitution, and loneliness in harrowing detail does she give up her assumptions about Marian's guilt.

Once again, however, Aurora errs, this time in her beliefs about Lady Waldemar: unlike Marion herself, Aurora assumes that Lady Waldemar's interference before the wedding signals responsibility for all that Marion has suffered, not just the breakup of her engagement. And then, Aurora's comment about the Parisian employer who dismissed Marian when her pregnancy became obvious (an adulteress herself, whose days are spent before her mirror) applies to Aurora's own behavior as well: "The devil's most devilish when respectable" (VII. 105).[15] The error born out of Aurora's unexamined respectability is greater in this second encounter with Marian, and it has to be corrected, not by an image of Marian Earle's language (Aurora's deliberate paraphrase of her first story), but by a transcription of Marian's language. Marian's second account is (except for Aurora's rare interjections) a dramatic monologue enclosed within Aurora's autobiography.[16] "You feel?/ You understand?" asks Marian, "no, do not look at me,/ But understand . . .

> We wretches cannot tell out all our wrong
> Without offense to decent happy folk.
> I know that we must scrupulously hint
> With half-words, delicate reserves, the thing
> Which no one scrupled we should feel in full. (VI. 1203-05, 1220-24).

The narrative structure of Book VI allows Marian's voice more autonomy in order to compensate for Aurora's judgmental, totalizing discourse.

Aurora's relationship with Lady Waldemar shows another dimension of Aurora's capacity for error. Lady Waldemar remains an unredeemed villain at the end of the book, but even Lady Waldemar - wealthy, glittering, amoral, and verbally crude - can be misunderstood. Her words, like Marian's stories, are embedded in Aurora's text - first in a long speech she delivers in person, in Aurora's London garret, and then in a letter at the end of the story. In Book III, Aurora describes Lady Waldemar's attempt to enlist her aid against Romney's marriage. The lady's veiled insults and patronizing flattery are ill-calculated, but, like so many of Robert Browning's monologists, she cannot help revealing herself more than she wishes. Although she may not be evil through and through, she has been single-minded in pursuit of Romney: "you eat of love," she says to Aurora,

> And do as vile a thing as if you ate
> Of garlic -- which, whatever else you eat,
> Tastes uniformly acrid, till your peach
> Reminds you of your onion. Am I coarse?
> Well, love's coarse, nature's coarse -- ah, there's the rub! (III. 450-55)

---

[15] This line about putative respectability resonates with Browning's scepticism of surface social propriety in the 1855 dramatic monologue "Respectability".

[16] Mermin points out that Barrett Browning, like other nineteenth-century women poets, "often use[s] dramatic monologues to allow female speakers to express passion, rage, and rebellion against social constraints" ("'The fruitful feud of hers and his'" 151), and it has been pointed out by Mermin and Knoefplmacher that Browning, too, explored female subjectivity through the same poetic form.

Marian's second story reveals Lady Waldemar's part in the dissolution of her engagement. Although Marian herself is unaware of Lady Waldemar's unscrupulous motives, Aurora hears enough details to become convinced, not only that Lady Waldemar persuaded Marian to leave England, but that Lady Waldemar also paid to have her abducted and raped. Again, Aurora has made too great a logical leap. Book IX opens with Lady Waldemar's scathing self-defense, in the letter for Aurora which Romney has just delivered: Marian, claims Lady Waldemar, was:

> Consigned to one I trusted, my own maid
> Who once had lived full five months in my house,
> (Dressed hair superbly) with a lavish purse
> To carry to Australia where she had left
> A husband, said she. If the creature lied,
> The mission failed, we all do fail and lie
> More or less -- and I'm sorry [. . .] .

"I had sooner cut/ My hand off," she adds, "Than crush her silly head with so much wrong" (IX. 85-91, 98-99, 101). The letter shows Lady Waldemar guilty of selfishness and triviality, but the erratic grammar of this passage lends credence to her insistence that she did not engage in gratuitous violence against a rival such as Marian. It is Aurora herself that Lady Waldemar hates:

> And yet, you loathed not Romney, -- though you played
> At 'fox and goose' about him with your soul;
> Pass over fox, you rub out fox, -- ignore
> A feeling, you eradicate it, -- the act's
> Identical. (IX. 153-57)

She continues,

> And, but for you, I might have won his love,
> And, to you, I have shown my naked heart;
> For which three things, I hate, hate, hate you. Hush
> Suppose a fourth! -- I cannot choose but think
> That, with him, I were virtuouser than you
> Without him. (IX. 164-69)

The language and narrative method show that, in her treatment of Lady Waldemar, Aurora has once again come dangerously close to inauthenticity: she has made hasty judgments, she has denied Lady Waldemar the respect she deserves as a fellow human being, and she has uncovered an emotional rift within herself. Although she is crude, Lady Waldemar is perceptive: in denying her love for Romney, Aurora has caused unnecessary suffering for herself and her cousin.

Aurora's relationship with Romney is more complicated. On the whole, her disapproval of him is justified. In his zeal to save the world through the gospel of Fourier, he proposes marriage to a destitute child of the working class whom he does not love, converts the family estate into a "utopian" community of beggars and the working poor, and channels all his human feelings into a "scientific" system more rigid than the traditional system of social class.[17] Romney's spectacularly obtuse dismissal of women's intellectual capacity, which he voices just before proposing marriage to Aurora the first time, typifies his blindness to other points of view. This world, he says,

> Uncomprehended by you, must remain
> Uninfluenced by you. -- Women as you are,
> Mere women, personal and passionate,
> You give us doating mothers, and perfect wives,
> Sublime Madonnas, and enduring saints!
> We get no Christ from you, -- and verily
> We shall not get a poet, in my mind. (II. 219-26)

Like Jane Eyre's arrogant missionary suitor St. John Rivers, Romney adds that he needs a wife to help him in his great social experiments - and that Aurora's intellectual gifts would be put to better use in service of the poor and in support of a man whose life is dedicated to the alleviation of suffering.

Nevertheless, as Aurora's aunt knows (and as Lady Waldemar and even Marian Earle realize), Aurora does love Romney, despite her denials. Romney and she are not only cousins, but orphans, and Aurora's earliest memories of him suggest a warmth vital to her survival, when she seemed close to death from loneliness and grief. And despite his attempts to rationalize emotion, it is clear that Romney (unlike St. John Rivers) also loves Aurora, who remembers from her childhood that:

> He would have saved me utterly, it seemed,
> He stood and looked so.

---

[17] The Brownings saw Nathaniel Hawthorne socially between 1853 and 1857, while he served as American consul in Italy. Barrett Browning would have been familiar with Hawthorne's critique of missionary zeal in the service of a similar ideology in *The Blithedale Romance* (1852), which ends even more disastrously than *Aurora Leigh*.

> Once, he stood so near
> He dropped a sudden hand upon my head
> Bent down on woman's work, as soft as rain --
> But then I rose and shook it off as fire,
> The stranger's touch that took my father's place
> Yet dared seem soft. (I.541-47)

Understandably, Aurora rejects the marriage proposal, but she blushes when her aunt says,

> I am not old for nothing; I can tell
> The weather-signs of love: you love this man. (II. 690-91)

"That treason of false witness in my blush," Aurora recalls, does not shake her insistence: "I think I loved him not, -- nor then, nor since,/ Nor ever" (II.709, 713-14). A little later, she also rejects Romney's assistance when her aunt's death leaves her penniless (since her father has been disinherited because he married an Italian, the entire estate is Romney's). Both decisions are made on rational grounds, and yet Aurora's self-analysis is duplicitous.

In a passage typical of Aurora's language under stress, her words go against the grain of the blank verse and betray her, long before the events at the end of the narrative force her to acknowledge her feelings. She remembers that when she rejected Romney,

> His eyes, the motions in his silent mouth,
> Were fiery points on which my words were caught,
> Transfixed for ever in my memory
> For his sake, not their own. And yet I know
> I did not love him. . nor he me. . that's sure. .
> And what I said, is unrepented of,
> As truth is always. Yet. . a princely man! --
> If hard to me, heroic for himself!
> He bears down on me through the slanting years,
> The stronger for the distance. (II. 502-11)

Seven years later, as she writes this part of the narrative, her grammar falters, and she gropes for the right words. Her first impression of Romney, when he appears on "the terrace of my tower" (VIII.2) after three years of separation, conveys the feelings for him she has denied since her first chilling arrival in England seventeen years before. A passionate lover of words (and as her uncritical emulation of the romantic poets suggests, inflated words) the young Aurora misconstrues Romney's language of understatement by taking it literally. He does want a helper in his work, but he understates his love rather than resorting to conventional romantic language. Romney's marriage proposal is insulting, but his earlier behavior has been affectionate and unselfish, and his ungenerous remarks mask real love. Graver than her misunderstanding of Romney, however, is Aurora's refusal to listen to her own heart, which would have decoded Romney's messages. When she is older, Aurora makes the opposite mistake: she takes Romney's meaning figuratively when he is expressing himself literally. The final conversation in Books VIII and IX reveals the extent to which Aurora is deaf to Romney's code. Romney admits his errors about Aurora's mental strength and the need for artists. His many references to darkness and light, blindness and sight, refer not only to error and truth, but to literal blindness and literal sight: "Overproud, of course," he says of himself,

> Even so! -- but not so stupid. . blind. . that I,
> Whom thus the great Taskmaster of the world
> Has set to meditate mistaken work,
> My dreary face against a dim blank wall
> Throughout man's natural lifetime, -- could pretend
> Or wish. . O love, I have loved you! O my soul,
> I have lost you [. . .] . (IX. 491-98)

Like that of Jane Eyre's Rochester, Romney's blindness is an indirect result of *hubris*, but it leads paradoxically to greater insight. (It will be recalled that the exacting mentor of Barrett Browning's early adulthood, the Greek scholar Hugh Boyd, was also blind. As well as his blindness, his behavior may have entered into her characterization of Romney.) Aurora's misconstruction of Romney's language pales, however, in comparison to her misjudgment of him as a man. When Romney understands that Aurora has coupled him in her mind with the wealthy and persistent Lady Waldemar, thereby characterizing him as emotionally defective or self-serving, for the first time he is outraged. For the first time, Aurora and Romney are able to see that Aurora's errors of the heart are equal to Romney's errors of the intellect. From each other, they have learned the lessons they could learn nowhere else.

At last, Romney has to explain that he cannot see the stars above them, that the fire at Leigh Hall and his struggle to save one of the lost souls he has harbored there (Marian Earle's alcoholic father) have cost him his sight.

Aurora finally accepts Romney, with his imperfections, as she accepts knowledge of her own error. They will share their lives and their work.

No perfect artist is developed here
From any imperfect woman [. . .]. (IX. 648-49)

she realizes, and even though perfection is not possible, there will be for Aurora and Romney a more profound art and a more consistent marriage of philosophy with action. As the autobiography of a fictional woman poet, the book is a form of action in a patriarchal world; as a novel poem by one of the most popular poets of the age, *Aurora Leigh* is both a theory of art and the practice of that theory.

This metafictional combination of theory and practice was not new to Barrett Browning, but *Aurora Leigh* is her most thorough synthesis of discursive, lyrical, and narrative elements in one work. Before, she had written essays - tough, scholarly, and theoretical - and she had written the emotional lyrics and narratives for which she was best known. In *Casa Guidi Windows* she had combined lyric subjectivity with literary theory to critique the way most poets, in her view, perceived and transmitted the cultural riches of the past. But until work progressed on *Aurora Leigh*, she had not developed a poetic practice which built upon the insights of the Casa Guidi project to combine her two strengths as a poet: lyrical risk with intellectual strength.

One of Barrett Browning's most underrated works is a series of critical papers published in 1842, "Some Account of the Greek Christian Poets," an investigation which, as we have already seen, contributed to Browning's dialogic religious poems. These minor voices, she admits at the beginning, are not a promising topic, so

it is right to premise [the account] with the full and frank admission, that they are not accomplished poets [. . .] . The instrument of the Greek tongue was, at the Christian era, an antique instrument, somewhat worn, somewhat stiff in the playing, somewhat deficient in notes which it had once, somewhat feeble and uncertain in such as it retained. (513)

Nevertheless, Barrett attacks her subject with verve, wit, and not a little sarcasm, sketching out a score of these minor poets and translating samples of their work. In spite of, or because of, her gleeful comments on their defects (and a few beauties), these poets lived briefly once more in the pages of the *Athenaeum*, a periodical of the day, and the exercise taught Barrett a lesson about literary history which she later recalled in *Aurora Leigh*: Eudocia, "wife of Theodosius, and empress of the world" was also a poet - an accomplished poet, it was said, who undertook to Christianize

Homer in a cento, a poem consisting of cannibalized quotations from an acknowledged canonical work,

> and the deed recoiled. For mark the poetical justice of her destiny. Let all readers mark it, and all writers, especially female writers, who may be half as learned and not half as fair, -- that although she wrote many poems [. . .] not one, except this cento, has
> survived [. . .] . She is punished by her [own] hand. (523)

Few Victorian poets were more scholarly and more aware of her literary past than Elizabeth Barrett Browning, but few were so convinced that the poet must live and write for the present. That is the lesson to be learned from the unhappy history of Eudocia, and the lesson that, in *Aurora Leigh*, Barrett Browning integrated into her own poetic practice.

The theory of *Aurora Leigh* is far from simple or conclusive. Crucial in the hero's evolution as a human being is her evolution as a poet. At no point in her career does Aurora Leigh write unselfconsciously; she continually considers what she writes, her models, her subject matter, inherited and new literary forms, the demands and rights of the reading public, the place of literature within its surrounding culture, and the intricate relationship between the poetic word and the political or religious deed. Among other things, Barrett Browning's novel poem narrates the evolution of a poetic theory from romanticism to realism, not teleologically, but projecting indefinitely beyond the ending of the work. All the characters change, Aurora Leigh most of all, and as she gains life experience, her theory of poetry becomes more relevant and profound.

The child Aurora wants to write poetry because, like the Romantic poets she has taken as models, she believes that poets "are the only speakers of essential truth" (I. 859). Although she never transgresses against the past to a Eudocian extreme, she has the impulse, and from the perspective of adulthood in Book I she writes in witty imitation of her youthful enthusiasm, her mushy and derivative style:

> O Life, O Poetry,
> -- Which means life in life! cognisant of life
> Beyond this blood-beat, passionate for truth
> Beyond these senses! -- poetry, my life,
> My eagle, with both grappling feet still hot
> From Zeus's thunder, who has ravished me [. . .] .
> I myself
> Half drunk across the beaker with their eyes!
> How those gods look!

> Enough so, Ganymede,
> We shall not bear above a round or two.   (I. 915-20, 927-28)

"Young men, ay, and maids," she concludes from her own experience, "Too often sow their wild oats in tame verse" (I. 948-49).

As she matures, Aurora's artistic essentialism is gradually mitigated, and her work takes on an existentialist coloration. The first stage in this process is recognizing her own interiority, "Disordered with all Adam in the blood/ But even its very tumors, warts, and wens/ Still organised by, and implying life" in order to transcend it (III. 341-43). But to support herself, Aurora must also write ballads for the popular press. Like Barrett Browning herself, Aurora is ambivalent about these productions because they show the weaknesses of her poetry - reliance on traditional poetic forms, indulgence in outworn romantic subjectivity, and repetition of feminine clichés about love and marriage. She would prefer to write philosophical poems, but the public will not read them. Her situation as an artist inspires an analysis of literary realism which moves her toward the conclusion that authentic and relevant art does not transcend real life. Instead, authentic art comes from and appeals to human nature as the poet finds it. Browning's sensuous Fra Lippo Lippi sees the Virgin in the Prior's pretty niece; Aurora Leigh finds traces of ideal male beauty in the rustic's face:

> Look long enough
> On any peasant's face here, coarse and lined,
> You'll catch Antinous, somewhere in that clay,
> As perfect featured as he yearns at Rome
> From marble pale with beauty [. . .] . (VII. 785-89)[18]

The characters are different, but the relationships suggested between the artist and the subject are the same. The same theoretical relationship between the poet and the proper subjects of poetry, which evolves in Books IV through VI of *Aurora Leigh*, is suggested over and over in *Men and Women* - by the positive example of the lusty painting monk, for example, the negative example of the "perfect painter" Andrea del Sarto, the comic self portrayal of Browning himself as he attempts to understand and preserve the art of the past, or in the satiric advice to a tedious "philosophical" poet rounding out "Transcendentalism: A Poem in Twelve Books":

---

[18] Antinous is a shortened name for the statue called the Belvedere Antinous, a representation of Mercury. It was regarded as a paragon of antique statuary.

So come, the harp back to your heart again!
You are a poem, though your poem's naught.
The best of all you showed before, believe,
Was your own boy-face o'er the finer chords
Bent, following the cherub at the top
That points to God with his paired half-moon wings. (46-51)

If at mid-career Aurora feels her great work is the philosophical poem no one reads, her poetry finally evolves into a mixed genre of self-awareness, truth-telling, and even the material of daily domestic life which interests her reading public.

This realist - and feminist - poetic is articulated most fully in Book V, although the poet does not fully understand the implications of her own theory until the end of the narrative. Poems should be about the poet's own time and place - a realist dictum, especially as realism was practiced by continental writers later in the century (Bieder 217) - and if the poet is a woman, she should write about the realities of women's lives. In an analysis which resonates with the relentless logic of Elizabeth Barrett's *An Essay on Mind*, Aurora Leigh holds that for poets,

Their sole work is to represent the age,
Their age, not Charlemagne's -- this live, throbbing age,
That brawls, cheats, maddens, calculates, aspires,
And spends more passion, more heroic heat,
Betwixt the mirrors of its drawing-rooms,
Than Roland with his knights, at Roncesvalles. (V.202-207)

To "flinch from modern varnish" and to dwell upon the epic past "Is fatal, -- foolish too" (V. 208, 210). By insisting on contemporary relevance, the masculinist realism of mid-century opened the back door to woman's world, the domestic interior, and Aurora Leigh boldly walks through.

In doing so, Aurora also finds that new poetic subject matter demands new poetic forms. For instance, why should a play have five acts? "And why not fifteen? why not ten? or seven?" (230):

What form is best for poems? Let me think
Of forms less, and the external. Trust the spirit,
As sovran nature does, to make the form [. . .] . (V.223-25)

Contemporary art is better if the form can somehow reflect the interior reality of the artist as well as the empirical world in which the artist lives: if it can turn "Inward evermore/ To outward, -- so in life, and so in art/ Which still is life" (V. 227-29).

In Bakhtin's terms, the great challenge for poetry is to fulfill the task of the novel in spite of the unitary nature of poetic language.[19] The work illustrates Barrett Browning's theory that the relationship between the narrator and the writer in this new form of literature - the novel poem - is a relationship between subjects, rather than between the literary subject (the writer) and the objects of scrutiny within the work.

It would be surprising not to find similarities in the phrasing of the Brownings' poetry. But another similarity between the two bodies of work at this time is both less obvious and more profound. Although she achieved a similar dialogic relationship between herself and her characters in a few of the shorter works throughout her career ("Mother and Poet," written during the last year of her life, is perhaps the best example), *Aurora Leigh* is the only major work in which Barrett Browning grants to her characters the kind of aesthetic and psychological autonomy that Browning's monologists almost always have. However, Browning's corpus is unique in the history of English non-dramatic poetry - no other poet except the Renaissance dramatists has matched his achievements in the presentation of a speaking subject other than the poet himself. It is therefore remarkable that in her great work, Barrett Browning was able to match this approach with such power. Moving radically beyond her claim for authority in *Casa Guidi Windows*, *Aurora Leigh* is Elizabeth Barrett Browning's best effort to escape from the closed circle of poetic authority, to engage in dialogue with the general reader, and to represent in poetry the drawing room as well as the epic battlefield. The split in her earlier poetry between passion and intellect, lyric and discursive, theory and practice, is mended.

Aurora Leigh also contains the clearest statement Barrett Browning ever made about the wonderfully complicated and complete nature of her marriage. It includes the "doctrine of love" held in common by both the Brownings. Aurora's assessment of her own work in Book IX repeats a theme heard throughout Barrett Browning's poetry:

O Art, my Art, thou'rt much, but Love is more!
Art symbolises heaven, but Love is God
And makes heaven. (IX. 657-59)

---

[19] Bakhtin's assessment of poetry seems to some readers negative and narrow, but, in fact, his definition of the novel is flexible enough to include such works as Byron's *Don Juan* and Pushkin's *Eugenii Onegin* as novels. There is no evidence that Bakhtin read either of the Brownings.

The words echo the poet's 1838 Preface to *The Seraphim and Other Poems*:

> Has not love a deeper mystery than wisdom, and a more ineffable lustre than power? I believe it has [. . .]. I assume no power of art, except that power of love towards it, which has remained with me from my childhood until now. (*Works*, 78, 80)

Some readers have claimed that *Aurora Leigh* ends in a conservative compromise of Aurora's autonomy and her art; that ultimately, through her art, she reinscribes a conservative ethic; or that Aurora values Romney's work over hers.[20] But despite the Carlylean rhetoric that Romney and Aurora substitute for Romney's hard-headed socialism *and* Aurora's single-minded commitment to poetry, the ending is less determinate and more open than such a reading allows.

Instead, Barrett Browning suggests that new forms are required for both art and life - the freedom of the novel poem parallels the marriage of equals, free from traditional gender roles and absolutely mutual. Just as Robert spoke in his own voice to Elizabeth in the last, dedicatory poem of *Men and Women*, surely the parting words of Elizabeth's poem represent her true feeling about partnership: that love and work are intertwined and infinitely satisfying. Romney looks into the future for both partners:

> Beloved, let us love so well,
> Our work shall still be better for our love,
> And still our love be sweeter for our work,
> And both commended, for the sake of each [. . .] . (IX. 924-28)

---

[20] DuPlessis, for example, writes that "Being an artist is, at the end, reinterpreted as self-sacrifice for the woman, and thus is aligned with feminine ideology. This work, then, created a powerful reference point, but it did not change the nineteenth-century convention of representation that saw the price of artistic ambition as the loss of femininity" (*Writing Beyond the Ending* 87). Similarly, David argues that "In common with many other Victorian poets and social thinkers, Barrett Browning constructs a pre-industrial Eden, the topos of benign authority, of joyful obedience, and of poetry, where the artist tends to copy order, rather than to create it" (*Intellectual Women and Victorian Patriarchy* 113.)

Afterword

When the Brownings returned to Casa Guidi in 1856, both were tired, and, although they did not know it then, their lives would never again settle into the easy rhythms of the early days in Italy. Elizabeth's health continued to decline, but she urged Robert into such an active social life without her that, while they were in Florence, he was gone from home almost every night of the week, sometimes taking Pen with him. Still, the family continued to move about Italy as always. Their longest absence from Casa Guidi was a trip to Rome in the fall of 1859, after which they spent much of the following summer in Siena.

But this time the change did not improve Elizabeth's health. The Brownings' days were filled with tension and disasters - friends and family members died, there were domestic upheavals as servants came and went. After struggling against asthma for years, John Kenyon finally succumbed in December of 1856 at his home on the Isle of Wight, only weeks after the Brownings had left him. Elizabeth's old friend and correspondent Mary Russell Mitford had died the year before, the still implacable Edward Moulton Barrett died suddenly of erysipelas in 1857, and uterine cancer killed her sister Henrietta in 1860, after months of terrible pain. Anna Jameson, who had been so kind to the couple during their chaotic honeymoon, died that same year at the relatively young age of sixty.

There were other painful experiences as well. After attending Elizabeth for nearly a decade, in 1853, Wilson had married the manservant Fernandino, in haste and with painful misunderstandings on both sides. Time only intensified the hurt feelings, and Wilson moved out of the household in 1857, pregnant for a second time, depressed, and ill. In 1858, when Browning's irascible old friend Walter Savage Landor's family could no longer bear his angry outbursts, Wilson became his caretaker in a lodging house which she established near Casa Guidi. Another source of friction was the Brownings' continued disagreement about spiritualism. Elizabeth trusted where Robert did not, but he could hardly enjoy feeling vindicated when her friend Sophia Eckley was revealed as a fraud. For years, the Eckleys had flattered and fawned, claiming to channel spirits, and preying upon Elizabeth's need to believe in a rational basis for spiritual experience.[1] But finally even she was forced to admit the couple's hypocrisy, and her vexation was heightened when she discovered that Sophia had also carried on an extramarital affair.

As for events outside the round of their domestic life, the Brownings were united in their deep concern with political and military events in Italy, which had reached a fever pitch. To some, the Risorgimento seemed doomed. The Brownings continued to worry as well about the political situation in France. Although Napoleon III seemed to operate from one day to the next, according to expedient, the Brownings hoped he would act on principle and support Italian efforts for unification and independence. Elizabeth, especially, was devastated by repeated setbacks on the political front as well as the battlefield. She trusted more than Robert to individuals who seemed to promise political freedom for the Italian people and therefore grieved more deeply at each political or military setback.

A note of ending and completion sounds in Elizabeth Barrett Browning's 1856 dedication of *Aurora Leigh* to Kenyon - because the poem is, she writes,

> the most mature of my works and the one into which my highest convictions upon Life and Art have entered;   that as, through my various efforts in literature and steps in life, you have believed in me, borne with me, and been generous to me, far beyond the common uses of mere relationship or sympathy of mind, so you may kindly accept, in sight of the public, this poor sign of esteem, gratitude, and affection[. . .] . (161)

She died five years after writing this, on June 28 1861, of the respiratory troubles which had confined and troubled her for so many years. After a night of chills, dreams, and difficult breathing, she faded from her

---

[1] Gayle Graham Yates' suggestion about Harriet Martineau's devotion to mesmerism, another pseudo-scientific theory about extra-material experience, provides a parallel for Elizabeth Barrett Browning's fanaticism about spiritualism:

> For so logical and analytical a writer to participate in such a mysterious and controversial medical process might seem bewildering. However, I think it makes sense as a link between[. . .] religious faith[. . .] and her need for something other than sheer theory and argument as a stabilizer for personal meaning in her life. (12-13)

Although Barrett Browning never abandoned her religious faith, as did Martineau, spiritualism did seem to provide a "scientific" basis for hoping that she might continue to commune with the dead -- her mother, her beloved brother, and the father who never forgave her.

husband's arms, and her last words affirmed the essential beauty of her relationship with him. "Are you comfortable?" he asked. "Beautiful" was her reply.[2]

Despite the depletion of energy and spirit, both poets continued to write between 1856 and 1861, although with less intensity. Barrett Browning devoted her efforts to shorter poems, which reveal her preoccupations with the conflicting demands of life and art. The work of her last five years includes both her most strident political poetry, collected in 1860 as *Poems before Congress*, and some of her most nearly perfect poems. One of these is "Mother and Poet," a dramatic monologue in the voice of Laura Savio, a poet of the Risorgimento whose sons died in the patriotic struggle she had, ironically, glorified in her poetry. "A Musical Instrument," based on Ovid's story of Pan and Syrinx, suggests, in a different way, that art is born of struggle, sacrifice, and violence. These works appeared in Barrett Browning's *Last Poems*, which Browning published in 1862. As for Browning, during this time he drafted a number of dramatic monologues, which became the nucleus for his 1864 collection, *Dramatis Personae*. One of them, "Mr. Sludge, 'The Medium,'" was an exposé of the spiritualism fad - the source of his deepest disagreements with his wife. Another was *Prince Hohenstiel-Schwangau, Saviour of Society*, a longer poem which was apparently first drafted in 1859-60, then destroyed and rewritten ten years later. The speaker is a fictional version of Napoleon III.[3]

But for Browning the poet, these years were mostly a period of incubation. The poems he wrote then were more heavily revised than his work at any other point in his career, and he used the time, too, to gather material for future poetry. In 1860, he unearthed "The Old Yellow Book" while rummaging in a Florentine market. It was a scrapbook of materials relating the seventeenth-century murder trial of Guido Franceschini, a degenerate nobleman who murdered his child bride Pompilia Comparini

---

[2] For a full account of Barrett Browning's last moments, see Forster's biography, 356-66.

[3] On the basis of Browning's dramatic monologue, which seems to diverge sharply from opinions EBB expressed during her lifetime, critics usually assume that the Brownings disagreed emphatically about the character of Napoleon III. In "The Case of 'Prince Hohenstiel-Schwangau': Browning and Napoleon III," however, Leo A. Hetzler argues persuasively that the Brownings agreed in the main about this political figure, that their mutually held views evolved in response to his activities in Europe, and that Browning's opinion had changed substantially by the time he rewrote his poem after his wife's death -- as hers probably would have done, had she lived longer.

and her parents, after they had compromised the betrothal bargain. The other player in the gruesome drama was a young priest, Giuseppe Caponsacchi; because Caponsacchi tried to save the Comparini, Guido's defense accused him of adultery with Pompilia in order to plead justifiable homicide. A few years later, Browning would turn this material into his masterpiece, *The Ring and the Book* (1868-69), a story of love and violence, spirituality and embodiment.

And it is with a series of such contrasts that Elizabeth is remembered in Book I, in Browning's famous tribute to her, which begins,

> O lyric Love, half-angel and half-bird,
> And all a wonder and a wild desire, --
> Boldest of hearts that ever braved the sun,
> Took sanctuary within the holier blue,
> And sang a kindred soul out to his face, --
> Yet human at the red-ripe of the heart --
> When the first summons from the darkling earth
> Reached thee amid thy chambers, blanched their blue,
> And bared them of their glory -- to drop down,
> To toil for man, to suffer or to die [. . .]. (I.1391-99)

Book I ends with a confession of faith that the poet's relationship with his lyric love will remain intact:

> What was, again may be; some interchange
> Of grace, some splendour once thy very thought,
> Some benediction anciently thy smile [. . .]. (1407-09)

These beautiful lines were an essential part of Browning's grieving. Naturally, so soon after her death, he would remember his wife in a rush of wings, blood, and fire. It is also natural that his delicate portrayal of Pompilia, whose tragic marriage and murder drive the action of the story, would resonate with his memories of Elizabeth.

But neither this passage nor the portrayal of the saintly girl represent Elizabeth Barrett Browning as she was, or as he came to remember her with the passage of time.[4] Browning's reconstructed memories - and a more

---

[4] According to Osbert Burdett, Barrett Browning's presence can be perceived in many of Browning's late works, in addition to the poems discussed here. These include especially the "Epilogue" of *Fifine at the Fair* (1872), Browning's version of the Don Juan story; "At the Mermaid" and "House," two poems in *Pacchiarotto and How He Worked in Distemper* (1876); *La Saisiaz* (1879), a pessimistic religious meditation; the short poetic preface to *Jocoseria* (1883); the "Prologue"

accurate representation of his wife's character - would emerge a decade after her death, in the early summer of 1861, when he wrote *Balaustion's Adventure*. "The most delightful of May-month amusements," he called it in the dedication to his friend Countess Cowper (*Poems* I 868), at whose home the poem was written.

Balaustion's Adventure is a double-framed, narrative-dramatic story which includes a translation of Euripides' *Alkestis* at its heart. (Donald Hair calls the work a collection of "nested plays" [*Robert Browning's Language* 226].) In private, Browning usually made light of *Balaustion*, calling it in a letter to Edith Story "my little thing" (Hudson, *American Friends* 164) and remarking to Isa Blagden as it was coming off the presses that he had had trouble getting copies of "the poor little Balaustion-book" (Browning, *Dearest Isa* 367). Because of Browning's own apparent insouciance about the work, its importance as a theoretical statement has been underestimated, and its significance as a moment in the relationship between the Brownings has been misunderstood. Indeed, the poem suggests that Elizabeth Barrett Browning's voice remained as audible in Browning's mind ten years after she died as it had ever been during her life.

But there are a number of reasons why Browning could have wished to avoid overburdening his new poem with too much attention. His heroine's version of Euripides' play (he calls it a "transcript" rather than a translation) is clearly a narrative adaptation of a dramatic work rather than a conventional translation. In scholarly terms, the *Alkestis* is also one of the easiest of the Greek plays to work with, for the available texts were complete and reliable, and the Euripidean canon is also relatively complete. Browning's attitude recalls that of Barrett Browning, who disavowed her first translation of *Prometheus Unbound*, made during a thirteen-day period during her last few weeks at Hope End in 1833, and then retranslated the play during the poets' courtship. Like her, Browning seemed hesitant to claim credit for a few weeks' work.[5] Browning may also have been unwilling to make great claims for *Balaustion* as a poetic work. In comparison to such weighty poems as *The Ring and the Book* or even the great dramatic monologues of Browning's middle period, *Balaustion's Adventure* can seem lightweight and light-hearted, so much so that Mermin

---

to *Ferishtah's Fancies* (1884); and "Speculative" and the "Bad Dreams" series in Browning's last volume, *Asolando* (1889).

[5] Despite Browning's modesty, H. B. Forman commented in a review of *Balaustion* that his *Alkestis* was "second to no English rendering of a Greek play, unless it be the [second] *Prometheus* of Mrs. Browning" (21).

has remarked upon its "mood of blithe holiday innocence" (*The Audience in the Poem* 66).

Browning's remarks about his poem may also reflect upon its content. The frame story - narrated by the fictional, eponymous Balaustion to four girlfriends some time after her adventure has taken place - is a comic novelistic figuration based on a minor incident in Plutarch's *Life of Nicias*. Nicias was a less than stellar general, whose uninspired leadership in the fifth century BCE contributed to the decline of Athenian supremacy and the ascendency of Sparta. In Browning's story, after Nicias' defeat, a band of Athenian sympathizers are driven by pirates into the harbor of Syracuse, a neutral power. Just as the Syracusans threaten to send the heroine and her shipmates back to the waiting pirates, a man in the crowd inquires about the latest plays. Balaustion, who has already roused the ship's crew to flee from the pirates with a song from Aeschylus, agrees to "tell" the latest play by Euripides. In the harbor of Syracuse, her storytelling once again saves the lives of her compatriots - and, not incidentally, reaffirms the cultural hegemony of Athens. If the historical events in the frame story are presented accurately, the social realities are not: in her free single status, her intellectual freedom, even her profound familiarity with the theatre, which would have been closed to her as a woman, Balaustion is a deliberate anachronism, though such an anachronism as Euripides might have appreciated. The frame story ends with Balaustion's marriage to Euthycles, a young man from Syracuse; in an understated comic touch, Browning has Euthycles so enraptured with her stories that he happily joins her shipmates in their political quest, as they sail from place to place, refusing to accept the defeat of Athens. Art engages eros.

Even the story Balaustion tells (and retells to her friends) is not a tragedy in the Aristotelian sense. When King Admetos offends Artemis, the death sentence meted out by the goddess is commuted through the substitution of his wife Alkestis, and Admetos agrees to the compromise, even though he protests that he loves his wife.[6] Alkestis is then rescued

---

[6] Due to Browning's eccentric spelling for Greek names, an effort to suggest to English readers the essential foreignness of Greek, my own choices for spelling are inconsistent. Browning suggests in the prefatory remarks to his translation of the *Agamemnon* that these unique transliterations from the Greek alphabet are more accurate than conventional spellings. They are not more accurate, as he must have known. However, Browning's spelling does create an impression of estrangement from the Greek stories which emphasizes the discontinuity of Greek from English, the difficulty of translations in general, and the discontinuities within Greek culture itself, which, he felt, had been minimized by the Victorian Greek revival.

from Hades by the hero god Herakles. Euripides has often been read as a feminist, and Balaustion takes full advantage of the feminist potential of the *Alkestis*, representing the ironies in Alkestis' perceptive speeches to and about her husband. In Euripides' version, sympathy for Admetos results from the tension between his self-pity and his self-control, and from Herakles' obvious regard. But, in Balaustion's version, Admetos is morally redeemed from his selfishness because Alkestis' impending death strikes him with unexpected remorse, and he learns to deserve her love. Their love contributes to the rescue because, by the time Herakles arrives in the underworld, it has already unsettled Koré, who prefers her shades dim and distracted, not focused still on the world of the living. For the goddess of the underworld,

'Two souls in one were formidable odds:
Admetos must not be himself and thou!' (2646-47).

In her commentary at the end of the narrative, Balaustion changes the story even more, suggesting that Admetos' love could have been powerful enough in itself to redeem his wife from death.

Like Browning, Euripides offended his contemporaries by altering traditional narrative materials and experimenting with received genres. For this play, Euripides developed an obscure story into something akin to a satyr play: not only missing is the more typical tragic denouement, in Herakles' hearty cheerfulness and love of feasting are preserved traces of the hero god's disreputable character in earlier versions of his story. Browning changes the character even more: the descriptions of Herakles - he of the "splendid smile" (2378) - suggest a genetic relationship between the Greek hero and the kenotic Christ, whose humanity is as arresting and powerful as his divinity:

For out of Herakles a great glow broke.
There stood a victor worthy of a prize [. . .].
                    Oh, he knew
The signs of battle hard-fought and well won,
This queller of monsters! (2273-75, 77-78).

But Browning's word choice also invests Herakles' labors with a spiritual dimension: "'For thou hast'," says Admetos, with Alkestis once again at his

---

When direct references to Browning texts call for his orthography, I use it. Otherwise, I use the more common spellings.

side, "'only thou -- raised me and mine/ Up again to this light and life!'" (2354-55).

Browning wrote *Balaustion* with two audiences in mind: readers such as Countess Cooper, and men of letters, including his friends Thomas Carlyle, Matthew Arnold, and Benjamin Jowett, the recently appointed master of Balliol (through whom he hoped to have Pen admitted to Oxford). Even readers who were not highly educated would have understood something about the nature of Browning's task in *Balaustion* because the Greek revival which began at Oxford had come to dominate English tastes more generally in the 1860s and 1870s. Still, the qualities of the work itself - the relative ease with which Euripides' play could be adapted, the relative simplicity of the project in comparison with Browning's other long poems, the happy content of both the frame story and the Alkestis story - do not entirely account for Browning's ready dismissal of *Balaustion's Adventure*, which is both philosophically and formally more complex than it may appear.

More problematic for Browning, no doubt, were the parallels between the plot of the poem and the plot of his own life: he had always carefully guarded his privacy. These similarities would have been obvious to friends and even to unknown readers who knew something of the Brownings' famous love story. On multiple levels, *Balaustion's Adventure* is a story of rescue. Balaustion saves her shipmates. In Balaustion's story of Euripides' play, Alkestis saves Admetos, and then Herakles saves Alkestis. Finally, in her interpretive conclusion, Balaustion imagines that the love shared by Alkestis and the newly sensitive Admetos saves them both. Browning never gave up the rescue fantasies which inform his earliest poems, but the theme evolved and matured over time, and, in *Balaustion's Adventure*, the fantasy has been detached almost entirely from traditional gender roles.

Browning's relationship with the remembered Elizabeth Barrett has been a consistent theme in the critical literature about this work, but despite the complicated web of rescues in the poem, much of the critical discussion has centered on one particular episode in Browning's life: his brief consideration in 1869 of marriage to the beautiful and wealthy Lady Louisa Ashburton, for Pen's sake, as he told her in brutally uncomplimentary terms.[7] Lady Ashburton rejected the proposal, as Browning must have expected her to do. In a frequent biographical reading of the poem,

---

[7] Joseph H. Friend calls the work "a cathartic projection of an inner conflict" (179). Miller unequivocally ascribes the inspiration for *Balaustion* to Browning's guilt about the unhappy affair with Lady Ashburton (269). Honan and Irvine follow suit in their more recent biography (445-51, 459-62). So does Erickson in *Robert Browning: His Poetry and His Audiences* (241-44).

Browning is to the whinging Admetos as Elizabeth Barrett Browning is to the noble, self-sacrificing Alkestis.[8] Although readers who interpret the poem as Browning's expression of guilt have grasped too tightly the autobiographical threads, they have not been completely mistaken: certainly, the presence of both Brownings can be felt in *Balaustion's Adventure*, as the name "Balaustion" in itself suggests. It means "wild pomegranate flower," and thus picks up once again the metaphorical thread representing life and passion found in the work of both poets, even before they met.[9]

The most significant self-referential aspect of *Balaustion* is not the biographical parallel, but the elaboration of the Brownings' theory and practice of poetry. As she synthesizes the poetic theories of both Brownings, the character of Balaustion represents what Prins characterizes as Browning's "intersubjective textual relationship with Barrett." *Balaustion's Adventure* is

> an act of the same mind that produced the correspondence between Barrett and Browning [. . .]. their letters are not really the product of one mind but produced by a dialogue between two minds [. . .]." ("Translating Greek Tragedy" 95, 100)

In a very early analysis of *Balaustion's Adventure*, written shortly after Browning's death, William Cranston Lawton departs from the conventional algebra of represented relationships in the work when he announces that Browning himself "is Balaustion" (372). What Lawton means, of course, is that Balaustion's opinions about people and poetry are Browning's own. Balaustion's voice as a storyteller echoes the colloquial tone and the conversational rhythms encountered in so many of Browning's other

---

[8] Reading Barrett Browning into Alkestis does not necessarily deny the resemblances between her and Balaustion as well. Friend does call the work "a complexly motivated product of Browning's art" (182) and calls Balaustion "an idealized and romanticized portrait of EBB as a young woman" (181). Erickson, too, sees Balaustion as a characterization of Barrett Browning in her role as Browning's reader (244).

[9] Employing the same methodology as in her important study of the interchange between "Saul" and *Sonnets from the Portuguese*, in "Elizabeth Barrett Browning and the Art of Collaboration," Sullivan has more recently investigated the exchange and permutation of the pomegranate metaphor in the Brownings' poetry. She concludes that, although "it is not possible to trace with any exactitude the specific order of reciprocity," their shared system of imagery reveals a powerful working relationship between the Brownings (54 and *pass.*).

poems, and *Balaustion's Adventure* is as clear and explicit an account of his poetic theory as can be found anywhere in his work.

But Balaustion "is" also Barrett Browning, not only as a personality - both are vivacious, courageous, tender in friendship, and passionate about politics - but in her theory and practice of literature. Balaustion is an ardent defender of what she believes is the best and truest art - and, like Barrett Browning, she believes that part of what makes art good and true is an ability to appeal to both public virtues and private emotions. Browning makes the comparison between Barrett Browning and his fictional character most explicit in the epigraph, a quotation from his wife's tribute to Euripides in "Wine of Cyprus":

> Our Euripides, the human,
>   With his droppings of warm tears,
> And his touches of things common
>   Till they rose to touch the spheres.

In another deliberate anachronism, Balaustion herself echoes these words in the conclusion:

> I know the poetess who graved in gold,
> Among her glories that shall never fade,
> This style and title for Euripides,
> *The Human with his droppings of warm tears.* (2668-71)

The Brownings' scholarship was an important bond between them from the very beginning. Balaustion does not, of course, represent the whole of either poet's complex and lifelong considerations about poetry and art. But by the time Browning published *Balaustion's Adventure*, his heroine's notions about the nature and function of poetry would have had a familiar ring to everyone who had been reading the Brownings' work carefully, for both poets had explored these themes throughout their lives.

In her youth, Elizabeth Barrett had been a tireless student of Greek. In addition to her two translations of *Prometheus Unbound*, she published numerous shorter pieces, leaving a number of finished translations which Browning included in *Last Poems,* and an even larger body of short translations from numerous authors which yet remain unpublished. By the time she was twenty-five, she had also memorized almost eight thousand lines of Greek - with a dedication and capacity obviously mirrored in Balaustion, who is able to remember songs from the plays she has heard - and, of course, whole plays (*Hitherto Unpublished Poems and Stories* 134-35). It is not surprising that the translation trope which suffuses *Sonnets from the Portuguese* reappears with such energy in Browning's remembrance of his wife. Balaustion, too, is "translating," as she changes the dramatic form of Euripides' work into the narrative form which can be delivered gracefully, by a single performer, to an audience whose sympathies are suspect. She is the third-person narrator of a chronologically ordered fiction, which she interrupts from time to time in order to judge the characters and assess their feelings. As the form of the story changes, the meaning of the new work is inevitably different from the old, but the intertextuality reveals new potential meanings in the older work as well.

At a moment early in their courtship, when Browning "tempted" Elizabeth Barrett to "Restore the Prometheus Πυρφορος [Fire-bearer] as Shelley did the Λυομευος [Bound]" (*Correspondence* 10.119), she responded that, despite the seductions of the historical past,

> I am inclined to think we want new <u>forms</u> . . as well as thoughts -- The old gods are dethroned. Why should we go back to the antique moulds. . classical moulds, as they are so improperly called. If it is a necessity of Art to do so, why then those critics are right who hold that Art is exhausted & the world too worn out for poetry. I do not, for my part believe this [. . .]. Let us all aspire rather to <u>Life</u> -- & let the dead bury the dead. If we have but courage to face these conventions, to touch this low ground, we shall take strength from it[. . .]. For there is poetry <u>everywhere</u>. . the "treasure" [. . .] lies all over the field. (*Correspondence* 10. 135)

In poems as early as "An Essay on Mind," Elizabeth Barrett had insisted that, in order to improve society and to be vital, the form and the content of poetry had to evolve in concert with other cultural changes, that cultural tradition was of use only if it were continually renewed. Barrett's opinions about poetry are articulated most fully, of course, in *Casa Guidi Windows* and *Aurora Leigh*, and it is no accident that the voice which speaks in those long poems resonates powerfully with the voice of Balaustion in her first adventure. Although the character of Aurora Leigh is not simply a stand-in for the poet herself, Aurora's theoretical statements do represent Barrett Browning's poetic theory. Every age, she says, has its own epos. Thus, the forms in which its heroes are represented must change. This important theoretical passage from *Aurora Leigh* bears repeating:

> What form is best for poems? Let me think
> Of forms less, and the external. Trust the spirit,
> As sovran nature does, to make the form;
> For otherwise we only imprison spirit

And not embody. Inward evermore
To outward, -- so in life, and so in art
Which still is life.   (V.223-29)

In *Casa Guidi Windows*, Barrett Browning relates the story of Michelangelo's beautiful snow statue, ordered in spite by Lorenzo the Magnificent. The artist's response turns the order upside down, for the spirit of the work lives on and inspires, though its external form melts away.

Similarly, Balaustion's position as the teller of a tale rather than participant in dramatic representation requires that, for her, received artistic forms work heuristically rather than prescriptively. As she explains to a man in the crowd, "a brisk little somebody,/ Critic and whippersnapper, in a rage/ To set things right,"[10]

What's poetry but a power that makes?
And, speaking to one sense, inspires the rest,
Pressing them all into its service; so
That who sees painting, seems to hear as well
The speech that's proper for the painted mouth [. . .]. (306-08, 318-22)

The world of Balaustion's art is dynamic: she loves Euripides --

Still, since one thing may have so many sides [. . .]
You, I, or anyone might mould a new
Admetos, new Alkestis. Ah, that brave
Bounty of Poets, the one royal race
That ever was, or will be, in this world!
They give no gift that bounds itself and ends
I' the giving and the taking: theirs so breeds
I' the heart and soul o' the taker, so transmutes
The man who was only a man before,
That he grows godlike in his turn, can give --
He also: share the poets' privilege,
Bring forth new good, new beauty, from the old. (2413, 2415-25)

To do justice to Euripides, Balaustion must build on the legacy he has turned over to her - and not simply preserve it. As Ryals comments, "*Balaustion's Adventure* is the poet's message to his age that, at a time when civilization seems on the verge of complete disruption, the spirit, if

---

[10] The man in the crowd is evidently a caricature of Alfred Austin, Browning's Nemesis.

not the forms, of the past can enliven the present and redeem the individual from despair" (*Browning's Late Poetry* 41).

These are also the terms of Fra Lippo Lippi's argument with the world. Contesting his masters' prescriptions - that he imitate Giotto and paint "no more of body than shows soul" (188) - Lippo articulates a new realism:

> For, don't you mark?we're made so that we love
> First when we see them painted, things we have passed
> Perhaps a hundred times nor cared to see;
> And so they are better, painted -- better to us,
> Which is the same thing. Art was given for that [. . .]. (300-04)

Giotto's forms reflected his own day; his truth was not identical to Brother Lippi's, but included within it. Browning is even more explicit in "Old Pictures in Florence":

> the Old and New are fellows:
> A younger succeeds to an elder brother,
> Da Vincis derive in good time from Dellos". (62-63)

From first to last, Browning had mined the dark corners of human experience and stretched out the limits of generic forms in order to represent what he found. Thus, *Balaustion's Adventure* is not only a theory of poetry, expounded by the heroine and demonstrated in her rendition of the *Alkestis*; the poem demonstrates something more, with its mixture of forms, layered narrative planes, and deliberate anachronisms. No less than *Sordello*, *Aurora Leigh*, and *The Ring and the Book*, *Balaustion's Adventure* is novelistic: it is permeated with characteristics which Bakhtin describes as "indeterminacy, a certain semantic open-endedness, a living contact with unfinished, still-evolving contemporary reality ("Epic and Novel" 7). It is also Browning's best tribute to the fellow poet who continued to give him courage and companionship, even in death.

The Brownings' relationship was no more static than their view of art, but it was constant. The attributes of Elizabeth Barrett which Browning loved most were the poetic sensibility and the critical intelligence about poetry which they shared. Neither poet flinched from contemporary reality, and neither was able or willing to take refuge in the idea of a cultural golden age. Each was the ideal audience for the other, and each enabled the other to develop the flower prefigured in the root.

Finally, illness, shared griefs, arguments, physical passion, the shared pleasures of Italy, even the shared experience of death - all mattered less to

Browning in 1871 than the voice of the beloved poet who still spoke to and through him even after her death. Browning's intertextual relationship with Barrett continued to change with the circumstances of his life and art, but she never ceased to be a living presence in his work.

Bibliography

Primary Works

Browning, Elizabeth Barrett. "The Art of Scansion." Ed. Alice Meynell. London: Clement Shorter, 1916 [private printing].
___. *Aurora Leigh*. Ed. Margaret Reynolds. Athens: Ohio Univ Pr, 1992.
___. *Aurora Leigh: Authoritative Text, Backgrounds and Contexts*, Criticism. Ed. Margaret Reynolds. NY: Norton, 1996.
___. *Casa Guidi Windows*. Ed. Julia Markus. NY: The Browning Institute, 1977.
___. *Elizabeth Barrett Browning's Letters to Mrs. David Ogilvy, 1849-1861*. Ed. Peter N. Heydon and Philip Kelley. NY: Quadrangle, New York Times Book Co., and The Browning Institute' 1973.
___. "Fragment of an 'Essay on Woman'." Ed. Kay Moser. *Studies in Browning and His Circle*. 12. (Spring/Fall 1984): 10-12.
___. *Hitherto Unpublished Poems and Stories, with an Unedited Autobiography*. Boston: The Bibliophile Society, 1914.
___. *Poems by Elizabeth Barrett Browning, Selected and Arranged by Robert Browning*. NY: Thomas Y. Crowell, 1893.
___. *Prometheus Bound and Other Poems*. Ed. Alice Meynell. London: Ward, Lock & Co., 1896.
___. *Works*. Intro. Karen Hill. Ware, Hertfordshire: Wordsworth Editions, 1994.
___. and Robert Browning. *The Brownings' Correspondence*. V. I-XIV+. Ed. Philip Kelley and Scott Lewis. Winfield, KS: Wedgestone Pr, 1984-.
___. *Letters of the Brownings to George Barrett*. Ed. Paul Landis with Ronald E. Freeman. Urbana: Univ Illinois Pr, 1958.
___ and Eliza Ogilvy. *Letters to Mrs. David Ogilvy, 1849-1861 with Recollections by Mrs. Ogilvy*. Ed. Peter N. Heydon and Philip Kelley. NY: Quadrangle, 1973.
Browning, Robert. *Browning's Essay on Chatterton*. Ed. Donald Smalley. Cambridge: Harvard Univ Pr, 1948.
___. *Dearest Isa: Robert Browning's Letters to Isabella Blagden*. Ed. Edward C. McAleer. Austin: Univ Pr, TX Pr, 1951.
___. *The Poems*. Ed. John Pettigrew, with Thomas J. Collins. V. I-II. NY: Penguin, 1981.
___. *Poetical Works*. V. I- General Ed. Ian Jack. Oxford: Clarendon Pr, 1983-.
___. *The Ring and the Book*. Ed. Richard D. Altick. NY: Penguin, 1971.
___. "Two Unpublished Browning Letters." Ed. Jackson J. Campbell. *Notes and Queries n. s.* 34 (March 1987): 41-42.

___ and Frederick Furnival. *Browning's Trumpeter: The Correspondence of Robert Browning and Frederick Furnival, 1872-1889.* Ed. William S. Peterson. Washington, DC: Decatur House Pr, 1979.

Sharp, Phillip David. "Elizabeth Barrett Browning and the Wimpole Street Notebook." MA Thesis. Baylor University, 1981.

___. "Poetry in Process: Elizabeth Barrett Browning and the Sonnets Notebook", Diss. Louisiana State University, 1985.

Secondary Works

Alaya, Flavia. "The Ring, the Rescue, and the Risorgimento: Reunifying the Brownings' Italy." *Browning Institute Studies* 6 (1978): 1-41.

Alfiere, Vittorio. *Saul. The Tragedies of Vittorio Alfieri: Complete, Including His Posthumous Works.* Ed. Edgar Alfred Bowring. V. II. Trans. C. Lloyd. Westport, CT: Greenwood Pr, 1970. 107-64.

Altick, Richard. "The Private Life of Robert Browning." *The Browning Critics.* Ed. Boyd, Litzinger and K. L. Knickerbocker. Lexington: University of Kentucky Press, 1965. 247-64.

Armstrong, Isobel. "The Brownings." *History of Literature in the English Language, Vol. VI: The Victorians.* Ed. Arthur Pollard. NY: Barrie and Jenkins. 292-94, 308-09.

___. *Language as Living Form in Nineteenth Century Poetry.* Englewood Cliffs, NJ: Barnes and Noble, 1982.

Auerbach, Nina. "Robert Browning's Last Word." In *Romantic Imprisonment: Women and Other Glorified Outcasts.* NY: Columbia University Press, 1986. 92-106.

Babcock Abrahams, Barbara. "The Novel and the Carnival World: An Essay in Memory of Joe Doherty." *MLN* 89 (Dec. 1974): 911-37.

Bakhtin, M. M. *Author and Hero in Aesthetic Activity. Art and Answerability: Early Philosophical Essays.* Ed. Michael Holquist and Vadim Liapunov. Trans. Vadim Liapunov. Austin: University of Texas Press, 1990. 4-256.

___. *Discourse in the Novel. The Dialogic Imagination: Four Essays.* Ed. Michael Holquist. Trans. Caryl Emerson and Michael Holquist. Austin: University of Texas Press, 1981. 259-422.

___. "Epic and Novel." *The Dialogic Imagination.* 3-40.

___. *Problems of Dostoevsky's Poetics.* Trans. Caryl Emerson. Theory and History of Literature, Vol. 8. Minneapolis: University of Minnesota Press, 1984.

___. "The Problem of the Text in Linguistics, Philology, and the Human Sciences: An Experiment in Philosophical Analysis." *Speech Genres and Other Late Essays.* Ed. Caryl Emerson and Michael Holquist. Trans. Vern McGee. Austin: University Texas Press, 1986. 103-31.

Barnes, Warner. *A Bibliography of Elizabeth Barrett Browning.* Austin: Humanities Research Center, University of Texas and Armstrong Browning Library, Baylor University, 1967.

Benjamin, Jessica. "A Desire of One's Own: Psychoanalytic Feminism and Intersubjective Space." *Feminist Studies/Critical Studies*.Ed. Teresa de Lauretis. Bloomington: Indiana University Press, 1986. 78-101.

Benstock, Shari. "Expatriate Modernism: Writing on the Cultural Rim." *Women's Writing in Exile*. Ed. Mary Lynn Broe and Angela Ingram. Chapel Hill: University of North Carolina Press, 1989. 19-40.

Bieder, Maryellen. "'El escalpelo anatómico en mano femina': The Realist Novel and the Woman Writer." *Letras Peninsulares* 5 (Fall 1992): 209-25.

Bieman, Elizabeth. "An Eros Manque: Browning's 'Andrea del Sarto'." *Studies in English Literature* 10 (1970): 651-68.

Bloom, Harold. "Browning's *Childe Roland*: All Things Deformed and Broken." *The Ringers in the Tower: Studies in Romantic Tradition*. Chicago: University of Chicago Press, 1971. 157-67.

Bornstein, George."The Arrangement of Browning's *Dramatic Lyrics* (1842)." *Poems in their Place: Intertextuality and Order in Poetic Collections*. Ed. Neil Freistat. Chapel Hill: University of North Carolina Pr, 1986. 273-88.

Burdett, Osbert. *The Brownings*. Boston: Houghton Mifflin, 1929.

Byrd, Deborah. "Combating an Alien Tyranny: Elizabeth Barrett Browning's Evolution as a Feminist Poet." *Browning Institute Studies* 15 (1987): 23-41.

Byron, Lord. *Childe Harold's Pilgimage. A Romaunt. Selected Poems and Letters*. Ed. William H. Marshall. Boston: Houghton Mifflin, 1968. 31-163.

Chadwick, Whitney and Isabelle de Courtivron, Eds. *Significant Others: Creativity & Intimate Partnership*. NY: Thames and Hudson, 1993.

Chesterton, G. M. *Robert Browning*. NY: Macmillan & Co., 1903.

Colby, Vineta. *Yesterday's Women: Domestic Realism in the English Novel*: Princeton: Princeton University Press, 1974.

Coleridge, Samuel Taylor. *The Complete Poems*. Ed. William Keach. NY: Penguin, 1997.

Collins, Thomas. *Robert Browning's Moral Aesthetic Theory, 1833-1855*. Lincoln: University of Nebraska Press, 1967.

Cook, Eleanor. *Browning's Lyrics: An Exploration*. Toronto: University of Toronto Press, 1974.

Craft, Christopher. "'Kiss Me with Those Red Lips': Gender and Inversion in Bram Stoker's *Dracula*." *Speaking of Gender*. Ed. Elaine Showalter. NY: Routledge, 1989. 216-42.

Crosby, Christina. *The Ends of History: Victorians and the Woman Question*. NY: Routlege, 1991.

Culbertson, Philip L. "Men and Christian Friendship." *Men's Bodies, Men's Gods: Male Identities in a (Post-) Christian Culture*. Ed. Björn Krondorfer. NY: New York University Press, 1996. 149-80.

Culler, A. Dwight. *The Victorian Mirror of History*. New Haven, CT: Yale University Press, 1985.

Cunningham, Valentine. "Tradition as Debris and the Debris of Tradition in the Poetry of Robert Browning." *Poetry and Epistemology: Turning Points in the History of Poetic Knowledge*. Papers from the International Poetry

Symposium. Ed. Roland Hagenbüchle & Laura Skandera. Eichstätt, 1983. Regensburg: Verlan Friedrich Pustet, 1986. 168-81.

D'Avanzo, Mario L. "King Francis, Lucrezia, and the Figurative Language of 'Andrea del Sarto'." *Texas Studies in Language and Literature* 9 (1958): 523-36.

David. Deirdre. "'Art's a Service': Social Wound, Sexual Politics, and *Aurora Leigh.*" *Browning Institute Studies.* 13 (1985): 113-36.

___. *Intellectual Women and Victorian Patriarchy: Harriet Martineau, Elizabeth Barrett   Browning, George Eliot.* Ithaca, NY: Cornell University Press, 1987.

DeVane, William Clyde. *A Browning Handbook.* 2nd Ed. NY: Appleton-Century-Crofts, 1935.

___. "The Virgin and the Dragon." In *The Browning Critics.* Ed. Boyd Litzinger and K. L. Knickerbocker. Lexington: University of Kentucky Press, 1965. 181-96 [first published in 1947].

Dowden, Edward. *The Life of Robert Browning.* London: Everyman, 1904.

DuPlessis, Rachel Blau. *The Pink Guitar: Writing as Feminist Practice.* NY: Routledge, 1990.

___. *Writing Beyond the Ending : Narrative Strategies of Twentieth-Century Women Writers.* Bloomington: Indiana University Press, 1985.

Erickson, Lee. *The Economy of Literary Form: English Literature and the Industrialization of Publishing, 1800-1850.* Baltimore: Johns Hopkins Press, 1996.

—. *Robert Browning: His Poetry and His Audiences.* Ithaca, NY: Cornell University Press, 1984.

Farrell, John P. *Revolution as Tragedy: The Dilemma of the Moderate from Scott to Arnold.* Ithaca: Cornell University Press, 1980.

Fleischman, Avrom. "Notes for a History of Victorian Poetic Genres." *Genre* 18 (Winter 1985): 363-74.

Forman, H. B. *"Balaustion's Adventure* [review.]." Reprt. for private circulation from *London Quarterly Review.* Jan. 1872.

Forster, Margaret. *Elizabeth Barrett Browning; The Life and Loves of a Poet.* NY: St. Martin's Press, 1988.

Franklin, Colin. *Elizabeth Barrett Browning at the Mercy of Her Publishers.* Waco, Texas: Armstrong Browning Library, 1989.

Friedman, Susan Stanford. "Gender and Genre Anxiety: Elizabeth Barrett Browning and H. D. as Epic Poets." *Tulsa Studies in Women's Literature* 5 (Fall 1986): 203-28.

Friend, Joseph H. "Euripides Browningized: The Meaning of *Balaustion's Adventure.*" *Victorian Poetry* 2 (Summer 1964): 179-86.

Froula, Christine. "Browning's *Sordello* and the Parables of Modernist Poetics." *ELH* 52 (Winter 1985): 965-92.

Frye, Northrop. *Anatomy of Criticism: Four Essays.* Princeton, N. J.: Princeton University Press, 1957.

Garber, Marjorie. *Vested Interests: Cross-Dressing and Cultural Anxiety.* NY: Routledge, 1992.

Gay, Penelope. "Desire and the Female Voice in Browning's *Men and Women* and *Dramatis Personae. AUMLA 71* (May 1989): 47-63.

Gibson, Mary Ellis. "The Poetry of Struggle: Browning's Style and 'The Parleying with Gerard de Lairesse'." *Victorian Poetry* 19 (Autumn 1981): 225-42.

Gilbert, Sandra. "From *Patria* to *Matria*: Elizabeth Barrett Browning's Risorgimento." *PMLA* 99 (March 1984): 194-211.

Gilligan, Carol. *In a Different Voice: Psychological Theory and Women's Development.* Cambridge, MA: Harvard University Press, 1982.

Graham, Colin. *Ideologies of Epic: Nation, Empire, and Victorian Epic Poetry.* Manchester: Manchester University Press, 1998.

Gridley, Roy E. *The Brownings and France. A Chronicle with Commentary.* London: Athlone Press, 1982.

Hair, Donald. *Browning's Experiments with Genre.* University of Toronto Department of English Studies and Texts 19. Toronto: University of Toronto Press, 1972.

___. *Robert Browning's Language.* Toronto: University Toronto Press, 1999.

Harper, J. W. "'Eternity our Due': Time in the Poetry of Robert Browning." *Victorian Poetry. Stratford-upon-Avon Studies* 15. London, 1972.

Hetzler, Leo A. "The Case of Prince Hohenstiehl-Schwangau: Browning and Napoleon III." *Victorian Poetry* 15 (Winter 1977). 335-50.

Hudson, Gertrude Reese. *Browning to His American Friends: Letters between the Brownings, the Storys, and James Russell Lowell 1841-1890.* NY: Barnes & Noble, 1965.

___. *Robert Browning's Literary Life: From First Work to Masterpiece.* Austin, Texas: Eakins Press, 1992.

Irvine, William and Park Honan. *The Book, the Ring, and the Poet: A New Biography of Robert Browning.* NY: McGraw-Hill, 1974.

Jack, Ian. *Browning's Major Poetry.* NY: Oxford, 1973.

James, Henry. *William Wetmore Story and His Friends.* 2 vols. London: Blackwood, 1903.

Janson, H. W. With Dora Jane Janson. *History of Art.* NY: Harry N. Abrams, Inc., [n.d.].

Jardine, Alice. *Gynesis: Configurations of Woman and Modernity.* Ithaca, NY: Cornell University Press, 1985.

Jehlen, Myra. "Archimedes and the Paradox of Feminist Criticism." *The Signs Reader: Women, Gender & Scholarship.* Ed. Elizabeth Abel and Emily K. Abel. Chicago: University Chicago Press, 1981. 69-95.

Johnson, Wendell Stacy. *Sex and Marriage in Victorian Poetry.* Ithaca, NY: Cornell University Press, 1975.

Kammer, Jeanne. "The Art of Silence and the Forms of Women's Poetry." *Shakespeare's Sisters: Feminist Essays on Women Poets.* Ed. Sandra M. Gilbert and Susan Gubar. Bloomington: Indiana University Press, 1979. 153-64.

Karlin, Daniel. *Browning's Hatreds.* New York: Oxford University Press, 1993.

___. *The Courtship of Robert Browning and Elizabeth Barrett.* NY: Oxford University Press, 1987.

King, Roma A., Jr. *The Focusing Artifice: The Poetry of Robert Browning.* Athens: Ohio University Press, 1968.

Knickerbocker, Kenneth L. "A Tentative Apology for Robert Browning." In *The Browning Critics.* Ed. Litzinger and Knickerbocker. Lexington, University Kentucky Press, 1965. 265-75 [first published in 1956].

Knoepflmacher, U. C.   "Projection and the Female Other: Romanticism, Browning, and the Victorian Dramatic Monologue. *Victorian Poetry.* 22 (Summer 1984): 139-59.

Kristeva, Julia. from *The Portable Kristeva,* 'Strangers to Ourselves'.. Ed. Kelly Oliver. NY: Columbia University Press, 1997. 264-94.

___. "Women's Time." *The Kristeva Reader.* Ed. Toril Moi. NY: Columbia University Press, 1986. 187-213.

Landow, George P. "Aggressive (Re)interpretations of the Female Sage: Florence Nightingale's *Cassandra." Victorian Sages and Cultural Discourse: Renegotiating Gender and Power.* New Brunswick, NJ: Rutgers University Press, 1990. 32-45.

Language and Literature catalog. Paul and Company: Publishers Consortium, Inc. 1995. 5.

Latané, David E., Jr. "Browning's *Strafford* and the History of the Present." *Critical Essays on Robert Browning.* Ed. Mary Ellis Gibson. NY: G. K. Hall, 1992. 226-42.

___. "The Diorama 'Showman' in *Sordello." Studies in Browning and His Circle.* 14 (1986): 25-27.

Lawson, E. LeRoy. *Very Sure of God: Religious Language in the Poetry of Robert Browning.* Nashville, TN: Vanderbilt University Press, 1974.

Lawton, David. "Browning's Narrators." *AUMLA* 71 (May 1989): 88-105.

Lawton, William Cranston.   "The Classical Element in Browning's Poetry." *Boston Browning Society Papers.* (1886-97). NY: Macmillan, 1897.

Leighton, Angela. "'Because men made the laws': the fallen woman and the woman poet." *New Feminist Discourses: Critical Essays and Theories on Texts.* Ed. Isobel Armstrong. NY: Routledge, 1992. 342-60.

Litzinger, Boyd and K. L. Knickerbocker, Eds. *The Browning Critics.* Lexington: The University of Kentucky Press, 1965.

Litzinger, Boyd and Donald Smalley, Eds. *Browning: The Critical Heritage.* The Critical Heritage Series. NY: Barnes and Noble, 1970.

Lootens, Tricia. *Lost Saints: Silence, Gender, and Victorian Literary Canonization.* Charlottesville: University Press of Virginia, 1996.

McCarthy, Mary. *The Stones of Florence.* NY: Harcourt Brace, 1963.

McClatchy, J. H. "Browning's 'Saul' as a Davidic Psalm of the Praise of God: The Poetics of Prophecy." *Studies in Browning and His Circle* 4 (Sept. 1976): 62-83.

McGann, Jerome J., Ed. *Historical Studies and Literary Criticism.* Madison: University Wisconsin Press, 1985.

___. "The Religious Poetry of Christina Rossetti." In *Canons*. Ed. Robert von Hallberg. Chicago: University of Chicago Press, 1984. 261-78.

McMahan, Anna Benneson. *Florence in the Poetry of the Brownings*. Chicago: A. C. McClurg, 1907.

Markus, Julia. *Dared and Done: The Marriage of Elizabeth Barrett and Robert Browning*. NY: Knopf, 1995.

___. "'Old Pictures in Florence': Through *Casa Guidi Windows*." *Browning Institute Studies* 6 (1978): 43-61.

Martin, Loy D. *Browning's Dramatic Monologues and the Post-Romantic Subject*. Baltimore, MD: Johns Hopkins University Press, 1985.

Maynard, John. *Browning's Youth*. Cambridge: Harvard University Press, 1977.

Mermin, Dorothy. *The Audience in the Poem*. New Brunswick, NJ: Rutgers University Press, 1983.

___. "Barrett Browning's Stories." *Browning Institute Studies* 13 (1985): 99-112.

___. "The Damsel, the Knight, and the Victorian Woman Poet." *Critical Inquiry* 13 (Autumn 1976): 64-80.

___. "The Domestic Economy of Art: Elizabeth Barrett and Robert Browning." *Mothering the Mind: Twelve Studies of Writers and Their Silent Partners*. Ed. Ruth Perry and Martine Watson Brownley. NY: Holmes & Meier, 1984. 83-101.

___. *Elizabeth Barrett Browning: The Origins of a New Poetry*. Chicago: University Chicago Press, 1989.

___. "Elizabeth Barrett Browning Through 1844: Becoming a Woman Poet." *Studies in English Literature* 26 (Autumn 1986): 713-36.

___. "'The fruitful feud of hers and his': Sameness, Difference, and Gender in Victorian Poetry." *Victorian Poetry* 33 (Spring 1995): 149-68.

___. *Godiva's Ride: Women of Letters in England, 1830-1880*. Bloomington: Indiana University Press, 1993.

Miller, Betty. *Robert Browning: A Portrait*. NY: Charles Scribner's Sons, 1952.

Munich, Adrienne. *Andromeda's Chains: Gender and Interpretation in Victorian Literature and Art*. NY: Columbia University Press, 1990.

Paz, Octavio. *Sor Juana: Or the Traps of Faith*. Trans. Margaret Sayers Peden. Cambridge: Harvard University Press, 1988.

Pearsall, Robert Brainard. *Robert Browning*. NY: Twayne, 1974.

Peckham, Morse. "Personalities and the Mask of Knowledge." *Victorian Revolutionaries: Speculations on Some Heroes of a Culture Crisis*. NY: George Braziller, 1970.

Peterson, Linda H. "Rereading *Christmas-Eve*, Rereading Browning. *Victorian Poetry* 26 (Winter 1988): 363-80.

Polette, Keith. "The Many-Walled World of 'Andrea del Sarto': The Dynamics of Self-Expatriation." *Victorian Poetry* 35 (Winter 1997). 493-507.

Pollock, Mary S. "The Anti-Canonical Realism of Elizabeth Barrett Browning's 'Lord Walter's Wife'." *Studies in the Literary Imagination*. 24 (Spring 1996): 43-53.

Prins, Johanna Henrica [Yopie]. "Translating Greek tragedy: Elizabeth Barrett and Robert Browning." Diss. Princeton University, 1991.

Reynolds, Margaret and Barbara Rosenbaum. "'Aeschylus' Soliloquy' by Elizabeth Barrett Browning." *Victorian Poetry* 37 (Fall 1997). 329-35.

Ridenour, George. "Robert Browning and *Aurora Leigh*." *Victorian Newsletter* 67 (Spring 1985): 26-31.

Riede, David G. "Genre and Poetic Authority in *Pippa Passes*." *Victorian Poetry* 27 (Autumn-Winter 1989). 49-64.

Rosenblum, Dolores. "*Casa Guidi Windows* and *Aurora Leigh*: The Genesis of Elizabeth Barrett Browning's Visionary Aesthetic." *Tulsa Studies in Women's Literature* 4 (1985): 61-68.

Rundle, Vivienne. "'The inscription of these volumes': The Prefatory Writings of Elizabeth Barrett Browning." *Victorian Poetry* 34 (Summer 1996). 247-78.

Ryals, Clyde de L. *Becoming Browning: The Poems and Plays of Robert Browning, 1833-1846*. Columbus: Ohio State University Press, 1983.

___. "Browning's *Christmas-Eve* and Schleiermacher's *Die Weihnachtsfeier*: A German Source for an English Poem." *Studies in Browning and His Circle* 14 (1986): 28-31.

___. *Browning's Late Poetry*. Ithaca: Cornell University Press, 1975.

___. "Levity's Rainbow: Browning's 'Christmas-Eve'." *Journal of Narrative Technique* 17 (Winter 1987): 39-44.

Schad, John. *Victorians in Theory: From Derrida to Browning*. Manchester: Manchester University Press, 1999.

Schwenger, Peter. "The Masculine Mode." *Speaking of Gender*. Ed. Elaine Showalter. NY: Routledge, 1989. 101-12.

Shaw, W. David. *The Dialectical Temper: The Rhetorical Art of Robert Browning*. Ithaca, NY: Cornell University Press, 1968.

___. *The Lucid Veil: Poetic Truth in the Victorian Age*. Madison, Wisconsin: University of Wisconsin Press, 1987.

Shelley, Percy Bysshe. "A Defense of Poetry." *Shelley's Poetry and Prose: Authoritative Texts and Criticism*. Ed. Donald Reiman and Sharon B. Powers. NY: Norton, 1977. 480-508.

Shires, Linda M., Ed.. "The Author as Spectacle and Commodity: Elizabeth Barrett Browning and Thomas Hardy." *Victorian Literature and the Victorian Visual Imagination*. Ed. Carol T. Christ and John O. Jordan. Berkeley: University California Press, 1995. 198-212.

___. *Rewriting the Victorians: Theory, History, and the Politics of Gender*. NY: Routledge, 1992.

Slinn, E. Warwick. *Browning and the Fictions of Identity*. NY: Barnes and Noble, 1982.

Smulders, Sharon. "Sincere Doubt, Doubtful Sincerity, and *Sonnets from the Portuguese*." *ANQ 8* (Fall 1995) <wysiwyg://bodyframe.1040/http://ehostvgw>.

Sotheby, Wilkinson, and Hodge. *The Browning Collections. Catalogue of Oil Paintings, Drawings & Prints; Autograph Letters and Manuscripts; Books* [of R. W. Barrett]. London: Dryden Press, 1913.

Starzyk, Lawrence J. "'The Coronation of the Whirlwind': The Victorian Poetics of Indeterminacy." *Victorian Newsletter* 77 (Spring 1990): 27-35.

Steiner, George. *After Babel: Aspects of Language and Translation.* NY: Oxford University Press, 1975.

Stempel, Daniel. "Browning's *Sordello*: The Art of the Makers-See." *PMLA* 80 (Dec. 1965): 554-61.

Stephenson, Glennis. *Elizabeth Barrett Browning and the Poetry of Love.* Ann Arbor, MI: UMI Research Press, 1989.

Stone, Marjorie. "Genre Subversion and Gender Inversion: *The Princess* and *Aurora Leigh.*" *Victorian Poetry* 25 (Summer 1987): 101-27.

___. "*Monna Innominata* and *Sonnets from the Portuguese*: Sonnet Traditions and Spiritual Trajectories." *The Culture of Christina Rossetti: Female Poetics and Victorian Contexts.* Ed. Mary Arseneau, Antony H. Harrison and Lorraine Janzen Kooistra. Athens: Ohio University Press, 1999. 46-74.

Sullivan, Mary Rose. "Elizabeth Barrett Browning and the Art of Collaboration." *Studies in Browning and His Circle.* 19 (1991): 47-55.

___. "'Some Interchange of Grace': 'Saul' and *Sonnets from the Portuguese.*" *Browning Institute Studies* 15 (1987): 55-68.

Sussman, Herbert. "Robert Browning's 'Fra Lippo Lippi' and the Problematic of a Male Poetic." *Victorian Studies* 35 (Winter 1992): 185-200.

___. *Victorian Masculinities: Manhood and Masculine Poetics in Early Victorian Literature and Art.* Cambridge Studies in Nineteenth-Century Literature and Culture 3. NY: Cambridge, 1995.

Taylor, Beverly. "'School-Miss Alfred' and 'Materfamilias': Female Sexuality and Poetic Voice in *The Princess* and *Aurora Leigh.*" *Gender and Discourse in Victorian Literature and Art.* Ed. Antony H. Harrison and Beverly Taylor. DeKalb: Northern Illinois University Press, 1992. 5-29.

Thale, Mary. "T. S. Eliot and Mrs. Browning on the Metaphysical Poets." *CLA Journal* 11 (1968): 255-58.

Thompson, Patricia. *George Sand and the Victorians: Her Influence and Reputation in Nineteenth-Century England.* NY: Columbia University Press: 1977.

Thorpe, James. "Elizabeth Barrett's Commentary on Shelley: Some Marginalia." *Modern Language Notes* 66 (Nov. 1951): 455-58.

Tucker, Herbert. "Wanted Dead or Alive: Browning's Historicism." *Victorian Studies* 38 (Autumn 1994). 25-39.

___. *Browning's Beginnings.* Minneapolis: University Minnesota Press, 1980.

Vasari, Giorgio. *The Lives of the Artists.* Trans. Julia Conaway Bondanella and Peter Bondanella. NY: Oxford University Press, 1991.

Vygotsky, Lev. "Interaction between Learning and Development." *Mind in Society: The Development of Higher Psychological Processes.* Ed. Michael Cole, Vera John-Steiner, Sylvia Scribner and Ellen Souberman. Cambridge, MA: Harvard University Press, 1978. 79-91.

___. "Tool and Symbol in Child Development." *Mind in Society.* 19-30.

Walsh, Susan. "'Doing the Aphra Behn': Barrett Browning's Portrait of the Artist." *Victorian Poetry.* 36 (Summer 1998). 163-86.

Walsh, Thomas P. "Companion Poems in *Men and Women*: The Love Gap." *Browning Society Notes* 24 (May 1997): 71-79.

___. "The Frames of Browning's *Men and Women*. *Browning Society Notes* 21 (1991-92): 32-39.

Waterfield, Giles. *Dulwich Picture Gallery*. [London: Dulwich Picture Gallery, n. d.].

___. *Rich Summer of Art: A Regency Picture Collection Seen Through Victorian Eyes*. [London]: Dulwich Picture Gallery, 1988.

Whiting, Lilian. *The Brownings: Their Life and Art.* NY: Haskell House Publishers, Ltd., 1972 [reprint of 1911 ed. n.p.].

Weinstein, Mark. *William Edmondstoune Aytoun and the Spasmodic Controversy*. Yale Studies in English 165. New Haven, CT: Yale University Press, 1968.

Woolford, John. *Browning the Revisionary*. NY: St Martin's Press, 1988.

Woolford, John and Daniel Karling. *Robert Browning*. Studies in Eighteenth- and Nineteenth-Century Literature. NY: Longman, 1996.

Yates, Gayle Graham. "Introduction." *Harriet Martineau on Women*. Ed. Gayle Graham Yates. New Brunswick, N J: Rutgers University Press, 1985.

Yetman, Michael G. "Exorcising Shelley Out of Browning: *Sordello* and the Problem of Poetic Identity." *Victorian Poetry* 13 (Summer 1975): 79-98.

Index

Kristeva, Julia 28, 138

Labé, Louise 87
Lamartine, Alphonse de 136
Landon, Letitia (L.E.L.) 19, 24, 27, 87, 89, 134
Landor, Walter Savage 60, 84, 203
Landow, George A. 134
Latané, David E. 77
Lawton, William Cranston 211
Leighton, Angela 145
Leopardi, Giacomo 133
Leopold, Grand Duke of Austria 129
Litzinger, Boyd 111
Locke, John 25, 54
logistoricus 116-117
Lootens, Tricia 5, 88
Lorenzo the Magnificent 214
Love Letters from the Portuguese (Anonymous) 90
Luther, Martin 139

Macready, William 38-39, 42-43, 56
Manzoni, Alessandro 133, 136
    I Promessi sposi 133
Markus, Julia 7, 124, 128, 136, 145, 148, 164, 169
Martin, Loy 11, 90, 95, 151, 160
Martineau, Harriet 204
Maynard, John 38, 60
Mazzini, Giuseppe 129, 139
McCarthy, Mary 127, 137
McGann, Jerome 119, 137
McMahan, Anna Benneson 148, 167
Medici, Cosimo de 129
Menippea 11, 111-117, 119-121
Mermin, Dorothy 2, 7, 18, 28, 33, 57, 89-91, 97, 125, 174-175, 192, 207
Meynell, Alice 83, 175
Michelangelo 71-72, 76, 137, 214
Mignaty, George 163
Mill, John Stuart 4-5, 38, 43, 45, 60
Miller, Betty 4, 52, 66, 108, 160-161, 210
Milnes, Moncton 84

Milton, John 25, 27, 44, 99, 125
Mitford, Mary Russell 8, 23, 27, 56, 82-84, 203
Monclar, Amédée de Ripert 37, 39, 43, 46, 48-49
Monti, Vincenzo 136
Moulton Barrett, Arabel 180
Moulton Barrett, Edward 3, 21-22, 24, 26, 64, 103-105, 157, 203-204
Moulton Barrett, Edward (Bro) 21-22, 65
Moulton Barrett, Henrietta 123, 138, 203
Moulton Barrett, Mary Graham-Clarke 21-22
Moulton Barrett, Samuel 82
Munich, Adrienne Auslander 68
Murillo, José 154

Napoleon III 60, 129-130, 147, 204-205
Narses 77
Nazianzen, Gregory 83
New Guelfs 133
Nonnus 111
Norton, Caroline 84

O'Neil, Patricia 1
Ogilvy, Eliza 164, 179-180

Parini, Guiseppe 56, 136
    Il Giorno 56
Paz, Octavio 87
Peacock, Thomas Love 16, 42
Peckham, Morse 54
Pellico, Silvio 133
    Le mie prigioni 133
Peterson, Linda H. 111, 115
Petrarch 88-90, 92-94, 97, 104, 133
philosophes 26
Pio Nono 125, 129, 140, 160
Plutarch 208
    Life of Nicias 208
Polette, Keith 160
polyvocality 2, 5